THE
SAS
AT WAR

By the same author
Castles in Colour
Weapons and Equipment of the Marlborough Wars
The Maginot Line – Myth and Reality
The Unknown Battle – Metz 1944
The Bitter End – Singapore 1942 (with Richard Holmes)
The Secret Hunters
Escape from Berlin

THE
SAS
AT WAR

The Special Air Service Regiment
1941–1945

ANTHONY KEMP

JOHN MURRAY

© Anthony Kemp 1991

First published in 1991
by John Murray (Publishers) Ltd
50 Albemarle Street, London W1X 4BD

The right of Anthony Kemp to be identified as the author of this work has been asserted
by him in accordance with the Copyright, Designs and Patents Act, 1988

British Library Cataloguing in Publication Data
Kemp, Anthony *1939–*
   The SAS at war, 1941–1945.
   1. World war 2. Army operations. Great Britain, army.
   Special Air Service Regiment
   I. Title
   940.541241

   ISBN 0–7195–4890–X

Typeset by Wearside Tradespools, Fulwell, Sunderland
Printed in Great Britain by
Butler & Tanner Ltd, Frome

Lieutenant-Colonel
Sir (Archibald) David Stirling KBE, DSO

This book is dedicated to the 'Originals' and all other men who served during the Second World War in L Detachment, SAS Brigade, 1 SAS Regiment, 2 SAS Regiment, the Mediterranean Special Boat Section, the Greek Sacred Squadron, the Special Interrogation Group, the Special Raiding Squadron, 3 and 4 French Parachute Battalions (*2ème et 3ème* RCP), the Belgian SAS Regiment and F Squadron, GHQ Liaison Regiment.

Contents

Illustrations

The author and publishers wish to thank the following for permission to reproduce illustrations: 1, 2, 7, The Imperial War Museum; 4, Douglas Mayne; 6, Reg Seekings.

Acknowledgements

Inevitably, a book of this nature cannot be written without immense help from others and I would like to be able to thank the many wartime members of the regiment who gave so generously of their time and their memories: Jim Almonds, the late Eric Barkworth, Bob Bennett, 'Tanky' Challenor, Johnny Cooper, Henry Druce, Roy Farran, John Fielding, Roger Flamand, the late Pat Hart, Dick Holmes, Quentin 'Jimmy' Hughes, Ray Keep, the late Dave Kershaw, Alastair McGregor, the Very Revd Fraser McLuskey, Lord John Manners, Nobby Noble, Peter le Poer Power, the late Fred Rhodes, Pat Riley, Mike Sadler, Reg Seekings, the late Sir David Stirling, David Sutherland, John Tonkin, Sir John Verney, Barney Waygood and Chalkie White.

Apart from wartime members of the regiment, many others opened doors and actively assisted the work of research. I am grateful to the following, several of whom allowed me to glimpse just what the 'Regiment' is: Miss Vera Atkins, Dave Cleary, Ian Crook, Johnny Crossland, Albert Dupont, George Franks, Prince Yurka Galitzine, Denise Gensigault, Trevor Harvey, Werner Helfen, Pat McDonnell, Joe McReady, Armand Malaise, Mayor of Moussey, Richard Moddiman, the late Dare Newall, Viscount Slim, 'Tanky' Smith, Roger Souchal and the comrades of the Groupe Mobile Alsace.

Finally, thanks to those who believed in a project that was not to be – Pippa Cross, who signed my expenses, and Gordon Stevens, who was a true companion along the path of discovery.

Introduction

On 5 May 1982 a small group of highly trained specialists stormed the Iranian Embassy building in London where terrorists were holding a number of hostages. Through no wish of their own, the assault party carried out their task in full view of the television crews who were covering the siege, and thus, for the first time, the Special Air Service Regiment found itself in the limelight. Ever since then the regiment and its activities have been the subject of intense speculation, analysis and often ill-informed criticism. Before Prince's Gate, the men from Hereford had been members of a small and virtually unknown unit of the British Army, and were quite content to leave things that way. They have never courted publicity and, indeed, actively discourage any form of prying into their organization, as secrecy and anonymity are vital to their role in the war against terrorism. The paradox is that there very nearly was no SAS available today to help in the defence of our society. Had it not been for the vision of a small group of senior officers in the aftermath of the Second World War, the regiment would have disappeared into limbo, sent there precisely because of its unorthodox methods.

The British armed forces have a long tradition of successful operations carried out by irregular or even clandestine units. Equally, they have a tradition of viewing such units with suspicion and doing their best to hinder their formation and activities. At the level of the individual soldier, the desire to opt out of large formations and engage in small-scale raiding with a few like-minded individualists is a strong one, going back in time perhaps to the delights of medieval cattle rustling. On the other hand, the bureaucracies that have organized our forces and those who have commanded them have generally displayed hostility to anything innovatory.

Much of the credit for fostering the offensive spirit and permitting the development of novel fighting methods during the Second World War must be given to Winston Churchill. An unorthodox man himself, his innovations were born of desperation, and when after the retreat from Dunkirk he issued his famous call for Europe to 'be set ablaze', he did so knowing that it would be a long time before Britain would be in a position to challenge Nazi Germany. Churchill's fertile mind was ever susceptible to fresh ideas to bring confusion to the Nazis, however impractical or crack-brained, and he took a keen personal interest in details of new weaponry and inventions. Thus it was that a whole clutch of small specialist units came to be formed, often the result of ideas of individuals who had the necessary push to struggle against the inertia of higher command. In terms of results, the contribution of special forces in general greatly exceeded the resources they expended.

Yet at the end of the Second World War, the armed forces ministries heaved a great sigh of relief as they either disbanded or absorbed into larger formations the various 'private armies' that had sprung up out of necessity. There was a feeling that once the war was over, one could get back to 'some proper soldiering'.

One such 'private army' was the Special Air Service. Founded in the Middle East in the summer of 1941, it was the vision of one man, David Stirling. It started off as a very small specialist raiding unit, was raised to the status of a regiment and ended the war as a somewhat unwieldy brigade. Though Stirling's SAS was abolished in 1945, its ideals did not perish and it was re-formed in 1947 as a Territorial Army unit. After a shaky start in Malaya in the 1950s, a regular regiment was raised which has since served with distinction in Aden, Oman, Borneo, the Falklands and Northern Ireland.

There have been several books charting the history of the regiment, but they have tended to be based on older published accounts which appeared after the war. As a result of a project to make a television documentary covering the period 1941 to 1947, enthusiastically supported by David Stirling and other senior members of the SAS Regiment, I was given facilities to carry out a large number of interviews, together with the director-designate of the series, Gordon Stevens. At the same time a start was made on researching into the documentary background in the public records, while other documents were obtained from those who were interviewed. The television project was abandoned, but I received encouragement to continue research from many of those I had contacted.

A myth has grown up that the wartime SAS never bothered with paperwork and that there was no documentation available to provide the basis for a more thorough study. But anybody who has ever had anything to do with the armed forces knows full well that you have to have an authorization even to get a replacement shirt button. As can be seen from the notes on sources at the end of the book it has been possible to trace a large quantity of documents.

At the time of disbandment in 1945, the papers of the two British SAS regiments were bundled up and sent to an army records office in Edinburgh, and were presumably shredded. The SAS, however, left its mark on the various higher headquarters which it came under at various stages of the Second World War, and there is a wealth of hitherto unexamined papers in the Public Record Office at Kew. Naturally there are tantalizing gaps. For example, there is little paperwork concerning the early period in North Africa, because during 'The Flap' when Rommel stood at the gates of the Nile Delta in June 1942, Middle East Headquarters burned the bulk of its records. Regular operational reports and analyses only seem to have been filed after the invasion of Sicily. Once the SAS became absorbed into the planning and execution of the landings in France in June 1944, its activities were influenced by HQ Airborne Forces, SHAEF (Supreme Headquarters Allied Expeditionary Force) and the 21st Army Group. Thus it has been possible to build up a reasonably comprehensive picture of how the SAS developed as a fighting force and what it achieved.

Where there are gaps in official records, I have had to fall back on other sources. Extensive use has been made of the series of interviews mentioned above, which provide a unique personal insight into the war as it was fought at an individual level. After such a lapse of time, however, even the best of memories can appear unreliable, and care has been taken to check dates and times wherever possible. A debt is also acknowledged to the writers of personal memoirs and other authors who have touched on the history of the regiment.

This is not an 'official history' as such and it represents entirely my own views rather than those of the SAS establishment, which bears no responsibility for any errors or omissions. No editorial control has been imposed by any outside source and all material used is within the public domain. The resulting text is offered as a tribute to those who, at great personal risk to themselves, were prepared both to dare and to win.

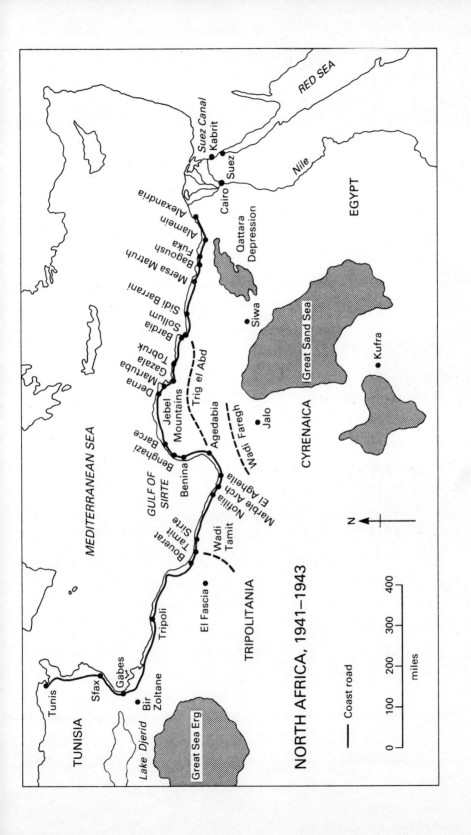

NORTH AFRICA, 1941–1943

— Coast road

miles
0 100 200 300 400

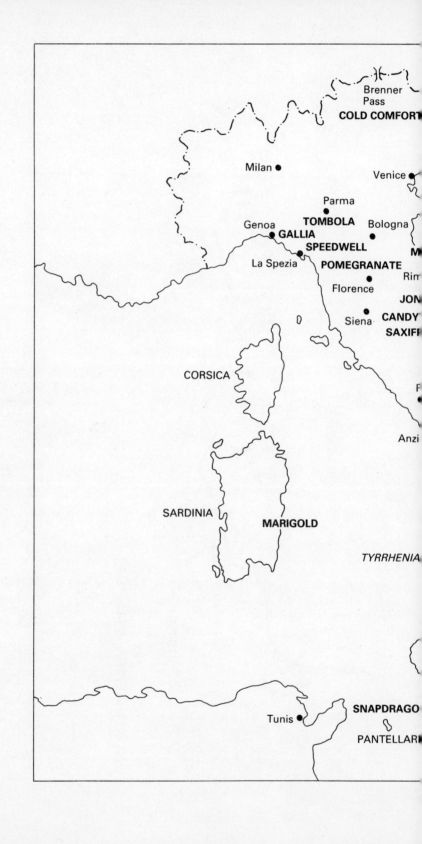

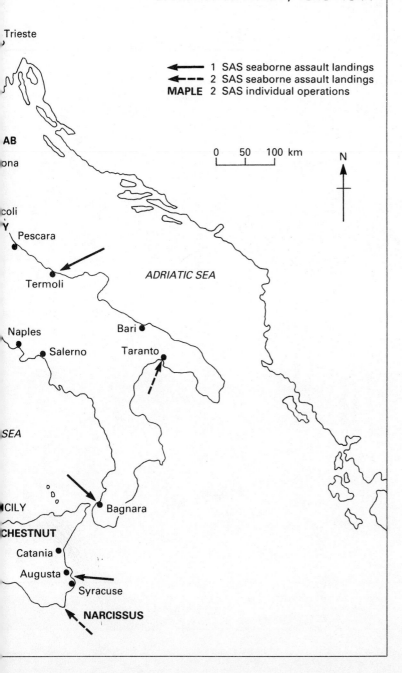

SICILY AND ITALY, 1943–1944

→ 1 SAS seaborne assault landings
⇠--- 2 SAS seaborne assault landings
MAPLE 2 SAS individual operations

0   50   100 km

N

Trieste

AB

ona

coli

Y

Pescara

Termoli

ADRIATIC SEA

Naples

Bari

Salerno

Taranto

SEA

Bagnara

CILY

CHESTNUT

Catania

Augusta

Syracuse

NARCISSUS

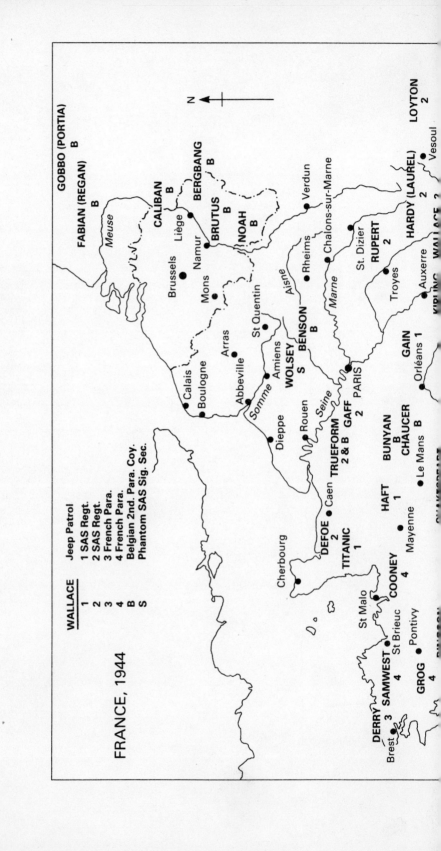

FRANCE, 1944

WALLACE   **Jeep Patrol**

1	1 SAS Regt.
2	2 SAS Regt.
3	3 French Para.
4	4 French Para.
B	Belgian 2nd. Para. Coy.
S	Phantom SAS Sig. Sec.

GOBBO (PORTIA) B

FABIAN (REGAN) B

CALIBAN B

BERGBANG B

BRUTUS B

NOAH B

Meuse

Liège

Namur

Brussels

Mons

Verdun

Rheims

Chalons-sur-Marne

St. Dizier

RUPERT 2

Marne

Troyes

Auxerre

Aisne

St Quentin

WOLSEY S

BENSON B

Arras

Amiens

Abbeville

Calais

Boulogne

Somme

Dieppe

Rouen

Seine

TRUEFORM 2 & B

GAFF 2

PARIS

GAIN

Orléans 1

HARDY (LAUREL) 2

KIPLING WALLACE 2

LOYTON 2

Vesoul

DEFOE 2

Caen

HAFT 1

BUNYAN B

CHAUCER B

Le Mans B

Mayenne

TITANIC 1

Cherbourg

COONEY 4

St Malo

St Brieuc

Pontivy

SAMWEST 4

GROG 4

DERRY 3

Brest

N ←

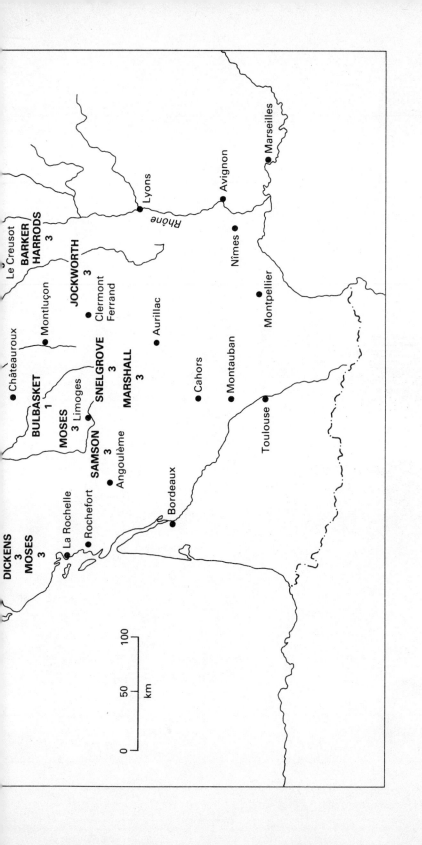

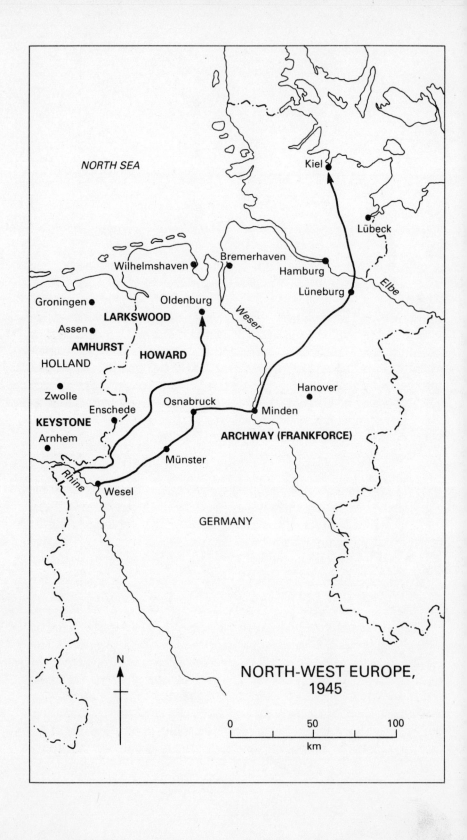

NORTH SEA

Kiel

Lübeck

Bremerhaven

Wilhelmshaven

Hamburg

Weser

Elbe

Groningen

Oldenburg

Lüneburg

LARKSWOOD

Assen

AMHURST

HOWARD

HOLLAND

Hanover

Zwolle

Osnabruck

Enschede

Minden

KEYSTONE

ARCHWAY (FRANKFORCE)

Arnhem

Münster

Rhine

Wesel

GERMANY

N

NORTH-WEST EUROPE, 1945

0   50   100

km

I

The Birth of an Idea

David Stirling was one of those individuals who combine within themselves the ability to dream and the ruthless singlemindedness to transform their ideas into action. Scion of an ancient family of Scottish gentry, the Stirlings of Keir, he was the founder of what was to become the Special Air Service Regiment as we know it today, although with typical modesty he always insisted on sharing the credit with others. In 1984 at the opening of new accommodation for the regiment at Hereford, appropriately named Stirling Lines, his speech included the following comment.

> I have always felt uneasy in being known as the founder of the regiment. To ease my conscience I would like it to be recognised that I have five co-founders: Jock Lewes, Paddy Mayne of the original 'L' Detachment, George Bergé who started the French S.A.S., Brian Franks who re-raised the S.A.S. flag after the war and John Woodhouse who created the modern S.A.S. during the Malaysian Campaign by restoring to the regiment its original philosophy.[1]

In the same speech, he described himself as 'something of a "cheekie laddie" and of dubious value to the army' in the spring of 1941. There was an element of truth in these comments and before charting the history of the regiment he raised, it is worth examining the background of this remarkable man, later known to members of the regiment either as 'Colonel David' or simply as DS. Born in 1915, one of a family of four boys and two girls, Stirling spent his childhood in Scotland. Like most young men of his background he excelled in outdoor activities –

deer-stalking, mountaineering and shooting. He was sent away to boarding school at Ampleforth and from there went to Trinity College, Cambridge, to read architecture. His one remarkable feature was his height, six feet and five inches. At Cambridge he showed little aptitude for study and tended to be diverted by horse-racing and other forms of gambling. A professional career as such seemed out of the question; his only ambition in life was to be an artist. After leaving Cambridge he went off to Paris to study drawing, but soon realized that he did not have sufficient talent. So instead he decided to climb Everest. With this in mind he spent most of the last two years of peacetime, training in Switzerland and then in the USA. While wandering in the Rockies on horseback in 1939, he heard that war had been declared and returned home to join two of his brothers (William and Hugh) in the Scots Guards.

Life as a second lieutenant in the Guards with little prospect of action did not appeal, although by the time the Germans invaded France in May 1940, Stirling was in Chamonix training with a force of experienced skiers who were to be sent to help the Finns. The first chance of real action came in the late summer of 1940 after the retreat from Dunkirk. Stirling volunteered and was accepted for one of the new Commandos, No. 8, which was raised by Captain Robert Laycock largely from Guards regiments. They moved north to Scotland for an intensive period of training, and he found himself in command of a section of young volunteers, many of whom were to serve with him later in the Middle East. One of them was Guardsman Johnny Cooper who had managed to join the Scots Guards while still under age and who was very impressed by his commanding officer: 'he was different from the officers I had come into contact with up to that time. This quietly spoken young lieutenant commanded far more respect and confidence, with his ability to put soldiers at their ease and his willingness to help.'[2]

Their training completed, No. 8 Commando together with two others embarked for the Middle East. They formed a composite unit known as Layforce, commanded by Bob Laycock, promoted to colonel, and their mission was to invade the island of Rhodes. The voyage out was a lengthy one via the Cape of Good Hope, and by his own admission Stirling spent most of it in his cabin gambling at cards. Two of his companions were Randolph Churchill and Evelyn Waugh. In a letter to his wife, the latter described Stirling as 'a gentleman obsessed by the pleasures of chance. He effectively wrecked Ludo as a game of skill and honour. We now race clockwork motor-cars.'[3]

On arrival, the various Commandos were billeted in camps along the Suez Canal and discovered that their mission had been overtaken by events. After the almost total defeat of the Italians in North Africa by General O'Connor in January 1941, the Germans had decided to send an Afrika Korps to bolster their allies. Commanded by the brilliant Rommel in a lightning campaign, the Afrika Korps threw the British forces into headlong retreat back to the Egyptian border, leaving only a garrison encircled in the coastal town of Tobruk. At the same time, the Germans swept through Greece and Yugoslavia.

Layforce was thrown into the action piecemeal and parts of it fought gallantly in Crete. No. 11 Commando became involved in fighting the Vichy French in Syria, while No. 8 Commando took part in a few unsuccessful raids along the North African coast, transported into action by the Navy. The latter on each occasion was either defeated by rough seas or spotted by enemy aircraft. Young David Stirling's frustration at his inability to have a crack at the enemy mounted, yet in a most extraordinary episode he was nearly court-martialled for cowardice. Feeling bored at being cooped up in the desert, he decided to feign temporary illness. 'This got me into the very comfortable American hospital, where I was well pampered. In a sense I was pretty ill, because I would go out at eight o'clock in the evening, having recovered from the appalling hangover caused by my previous night's activities in Cairo, and re-establish my illness by that night's activities.'[4]

Hearing that there was the prospect of action with No. 8 Commando, he reported back for duty. Returning from a training exercise one night, Stirling tripped over the guy ropes of his tent and cut his eye quite badly, which entailed a return to hospital. This, combined with the previous episode, created suspicion that he had been malingering to avoid going into action and resulted in his being charged with cowardice. The charges were eventually dropped after an investigation, but had he stayed with the Scots Guards his career would inevitably have been wrecked.

The 24-year-old David Stirling was no rough and ready brawling cut-throat though, in spite of his thirst for coming to grips with the enemy. Always immaculately dressed, he was remembered for his invariable courtesy and charm as he moved through the hotel bars and restaurants of cosmopolitan wartime Cairo. His height he tended to disguise with a slight stoop, and he made no secret of his contempt for the desk-bound staffs who had mushroomed far behind the lines.

As Layforce was now spread out all over the Middle East, it was decided to disband it and use the manpower to bolster other units. Shortly before this, however, fate took a hand in the so far uneventful war of Second Lieutenant Stirling. A brother officer, Jock Lewes of the Welsh Guards, had discovered some parachutes which were destined for transport to India, and obtained permission from Laycock for himself and Stirling to experiment with them, together with four other Guardsmen. The following is a report of the first parachute jump in the Middle East, written by Guardsman D'Arcy, Irish Guards, who later served with the Special Boat Section.

He [Lewes] and his party first went to an R.A.F. headquarters located somewhere near Fuka. There he discussed the details with an R.A.F. officer who, although none of the party had jumped before, was most helpful. He showed us the parachutes we were to use. From the logbooks we saw that the last periodical examination had been omitted, but Lt. Lewes decided they were okay.

Next day, along with Lt. Stirling and Sgt. Storrie, who were hoping to do a job in Syria, we made a trial flight. The 'plane used was a Vickers Valentia. We threw out a dummy made from sandbags and tent poles. The parachute opened okay, but the tent poles smashed on landing. Afterwards we tried a ten foot jump from the top of the 'plane and then a little parachute control.

The following afternoon we flew inland in the Valentia, which was used to deliver mail. We reached the landing field towards dusk, landed, fitted on our parachutes and decided to jump in the failing light. We were to jump in pairs. Lt. Lewes and his servant, Guardsman Davies first, the R.A.F. officer to despatch. The instructions were to dive out as though we were going into water. We hooked ourselves up, circled the field, and on a signal from the R.A.F. officer, Lt. Lewes and Davies dived out. Next time round I dived out and was surprised to see Lt. Stirling pass me in the air. Lt. Lewes made a perfect landing. Next came Davies, a little shaken. Lt. Stirling injured his spine and also lost his sight for about an hour. Next, myself, a little shaken and a few scratches, and lastly Sgt. Storrie, who seemed okay. Guardsman Evans was unable to jump as the pilot decided to land owing to the approaching darkness.[5]

The aircraft that this intrepid group had used was a large lumbering biplane dating back to the early 1930s. It seems incredible that they were allowed to go up and jump out without any rudimentary training in landing techniques. The static lines which pulled open their parachutes had simply been tied to the metal legs of the seats inside the fuselage. What had happened was that Stirling's static line had snagged on the tail section as he exited from the door, and two panels were ripped from the parachute, causing him to descend too rapidly. He was carted off to the Scottish Military Hospital in Alexandria, while the remainder of the group made a second jump the following day without any further serious mishaps.

In fact, both Stirling's legs were temporarily paralysed and he suffered quite a severe back injury which was to keep him immobilized for the best part of two months. This period of enforced idleness, however, was not wasted, as Stirling's ever-fertile brain analysed the progress of the war in the Middle East and drew its own conclusions. Layforce having virtually ceased to exist, there was no longer any credible raiding force at the disposal of the Commander-in-Chief. The advent of Rommel had changed the balance in favour of the Axis powers, and everywhere British forces were on the defensive. In the desert, an offensive in June to relieve Tobruk, code-named 'Battleaxe', failed and the commander-in-chief, Wavell, was sacked. He was replaced by General Auchinleck on 2 July.

The outline of what was to become the Special Air Service was roughed out in pencil on sheets of paper in hospital during June and July 1941. Though unable to sally out to sample the night life, Stirling was not alone, as he had a constant stream of visitors with whom he discussed his ideas, including Jock Lewes who came to see him before departing for Tobruk. But in spite of his obsession with the failures of the past, his essential irreverent humour remained undimmed.

I remember Evelyn Waugh coming in, a great chum of mine in those days. The matron had told him that they had removed one of my legs and were going to have the other one off the following day. He sat on the edge of the bed with his usual cynical observations, but he kept looking out of the corner of his eye. I was very proud of having got movement back in my second leg and was twiddling my toes, but he thought that he was seeing a bloody ghost. Then he couldn't stand it any longer and said, 'What the hell's happening here? Matron told me that you would have both legs removed. What's that twiddling at the end of the bed?'[6]

The original document no longer exists, as far as can be determined, but in November 1948 David Stirling wrote a confidential memorandum on the origins of the regiment he founded, on which much of the following section is based.[7] The proposal by the then second lieutenant was addressed directly to the Commander-in-Chief Middle East, as Stirling knew full well that 'going through channels' would be a total waste of time.

There was no way you could put it in except to the C-in-C. Never at MEHQ [Middle East Headquarters]. There was layer on layer of fossilized shit. The energetic soldiers who had survived the first war were in active command, but there was a great residue of staff officers from the first war who did not fight, who determined the spirit of the administration. It was ludicrously swollen, unnecessarily big and wholly obstructive to anything that looked like a new idea.[8]

He started off by pointing out that Rommel's lines of communication, stretched out along the coast, were extremely vulnerable to a determined attack. The Commando raids, however, had been too unwieldy and had thus lacked the element of surprise. In addition, the Navy was far too hard pressed to find the shipping to transport a large Commando force.

I argued the advantages of establishing a Unit based on the principle of the fullest exploitation of surprise and of making the minimum demands on man-power and equipment. I argued that the application of this principle would mean in effect the employment of a sub-unit of five men to cover a target previously requiring four troops of a commando, i.e., about 200 men. I sought to prove that, if an aerodrome or transport park was the objective of an operation, then the destruction of 50 aircraft or units of transport was more easily accomplished by a sub-unit of five men than by a force of 200 men.[9]

Stirling went on to suggest that a force of 200 men, properly selected, trained and equipped, and organized into five-man sub-units, should thus be able to attack thirty different objectives simultaneously on the same night – compared to only one target using the Commando technique. The corollary to this was that a unit operating according to such principles would have to be trained to arrive on the scene of an operation by every practical method from land, sea or air.

I insisted that the Unit must be responsible for its own training and operational planning and that, therefore, the Commander of the Unit must come directly under the C in C. I emphasised how fatal it would be for the proposed unit to be put under any existing branch or formation for administration. (I was determined to combat in advance any risk of being taken over by G(R), the Middle East equivalent of S.O.E., which was already showing signs of being the monstrous and inefficient octopus it later became; or coming under the control of the Director of Combined Operations.) I pointed out that the head of any such branch or formation would have less experience than myself or my successor in the medium in which we proposed to operate.[10]

Future events were to prove just how right Stirling had been in making the latter observations and how his basic principles were to be constantly watered down by interference from outside bodies trying to get their hands on the SAS Regiment, which achieved its greatest successes when left to its own devices. It is interesting to note that the concept of the five-man sub-unit was reduced to four and even three as the result of operational experience in the desert.

Stirling himself realized that if he was to stand any chance of getting his radical ideas accepted, he had to 'sell the proposal' to the Commander-in-Chief. To do this he put forward in his submission a detailed plan for the employment of his unit in the offensive being planned by Auchinleck to take place in November, which was no secret in Cairo at the time. What Stirling instinctively realized was that the German and Italian air forces posed a very real threat to an advance by the Eighth Army and that if those enemy aircraft could be neutralized on the ground, the offensive would stand a much greater chance of success. His aim was to drop five parties by parachute two nights before the offensive to attack the five enemy forward airfields around Timimi and Gazala. They would use incendiary-cum-explosive bombs to disable the aircraft and then retire to a pre-arranged rendezvous point in the desert where they could be picked up by a patrol of the Long Range Desert Group (LRDG).

This group needs a brief introduction at this stage, as its activities were interwoven with those of the SAS during its early period of operations in the Middle East. In the years prior to the Second World War, a small group of pioneers had spent long periods exploring the Libyan desert in vehicles. One of those men was Major R. A. Bagnold and in June 1940 he was authorized to form a reconnaissance unit to collect information from behind enemy lines. Using 30-cwt. Chevrolet trucks, the LRDG patrols ranged thousands of miles deep into Libya radioing back vital information to their base and perfecting the art of desert navigation.

The story of how the convalescent David Stirling got his proposal into the hands of General Auchinleck was told to the journalist Virginia Cowles in 1958, and is based on Stirling's memory of events not too long after they occurred.[11] It was a perfect example of sheer brazen cheek. He took a car to the front entrance of MEHQ and, still on crutches, told the sentry that he had left his pass behind. That failed to gain him entry. Then he noticed a gap in the wire through which he squeezed his vast height, leaving the crutches behind. Limping across the courtyard he was noticed by the sentry who promptly raised a hue and cry. The second lieutenant disappeared inside the main building intending to call on the Commander-in-Chief – without an appointment needless to say – but realized that he was in difficulties. He hobbled through the first available door, which was marked Adjutant General, and saw a red-faced major seated behind the desk. He started to explain what it was he wanted, with sentries shouting along the corridors outside, but was cut short. The red-faced major had a good memory for faces and well recalled that when he was lecturing to the officers of the Scots Guards at Pirbright in 1939, a certain young gentleman had persistently slept through his talks, having spent the previous nights at wild parties in London.

Mumbling apologies, Stirling retreated into the corridor and decided on one more attempt. He pushed through the door of the Deputy Chief of Staff, who at that time was General Neil Ritchie, and handed him his pencil-written memorandum. To his everlasting credit, Ritchie, instead of having the intruder thrown out, read it through carefully and promised to hand it personally to Auchinleck. He said that he thought the proposal could well be what they wanted and promised a definite decision within two days. In the meantime he authorized a start to be made with planning and summoned, of all people, the red-faced major to his office. The latter, to his chagrin no doubt, was ordered to assist Stirling with working out details of supplies and equipment for the new force.

In a further interview with Ritchie, Stirling was authorized to recruit a force of six officers and sixty men from the remnants of Layforce and was promoted to captain. He was to plan the operation with the Director of Military Operations at MEHQ and was allotted an area near the Suez Canal at Kabrit as a base. This embryo raiding force was to be called

8

L Detachment, Special Air Service Brigade. Such a brigade did not exist, but had been dreamed up by Brigadier Dudley Clark, who at the time was in charge of an outfit dealing with deception plans. One of his ideas was to convince the Italians that there was a large airborne force in the Middle East. To do this he had been dropping dummies by parachute near Italian prisoner-of-war camps, and the advent of some real parachutists was an obvious gift.

Stirling's first job was to start recruiting and there were two particular officers he had in mind. The first was Jock Lewes who was in Tobruk, where he had been successfully carrying out small raids against the surrounding enemy outposts. Travelling there by boat, Stirling found Lewes in bed, suffering from desert sores, but managed to persuade him to join L Detachment, bringing with him one or two of his own men. Before the war, Lewes had been President of the Oxford University Boat Club, and was quiet and studious, in contrast to most of the young officers who had been with the Commandos.

The other officer was Blair Mayne, known as Paddy. An Ulsterman and pre-war Irish rugby international, Paddy had been in No. 11 (Scottish) Commando, which was part of Layforce. He had tasted action in a raid along the Litani river in Syria against Vichy French forces in June 1941 but when Stirling went to interview him he discovered that Paddy was under close arrest for striking his commanding officer in the mess. Stirling managed to obtain his release, but had quite some difficulty in persuading Paddy to join him. 'He had every reason not to take me seriously as a soldier as he knew how idle I had been in prior days in Layforce.'[12] Mayne was another immensely tall man endowed with tremendous physical strength. To the men under him he was a most considerate and loyal officer, but he had a darker side to his character. Often morose and withdrawn, his drinking bouts frequently ended in mindless violence. Yet when in action he was the perfect fighting machine with a total disregard for his own personal safety.

Many members of the Guards Commando were in a camp at Genefa on the Great Bitter Lake and that was where Stirling went in search of the bulk of his sixty other ranks. Bob Bennett, Grenadier Guards, was one of those frustrated warriors who were called in to a large marquee. 'He put the proposition to us that he was forming a unit that would operate behind the lines. He realized that we felt disgusted at what had been achieved in the commandos and that he had had this brainwave of small parties behind the lines.'[13]

Stirling's old troop from No. 8 Commando had been absorbed by the

2nd Battalion Scots Guards who were in the desert at a place called Bug Bug, from where Johnny Cooper was recruited. 'The majority of the old No. 3 Troop volunteered and I crawled out of my foxhole to put in my application'. Initial selection was based solely upon Stirling's impressions of the men at brief interviews. He had no great difficulty in getting together the numbers he required, and simply told them that if they failed to make the grade in training, they would have to return to their original units. Thus the 'Originals' were in a sense on probation from the moment they clambered into the lorries which took them to Kabrit.

On arrival we were bemused to find only two medium sized marquees and three 180lb tents piled up in the middle of the strip of desert allotted to us. . . . Our lorry stopped outside one of the marquees and out strode the portly figure of C.Q.M.S. Gerry Ward, who was eventually to become our quartermaster. He ordered us to collect picks and shovels and to start digging holes already marked out for the tentage. . . . So we set to under our section corporal, Jimmy Brough, and slogged away until we had completed ten such excavations, wondering where the tents were that were to fill them.[14]

They soon found out. That evening the new recruits to L Detachment were informed that their first operation was to steal their camp. Nearby was the base camp for the New Zealand Division that was away fighting in the front line. After dark the men of the SAS crept in and obtained the necessary tentage and equipment to set themselves up, including even a piano for the officers' mess. They were driven to this by the obstructiveness that Stirling met with. It was not enough to have the Commander-in-Chief's approval to set up his unit. He continued to have to battle with the various staff departments where he had already made enemies. 'I found during this and subsequent stages, that the A.G. [Adjutant General's] Branch was unfailingly obstructive and uncooperative.'[15]

But in spite of every difficulty placed in his path, by the end of July 1941 David Stirling had got roughly what he wanted. He had three months to train and equip his force before their first operation in November. In the eyes of higher headquarters, L Detachment was so small that it was simply expendable. If they proved that they could deliver what they promised, well and good. If not, any that survived could simply be posted back to their parent units and the whole scheme could be rapidly forgotten.

At this stage, David Stirling might perhaps have allowed himself a moment or two of self-congratulation. After all, he had managed to defeat the system and was in sole command of a small military unit. His immediate priority, though, was to weld a disparate group of men into a cohesive fighting force. He had no track record himself in combat and the men he was to lead in battle were a pretty tough crowd, all of them individualists and likely to be highly critical of any officer who did not come up to their own standards. Looking back after forty-five years had elapsed, he had the following to say about the 'Originals' of L Detachment.

In a sense they weren't really controllable. They were harnessable and all had a sense of individuality. The object was to give them a sense of purpose and once they were harnessed to that proposition, they policed themselves, so to speak. And that goal had to be a very exacting one. . . . That bag of vagabonds had to grasp what they had to do in order to get there, which included discipline. Although most of them were escaping from conventional regimental discipline, they didn't fully appreciate that they were running into a much more exacting type of discipline.[16]

There is no real common denominator that can be used to classify the 'Originals', the first fifty-odd recruits to the SAS, some of whose names will constantly crop up during the course of this book. Most of them had done their basic training in one of the Guards regiments and most had completed the Commando course. Few had any experience of combat, although Dave Kershaw had served as a volunteer during the Spanish Civil War. Johnny Cooper was the 'baby' of the unit and was only 18 at the time. A slim, wiry youth, he was one of the few who could claim a 'middle-class' upbringing. Bob Bennett was a typical Cockney with a dry sense of humour, who had volunteered for anything that was going just to get away from the parade-ground atmosphere of the Grenadier Guards. He gained a reputation as a practical joker, yet at the same time could be quite morose. Pat Riley, large, square and solid, the sergeant-major who ruled by tact, was actually an American citizen, having been taken there as a child. There were Sergeant Rose, whom everyone remembered for his fine singing voice, and Bob Lilley, married and at nearly 40 one of the oldest operatives. Reg Seekings, a short, stocky and pugnacious East Anglian, had achieved a considerable reputation in the boxing ring. Nobody could put one over on him. 'Gentleman' Jim

Almonds, immensely tall and a little less boisterous than some of the others, had seen action at Tobruk together with Pat Riley and Jock Lewes.

The principles of training laid down by Stirling differed from those in the Commandos, where a group of volunteers, once recruited, were nursed up to the required standard. 'L Detachment on the other hand, had set a minimum standard to which all ranks had to attain and we had to be most firm in returning to their units (R.T.U.) those who were unable to reach that standard.'[17] Even today, RTU is the ultimate sanction applied in the SAS. Stirling also insisted on a Brigade of Guards standard of turnout and behaviour even when off duty.

> There had grown up in the Commandos a tradition that to be a tough regiment it was necessary to act tough all the time in the barracks and on leave, and they were liable to be badly dressed, ill disciplined and noisy in the streets and restaurants of Cairo. We insisted with L Detachment that toughness should be reserved entirely for the benefit of the enemy.[18]

There is very little in the way of documentation in the public records about those early days of L Detachment and the story of their first three months has to be pieced together from their own memories. Stirling himself spent a lot of time in Cairo wheedling supplies and planning the first operation. He placed Jock Lewes in charge of training, describing him as 'the best training officer I have ever been associated with or heard of during the war'.[19] Lewes instituted a pretty strict regime which at times tended to be resented, although it brought results. Reg Seekings, who came from No. 7 Commando, remembers an incident right at the beginning when they got fed up with erecting tents, that nearly erupted into a minor mutiny. 'Jock Lewes had a word with us. He told us we'd got a yellow streak a yard wide down our backs. Christ, I don't know how he survived. He said: "Right, prove me wrong. I'll do anything that you do and you do anything that I do." '[20]

The first priority was to get parachute training underway, and as there were no facilities in the Middle East everything had to be improvised. A letter requesting help was sent to Ringway, near Manchester, where airborne troops in Britain were trained, but no reply was received. Eventually some instructional material did arrive, but not until October, by which time the whole detachment had qualified. Ultimately Captain Peter Warr was sent out from England and remained a chief parachute instructor. Lewes had some towers made of scaffolding poles from which men could swing from ropes to simulate the final drop of landing. What caused a crop of broken limbs, however, was his brainwave of making men do backward rolls out of a 15-cwt. truck speeding across the desert at 30 miles per hour. With a considerable number of men in plaster, he resorted to constructing a sled which sped down an incline on rails, from which the trainee rolled off sideways. All this was to prepare the men for their first actual jump from an aircraft.

Stirling had managed to get the use of a Bristol Bombay, an aged and under-powered troop-carrier, from 216 Squadron RAF. It was converted for parachuting by having a rail bolted along the fuselage on to which the rings at the end of the static lines were fixed by a dog-lead clip. The group to jump, known as a stick, hooked up and shuffled in a line to exit from the side door. On the day appointed, the aircraft took off with the first stick, all of whom landed successfully. Then disaster struck. The first two men to exit from the following party were killed when their parachutes failed to open, but luckily the RAF dispatcher managed to stop the rest from jumping. Stirling called all the men together on the ground and promised that modifications would be made, but that jumping would continue at first light the following morning. It transpired that somehow the clips had twisted and become detached from the rail, causing the only fatal accidents during the entire training programme. Stirling also authorized the issue of fifty cigarettes to each man. It was a very nervous group, their fingers stained with nicotine, who assembled on the airfield the next day, but Stirling himself jumped first, followed by the rest of the detachment.

Parachuting, however, was only a small part of a most intensive programme. There were lectures on quite advanced medical care, on intelligence-gathering, signalling and demolitions. On the range, the men had to familiarize themselves with every form of weapon including German and Italian ones. There was strenuous PT and swimming in the Suez Canal. To train their memories, Kim's game was used. The men were taken into a tent and allowed to look at a group of objects for a short period after which they had to recall every detail they had observed.

Jock instilled into us that the end product of our training was for us to become independent in every way, operating either alone or in very small groups. We would have to develop an ingrained self-confidence in our ability to navigate across featureless terrain without any back-up whatsoever and using maps that gave little or no detail. We would have to survive on minimum sustenance and to control the use of food and water during the hot periods of the day, using the cover of darkness for offensive activity.[21]

Reg Seekings recalled,

It was practically a twenty-four-hour programme and we'd be out at night, reading the stars and familiarizing ourselves with them. We'd have our packs loaded with various weights and we'd march 100 yards measuring the length of pace, the time it took. Then we'd go on a ten-to twenty-mile march and when we came back it would all be weighed again. Then we'd again pace 100 yards, counting the paces and the time it took, so that we could do dead reckoning on our march in.[22]

All who went through that regime of training remember the extremes of fatigue and of being pushed to their limits. Even the food in camp was of poor quality and there was little opportunity for relaxation. Lewes drove them hard, but when not training he was wrestling with a different problem. In order to achieve their aims, the various sub-units of L Detachment would have to be able to carry enough explosive in their packs to destroy considerable numbers of aircraft on the ground. What was needed was a small bomb capable of blowing a hole through the wing of an aircraft and igniting the fuel in the tanks inside. There were high-explosive and incendiary bombs of various types available, but no combination weapon. A senior officer in the Royal Engineers poured scorn on the idea and said that it was impossible.

Jock Lewes organized a primitive laboratory in a hut and set to experimenting with various mixtures of plastic explosive, thermite, oil and aluminium filings. Finally he perfected what became known as the Lewes bomb, and a demonstration was arranged before an invited audience, including the senior Royal Engineer. Jock set up an old aircraft wing with a tin of petrol inside to simulate a fuel tank, which he propped up on some oil drums. He then placed one of his bombs on top of the wing and detonated it. There was an explosion and a flash as the device punched a neat hole through the metal and ignited the petrol inside with a satisfactory whoosh of flame. His point had been proved with spectacular success. The bomb weighed no more than a pound and a man could carry up to thirty of them.

The end of all this intensive training was a final exercise as a sort of passing out examination, to test all the various skills learned:

> We were to mount a dummy attack on the R.A.F. airfield at Heliopolis, just outside Cairo, a distance of about a hundred miles across open desert. . . . Supplies were to consist of four water bottles each, three pounds of dates and a few glucose sweets. The entire unit set out from Kabrit at night, carrying weights to simulate the bombs which we would have to cart along with us on a real raid. During the day we lay up in the desert, camouflaging ourselves with pieces of hessian sacking against the R.A.F. patrols who were out looking for us from the air.[23]

The various small patrols converged on the target and on the fourth night out mounted their attack, moving in from different directions. They plastered a considerable number of parked aircraft with sticky labels marked 'bomb': the station commander reportedly was furious the following morning. His guards had been unable to intercept a single raider, in spite of having been warned of the exercise.

L Detachment was thus judged ready for operations, and to wind down were given a few days' leave to be spent in Cairo. Previously they had lacked an identity, but the training period had welded them together into a cohesive fighting force with an intense pride in themselves and their unit. Accounts differ as to when the unit insignia was first worn, but several of the 'Originals' maintain that it was at the end of the training period and before the first operation. The design of the cap badge had been the result of a competition which was won by Sergeant Bob Tait who came up with the winged dagger emblem. The motto, 'Who Dares Wins', is credited to Stirling. The only fly in the ointment was the headgear which was issued – white berets.

'Wearing a white beret in among Australians, New Zealanders and every type of nationality out there brought some great wolf whistles, which were naturally not received in the right manner. It was a question of: You pick your partner and I'll pick mine.'[24] The offending headgear was soon withdrawn, to be replaced initially by a khaki forage cap and then by the famous sand-coloured beret. A set of wings was also introduced, said to have been designed by Jock Lewes. Their pattern was inspired by a fresco of an ibis in the foyer at Shepheard's Hotel. The right to wear them over the left breast pocket instead of on the sleeve was granted to those who had taken part in three trips behind the lines.

It was quite unheard of in the Army for such a small unit to have its own self-designed insignia, but some months later Stirling, quite undismayed, wore his cap badge on parade when General Auchinleck came to inspect them at Kabrit. The Commander-in-Chief returned Captain Stirling's salute with a broad smile on his face, which the latter took to be tacit official approval.

Operation Crusader, Auchinleck's offensive to push Rommel back out of Cyrenaica, was to be the largest armoured operation undertaken by British forces at that time. It was to be mounted by the Eighth Army, commanded by General Cunningham, and the main objectives were to relieve the garrison of Tobruk and to secure advance airfields from which the convoys to Malta could be protected. It was to start on the night of 17 November, and L Detachment's role in this was to be small but potentially crucial. David Stirling's final plan was for his force to embark in five Bristol Bombay aircraft of 216 Squadron on the night of 16 November and drop near their targets. They would lie up the following day along the rocky escarpment which ran parallel to the coastal plain to observe their targets, the airfields at Timimi and Gazala. Then that night, just before the offensive was due to start, they would slip down and place their bombs on the parked enemy aircraft. Once this had been accomplished, the various parties would proceed on foot to an agreed rendezvous in the desert, about forty-five miles inland, where they would be picked up by a patrol of the Long Range Desert Group. It can be seen that this was essentially the plan put forward by Stirling in his original submission for the attack.

L Detachment was divided into five aircraft loads, commanded by Stirling, Mayne, Lewes, McGonigal and Bonnington. Captain Thomas went with Bonnington's stick, but there is confusion as to whether the remaining officer, Lieutenant Bill Fraser actually took part. According to Virginia Cowles, he dropped with Lewes's party, but others say that he was left at Kabrit as a result of injuries during training and met up with the survivors later.

L Detachment, carrying their weapons, bombs and personal equipment, proceeded to the forward airfield at Bagoush in high spirits. All of them were ready for action after the long period of training, but when they arrived they found that a gale had brewed up. Stirling, who had come direct from Eighth Army Headquarters, was on the horns of a dilemma. The most obvious solution was simply to cancel the operation as the weather was totally unsuitable for parachuting. The men would risk being scattered on landing and the pilots would find it difficult to navigate because of the sand being blown about by the wind. There were, however, two very good reasons why the operation had to go ahead regardless. The first was that Stirling had promised his men that they would never be subjected to the indecisions of the Commando days when operation after operation was planned and then cancelled at the last minute. Second, failing to take off would give L Detachment's detractors at headquarters just the ammunition they were looking for to disband the unit.

The RAF clearly regarded the group as a suicide squad, but laid on a slap-up meal. Reg Seekings felt that they were being treated like condemned men going to the gallows, but he did manage to buy a tin of Craven A cigarettes. Stirling called the officers together and put the situation to them. The decision to go ahead was unanimous. Without further hesitation they gathered their sticks together and boarded the five Bristol Bombays, squeezing themselves into the fuselages among the piles of equipment that were to be dropped with them. The aircraft took off into the darkness. Inside it was both noisy and freezing. According to Seekings, the doors had been removed and part of the interior was taken up by a huge extra fuel tank. After about two hours flying over the sea, they swung in over the coast and were given a welcoming burst of anti-aircraft fire. The pilots took evasive action which tipped men and equipment all over the place. Then the red lights came on and L Detachment sprang out into the pitch-black night, unsure of exactly where they were. The problem was that none of the pilots were really confident of their navigation, the sand storm having obliterated the landmarks they were relying on. It was a recipe for disaster.

Stirling jumped as the first man of his stick and in the darkness made a bad landing as he could not see the ground. He was knocked unconscious for a brief period but luckily nothing was broken. It took him nearly an hour to assemble the rest of the stick who had been dragged all over the desert by their parachutes. One man could not be found, several others were slightly injured, but worst of all vital supplies were missing. They had some Lewes bombs, but no detonators, and thus could not carry out their mission. Then and there he resolved that never again would containers be dropped with essential parts missing from the load. With deep regret he decided that he would have to abort his part of the mission. He ordered Sergeant Yates to take the bulk of the party to the rendezvous, while he himself set off to reconnoitre the escarpment with Sergeant Tait.

Johnny Cooper dropped with Jock Lewes's stick, which fared no better.

As it was impossible to see the ground I kept my legs braced, but when I hit the desert I suffered a tremendous jolt right through my body. Before I could gather myself properly, I found myself being dragged across the desert at more than thirty miles per hour by the wind.... Finally I managed to get out of the harness and, luckily for me, the parachute that was dragging me along got tangled in a camel thorn bush. I managed to roll clear just as it flew off into the air, never to be seen again.[25]

It also took them an hour to assemble in the darkness and likewise they discovered that most of their supply containers were missing.

Reg Seekings, who was with Paddy Mayne, was also dragged across the desert at such a speed that his arms and face were skinned. He ended up in a thorn bush where he finally managed to break free from his billowing parachute. Paddy quickly took command, but with most of their gear missing and two men so badly injured that they had to be left behind, there was nothing for it but to try to make the rendezvous with the LRDG. They trooped off into the night, short of food and water, but incredibly a freak rainstorm burst, turning the desert into a lake.

It was at this stage that the intensive training in navigation paid off. When dawn broke, the rain ceased and the various parties were able to take stock of their positions. Stirling and Tait managed to make it north to the escarpment where they spent some time observing enemy traffic on the coastal road below. The remainder made for the Trig al Ab, a desert track running inland about thirty miles south of the coast. Lewes's group found the track, and on the second night out stumbled on the signal lights placed by the LRDG. They whistled the recognition signal, 'Roll out the Barrel', and were welcomed into the camp with tea laced with rum. Shortly afterwards Stirling and Tait turned up, and finally Paddy Mayne's depleted group. They waited for another thirty-six hours, but no further stragglers arrived. There was no sign of either Bonnington's group or that led by McGonigal. Only four officers and eighteen other ranks survived to fight on. On the face of it the first SAS operation had been a total disaster.

2

Early Raids in the Western Desert

It was a pretty despondent group that sat around the fire of the LRDG patrol, each sunk in his own thoughts. Paddy Mayne was mourning the loss of his close friend and fellow Ulsterman, Eoin McGonigal, and all the others had lost mates with whom they had shared the hardships of training and the pleasures of drinking and rampaging on leave. It was only later that the fate of the missing aircraft became known. The one carrying Bonnington's party had been damaged by anti-aircraft fire. With a defective engine, little fuel and no instruments, the pilot decided to land, imagining that he was back over British-held territory. With great skill he managed to get the overladen aircraft down on the desert, but at dawn they discovered German traffic on a nearby road. There was nothing for it but to attempt a take-off and try to make for Tobruk. The parachutists climbed on board and the Bombay lurched back into the sky. It was soon hit again by gunfire and the long-range tank in the fuselage caught fire. With most of the control surfaces shot away, they were easy meat for a Messerschmitt. The Bombay crash-landed in the desert, killing two of the crew and one of the SAS men. The rest miraculously survived their injuries in various prisoner-of-war camps. What happened to McGonigal's stick has never been satisfactorily established. It is probable that they either crashed or were shot down, although Stirling states that there was evidence that at least some of them may have reached their target. On one of the target airfields, eighteen enemy aircraft were later found to have holes all over them.[1]

Stirling himself was obviously downhearted, but he did not show it. Captain David Lloyd-Owen's LRDG patrol also turned up at the rendezvous and he recalls his first meeting with him. '"My name's

Stirling," he said, almost as though we were meeting for the first time outside his Club in London. "Have you seen any of my chaps?"[2]

The remainder of L Detachment finally clambered on to the trucks of Jake Easonsmith's patrol and were taken to the LRDG base at Siwa Oasis, just to the north of the Great Sand Sea. During that drive there was much discussion about the future, which looked pretty grim. Such a failure could well result in L Detachment simply being wound up. But Stirling, the incurable optimist, was already making new plans. He realized full well that he stood no chance of getting further reinforcements, and anyway he would not have time to train them. Therefore they would have to carry on with the remaining group. Several people have claimed the credit for the idea that if the LRDG could pick them up after a raid, it could also deliver them to within easy walking distance of future targets. It is probable that the actual idea was the synthesis of discussions, but it was the one that Stirling adopted, starting a fruitful partnership with what became known to L Detachment as 'The Desert Taxi Service'. The latter had a less favourable nickname for the SAS, whom they referred to as the 'Parashites' for a while.

Leaving Paddy Mayne to bring up what he could in the way of supplies from Kabrit, Stirling set off from Siwa to Eighth Army Headquarters, which he found in turmoil. After initial successes, Cunningham's offensive had been outflanked by Rommel and brought to a standstill. While he was still at headquarters, the unfortunate Cunningham was sacked by Auchinleck and replaced by General Ritchie. One slight advantage of all this was that nobody had time to consider the fate of L Detachment. Stirling had a lucky encounter, however, with Brigadier John Marriott, a Scots Guards officer whom he had known in Cairo. Marriott's wife, Momo, was a celebrated hostess and a friend of Randolph Churchill, who naturally would have introduced his set of companions. It was Marriott who suggested that Stirling should make himself scarce for a while and recommended him to Brigadier Denys Reid. The latter was at Jalo Oasis, in command of a motorized force that was to operate on the southern flank of the Eighth Army.

Thus Stirling took himself to Jalo where he was joined by his depleted force who were flown in. The oasis lay 150 miles south of Benghazi and the enemy airfields strung out along the Gulf of Sirte. It had the additional advantage that it was well out of the way of prying headquarters staff and was being established as a forward base for the LRDG. 'Jalo itself was a typical Foreign Legion outpost, straight out of

Beau Geste. Rolling white sand dunes surrounded by a large oasis of swaying palm trees with a square fort in the middle. This guarded a series of artesian wells producing evil-looking but supposedly potable water which had a distinctly salty flavour.'3

Reid's column had captured the oasis from the Italians on 25 November, and his orders were to move from there towards the coast south of Benghazi to link up with a new offensive planned by Auchinleck and Ritchie. Being short of supplies he had to wait, but estimated that he would arrive in his operating area on 22 December. If L Detachment could eliminate the enemy aircraft on Agedabia airfield the night before, his final approach would be a lot safer. Stirling was more than happy to oblige, especially as Major Steele's LRDG squadron was prepared to take the raiders out and bring them back. The existence of L Detachment at Jalo was not mentioned in radio traffic, just in case somebody decided to order them back to Kabrit. Like a band of outlaws, the men checked their weapons and the officers pored over their maps.

Stirling, typically, was not content with just a small raid to prove the potential of his decimated force. With his vision of what they could achieve, he planned a whole series of assaults on airfields along the coastal strip. He and Paddy Mayne, taking nine men with them, would leave first to attack Sirte and Tamit. Lewes would lead his group to Agheila two days later as they would have less distance to cover. These raids were planned for the night of 14 December. Fraser would then leave for Agedabia as agreed to carry out his attack on the night of 21 December. This was not the concept of a cautious or beaten man. Stirling was going for broke.

No after action reports seem to have been filed for any of these early raids, which is not surprising considering the impromptu nature of their planning and execution. Thus the following account is a synthesis of interviews with those who took part and earlier published sources, all of which tend to differ slightly. The Stirling and Mayne groups left Jalo piled on top of the seven trucks of Gus Holliman's patrol at dawn on 8 December. His men were all Rhodesians, tough, self-reliant and taciturn men to whom the open-air life was second nature. The navigator was a young sergeant named Mike Sadler who had emigrated to Rhodesia before the war and who was arguably the best at finding his way around the Libyan desert. He later joined the SAS, serving with them until the end of the war.

The idea of a small group of men setting off into the desert to travel hundreds of miles behind the enemy lines was not such a hare-brained scheme as might be thought. There were no enemy ground forces to contend with except in the immediate target areas and the civilian population was minimal, restricted to the odd encampment of nomadic Arab tribesmen. The real threat came from air observation, as both the Italians and the Germans flew regular patrols over the desert, especially after a raid had been carried out. The actual casualties suffered by both the SAS and the LRDG were mainly caused by bombing or strafing when caught in the open desert. Assuming adequate water supplies and reliable vehicles, it was quite feasible to deposit a five-man raiding team within easy walking distance of their target and recover them afterwards. All the fighting in the campaign in North Africa by the main armies involved took place along the narrow strip between the sea and the escarpment that bordered the trackless wastes to the south.

The typical LRDG truck of the period was a 30-cwt. Chevrolet pick-up with two-wheel drive, painted a mixture of pink and light green, which had proved to be the best camouflage. It was armed with a Lewis gun on the back and carried a vast load of food, petrol, ammunition and other stores, enabling it to remain out in the desert for periods of up to three weeks. Space for a raiding party was limited, and jolting across the sand perched up on the back was extremely uncomfortable.

The journey of the first group was fairly uneventful until they were within about sixty miles of the coast at Sirte, when the going became more rocky and uneven. This slowed the patrol down, and they were located by an Italian spotter aircraft which dropped a couple of small bombs wide of the mark. Holliman decided that they had to take cover, so they scuttled into a patch of scrub and camouflaged themselves with nets. Inevitably more aircraft appeared, dropping a hail of bombs and then strafing with machine guns for good measure, but, amazingly, no damage was done.

Stirling, however, was worried that their cover was blown and decided on a change of plan. A recce of the area had shown that there was another airfield thirty miles from Sirte at Tamit. He decided to split the party, sending Mayne to attack this new target, while he dealt with Sirte itself.

Stirling, accompanied by Sergeant Jimmy Brough and two privates, Charlie Catell and Johnny Cooper, was driven by Holliman to within three miles of the target. A rendezvous was arranged on the coast road after the attack. With rucksacks on their shoulders and clutching their weapons, the group of desperadoes trudged up the main coast road, clearly silhouetted by the headlamps of passing enemy traffic. After a while, deciding that discretion was preferable, they moved off some distance into the desert parallel to the road. They duly arrived at the perimeter wire of the airfield and to their left they noticed a pair of Italian sentries manning a roadblock. It was then that Brough discovered they were in the middle of a minefield. A commotion ensued when Stirling loudly asked him what the hell was going on, and the alerted Italians began shouting. Realizing that there was little chance of getting into such a defended area undetected, they decided to make for the rendezvous, contenting themselves with placing their bombs on vehicles parked for the night alongside the road. They were consoled by the sight of a series of brilliant flashes and explosions in the night sky to the east, which they took to mean that Paddy Mayne had found his prey.

As indeed he had. His party made their way on to the airfield without difficulty and what followed was a foretaste of Paddy Mayne's style. They simply wandered around in the dark, placing their bombs on the parked aircraft until they ran out of them. But then, instead of making a hasty retreat, they lurked around the airfield buildings to wait for the explosions. Sure enough, the twenty-minute time pencils activated the detonators and up went the aircraft. It was then that Mayne noticed light coming from under a door. Kicking it open he saw a group of officers, probably pilots, and emptied the contents of a tommy-gun into them. As the raiders then slipped away across the airfield, an undamaged aircraft loomed out of the darkness. There were no bombs left, so Mayne leaped up on to the wing and, reaching into the cockpit, wrenched out the instrument panel with his bare hands. Still clutching this souvenir, he and his group made their rendezvous and met up with Stirling back in the desert. They then all travelled back to Jalo in high spirits. Mayne himself claimed twenty-four aircraft and some bomb and petrol dumps destroyed.

Jock Lewes came in a few days later with a different tale to tell. Arriving at Agheila they discovered that all the aircraft based there left at night, so something else had to be improvised. He had taken a captured Italian Lancia lorry along on the trip, as he had heard that there was a roadhouse at Mersa Brega used by groups of officers for meetings. His idea was to infiltrate the Lancia, which was armed with a Breda machine gun on the back, into an Italian convoy and shoot the place up, with a view to grabbing some prisoners. 'Gentleman' Jim Almonds was part of Lewes's group on the raid.

The chief target we came to that night was a staging post for enemy convoys along the route. We pulled into the car park alongside the other trucks outside the place and most of the drivers were inside. Some of the boys got off and placed bombs on the trucks. The idea was that when that was done, on a signal I was to open up with the Breda and shoot up the café. But, although we had tested it during the day, the drop in the temperature at night was so great that the oil in the mechanism became sluggish and thick. I cocked the old gun and squeezed the trigger, and it just went forward too slowly to fire a round. And so we used the small weapons we had.[4]

After creating the maximum of confusion, they piled into the Lancia and set off back along the road for their rendezvous with the LRDG, accompanied by an Italian whom they had taken prisoner after he had foolishly asked Lewes for a light while the latter was placing a bomb on his truck.

Bill Fraser, accompanied by Sergeants Tait and DuVivier and Privates Byrne and Phillips, arrived back at Jalo four days after the others, able to claim the greatest success. They had reached Agedabia without difficulty. Both DuVivier and Byrne wrote accounts of the raid fairly soon afterwards, and although they disagree on details, the main story is clear.[5] They were left by the LRDG about ten miles south of the target, and marched through the night to a point where they could observe the target during the following day. Byrne said that they each carried a water bottle, a compass, a revolver, eight Lewes bombs, a tin of chocolate, and a mixed ration consisting of raisins, lumps of cheese and broken biscuits. In addition, he had a tommy-gun and four spare magazines. That night they simply marched on to the airfield and set their bombs on a plentiful supply of aircraft. The first bombs went off while they were still walking around, and although the garrison fired away merrily, in the mêlée no shots came near the raiders. Byrne says that they added to the confusion by jumping up and down and shouting with glee. Reluctantly they headed away into the darkness and made the rendezvous rather late, but luckily the patrol had waited for them.

As they drove off, the LRDG boys said that they had heard and seen everything and had just had to stay to the end. Then, as dawn broke, they encountered the leading vehicles of Brigadier Reid's E Force. Soon engulfed by the column, they waited until Reid himself came up. He asked Fraser how many aircraft he had destroyed and when told thirty-seven, he said, 'I am proud to shake the hand of someone who has done something so well worthwhile.' Sadly, however, the return trip was marred by the death of two members of the Rhodesian patrol, killed in an attack by two Blenheims, in spite of their having spread out the correct air recognition signals.

Fraser's party arrived back on 23 December, but there was only time for a brief celebration, as Stirling, Mayne and Lewes were off the following morning for another series of raids. Celebration was in order, however. The SAS themselves had suffered no casualties and had destroyed sixty-one enemy aircraft, plus stores, petrol and vehicles. Put in perspective, that was equivalent to the achievement of the whole of Fighter Command during a day at the height of the Battle of Britain, but with only a handful of men and stores involved. Certainly David Stirling's theories had been vindicated in a spectacular way, but that was only the beginning. He was not the man to sit back and boast. In spite of Fraser having only just got back, he was invited to accompany them, and just as naturally agreed. The plan was to return to the same group of airfields, on the assumption that the garrisons would hardly expect them back quite so soon.

On Christmas Day 1941, Gus Holliman and his patrol, together with the Mayne and Stirling parties, set off once again into the desert. It was on this trip that a remarkable partnership came together for the first time. Stirling's own team included two men, Reg Seekings and Johnny Cooper, who had asked if they could be together. They were to stay with him throughout the desert campaign. Several subsequent accounts have referred to Cooper as 'David Stirling's driver', but in fact Stirling always insisted on doing the driving himself. The truth was that Cooper learned the skills of navigation and acted within the team in that capacity in the future.

That particular trip was more or less a carbon copy of the previous one. They had a relatively easy passage to the escarpment, where they split up. Holliman agreed to drive Stirling's team down on to the road and along it until they were within easy striking distance of the airfield at Sirte. Unfortunately they were again delayed by rough terrain, and when they got to the road they found it choked with German armour heading for the front. Ritchie's Eighth Army had gone over to the offensive and Rommel was in retreat towards Agheila. Thus they were forced to remain in hiding and at half past two they saw the glow of the fires that Mayne had lit at Tamit lighting up the horizon. This was particularly frustrating for Stirling, who had yet to score. By the time the traffic ceased, they were far too late to carry out a proper raid on the airfield and had to content themselves with shooting up transport along the road. Paddy Mayne, however, had managed to add a further twenty-seven aircraft to his bag.

The two groups returned safely to Jalo, where they had to wait some time for news of Jock Lewes and Bill Fraser. When it came, it was bad. Lieutenant Morris of the LRDG limped into Jalo in the one remaining truck of his original patrol of six, crowded with men. His tale was a sad one, backed up by the men of Lewes's troop. They had been dropped near their target, Nofilia airfield, and the following day had hidden themselves to observe the defences. They got on to the airfield that night and started to place their bombs, but as the aircraft were widely dispersed, this took time in the dark. Before they were finished, the first charges went off and the place became a hornets' nest. They were forced to beat a hasty retreat and arrived at their rendezvous with Morris's patrol on time. From there they set off to the landing ground which was Fraser's target.

On the way they were spotted by an Italian aircraft which came in and strafed them. Jim Almonds leaped off his truck and set up a bren, but Lewes stayed where he was. Afterwards his men felt that he had waited too long before baling out. He was hit several times and died shortly afterwards. Then further enemy aircraft arrived and bombed and strafed the patrol for several hours. When the attack ceased they managed to cannibalize parts to get one truck going and set off for the rendezvous with Fraser, only to find nobody there.

The death of Jock Lewes was keenly felt and it meant that Stirling was down to only one officer besides himself, assuming that Fraser was missing. Lewes had spent only a short time with the unit, but had impressed everyone with his absolute dedication to his work. Stirling may have laid down the principles, but it was Lewes who had trained the men to put them into practice. It is a paradox that very little is known about him as a person; although he was respected by the men, he kept his distance. Often when a member of a close team of people dies, all sorts of incidents and anecdotes are remembered. Yet when asked, those who served with him find it difficult to sum him up. John Steel Lewes was buried in the desert and is listed on the El Alamein memorial as having no known grave.

Stirling naturally realized that Lewes would be difficult to replace, and was deeply saddened by his death. Yet he could return to Cairo with a justifiable sense of pride in knowing that he had delivered what he had promised. There was a vital need to recruit fresh men and to replenish stores. L Detachment headed back to Kabrit for a well-earned rest and some leave.

It is at this stage in the history of the unit that its existence starts to register gradually in official records for the first time. While they were *en route* back to base at the end of December, there was a most puzzling exchange of correspondence between staff officers at MEHQ and Eighth Army Headquarters that sheds some light on how Stirling went about his business. The reference to a proposed parachute operation is strange, because there is no evidence that Stirling was planning any such thing at the time, yet the correspondence is dated 30 and 31 December 1941, when Stirling was in the desert. The following is the text of a letter from a Colonel M. B. Jennings at MEHQ to Colonel Thirburn at Eighth Army Advanced Headquarters.

We have been in great difficulty during the last thirty six hours over an alleged parachute operation which you have in view. Stirling appears to have told someone in R.A.F. Ops. about it, but of course not the right man. Stirling never breathed a word about it to anyone on the Ops. side here. Stirling's R.A.F. confidant made arrangements for converting the aircraft but did nothing about telling any of his colleagues planning the operation. The result was that yesterday they turned on us for information as to the number of men to be dropped, the weight of stores and the mileage and so on, all of which was essential for them to know if they were to fit out the aircraft properly. We all know Stirling's weakness for laying on his plans by the queerest methods. His ideas of organisation are elementary to say the least. I have an idea, however, that he is apt to think out his own operations, try to lay them on without any authorisation from your HQ and then come and offer it to us on a plate. He probably tells you that it is all arranged at this end, whereas in point of fact nothing has been laid on except by verbal arrangement with him, and then we have a frightful period such as is now going on. I fully realise the need for extreme secrecy in this type of operation. Nevertheless the present system cannot continue. I am therefore arranging with R.A.F. that they will not deal with Stirling direct unless he is armed with a written request from GHQ. This branch in its turn will not cooperate until he can produce a written request from you. . . . I am sorry to worry you over this but the result of the present system is that John Merer and I are barely on speaking terms.[6]

27

The reply from the Eighth Army Advanced Headquarters dated the following day was couched in similar terms.

I was very annoyed over the whole business this end, when it transpired that nobody had any information on the subject either. I realised then what had happened. When your first telegram arrived at about two a.m. a few nights ago requesting destination for the modified aircraft, I thought that Stirling had spoken to B.G.S. here and fixed his requirements with you. I am sorry you had all this bother. We cannot clear the matter up until Stirling returns from his present party in three days time. . . . I have sent for Stirling to report here on his return when I shall make the new procedures clear to him. I hope it will work but I have found that his natural impetuousness and importunity make it difficult for him to stick to any procedure![7]

The only conclusion that can be drawn from the above correspondence is that Stirling must have had some sort of operation in mind using parachutes during the period when he was returning from his second visit to Sirte. However, he would not have been around to negotiate with the RAF and would have had to rely on a tenuous radio link with the LRDG main base. He carried out the raid on the night of 24 December and would have taken at least three days to return to Jalo. There was never any mention of further plans for parachuting after the first operational disaster, and the correspondents agree that he was away in the desert. The dates on the letters are quite clear, but a vague possibility is that they refer to the first actual parachute operation and that the dates are confused – by perhaps a month. The mystery remains, but the letters are worth quoting as they reflect the attitude of middle-ranking staff officers to Stirling at the time.

He arrived back in Cairo with an action-packed programme to be fulfilled, leaving little time for the bar at Shepheard's Hotel or for swanning around the night-clubs. The priority was to get hold of some more men, although they would first have to be trained up to SAS standards before being of any use on operations. He had little more than a week, as his intention was to return to Jalo by 10 January. The first call was at MEHQ where Stirling, sporting a full black beard, was shown in to see Auchinleck. The latter had been informed of L Detachment's successes and was amenable to the further plans for action which Stirling was ready to put to him.

At that time, Rommel was in retreat and the Eighth Army expected to enter the major port of Benghazi any day. Stirling, the strategic thinker, had already reasoned that the Afrika Korps would have to re-route their supply lines and that the small port of Bouerat, 300 miles to the west, would become extremely important. He suggested to Auchinleck that he raid Bouerat and destroy any shipping and port facilities. The Commander-in-Chief agreed to the plan and also authorized Stirling to recruit a further six officers and up to forty men. As an added bonus, Stirling was immediately promoted to major. Incidentally, both Stirling and Mayne were awarded the DSO for the series of raids carried out in December 1941.

In Cairo, Stirling based himself at the flat of his brother, Peter, who was an official at the British Embassy. From there he sallied forth about his many errands, meeting the usual obstructiveness whenever he asked for anything. Peter was a few years older and shared David's passion for gambling and the good things in life. His flat became a haven for a clique of young men of similar tastes whom the war had thrown together in Cairo. It was presided over by an Egyptian *suffragi* known as Mo, who was a mixture of hall porter, diplomat, negotiator and general factotum.

The sitting room sofas were a nondescript grey, dotted with cigarette burns and stained with a grimy black line at head level. Haphazardly placed photographs of King George and Queen Elizabeth, cut from a magazine, had been hastily glued to the wall before the landlord came to lunch – to hide the marks of indoor revolver practice. On a table in the hall was a pile of letters, addressed to officers who might be dead, or in prison camps, or coming back at any moment. . . . The bathroom was piled high with uniform cases, captured German ammunition, and a pair of elephant tusks, while a fluctuating assortment of bedrolls, kit-bags and camp beds were strewn about the bedrooms. . . . The food was delicious, the drink unlimited; and in spite of the dated dance records and battered furniture, the flat was considered one of the smartest places to be seen in Cairo.[8]

One highly motivated recruit Stirling did manage to persuade to join him was Fitzroy Maclean, who had served as a diplomat in Russia before the war. By bending the rules which restricted travel to a few miles around Moscow, he had managed to undertake a number of journeys to such places as Samarkand, wonderfully described in his book, *Eastern Approaches*. When war broke out, the Foreign Office refused him permission to enlist, so he resigned and stood for Parliament. Winning his seat as Member for Lancaster, he promptly joined the Cameron Highlanders and was unemployed in Cairo when he met Stirling. A group of Free French troops provided a further source of manpower. They had already been parachute-trained at Ringway near Manchester and were led by the redoubtable Commandant Bergé, whom Stirling later acknowledged as a co-founder of the SAS.

The Frenchmen were keen to join up, but the snag was persuading the French authorities in the Middle East to permit them to come under British command. Stirling said that he had to fly up to Beirut where he met a very senior French general, who promptly said 'Non'. Stirling expostulated that this was as bad as the 'bloody English at M.E.H.Q.', whereupon the general enquired as to his nationality. Stirling replied that he was Scottish and, in the spirit of the 'Auld Alliance', agreement was given. There was, however, a senior general, Catroux, representing the Free French in Egypt at the time, and it is more probable that it was he who interviewed Stirling.

The French proved to be a highly motivated and very brave addition to the ranks of the SAS, but in some ways they were a mixed blessing. They were so keen to get to grips with the enemy that they disregarded much of the training in stealth and guile. As a result they suffered many casualties.[9] It is interesting that they became an integral part of the SAS, wore British uniform and insignia, yet tended to remain a separate squadron – mainly because of the language problem.

At Kabrit in the meantime the L Detachment men were busily making ready for the departure back to Jalo, from where they were to head for Bouerat. As he only had one experienced officer left, Stirling had no option but to tell Paddy Mayne, newly promoted to captain, that he would have to stay behind to supervise the training of the new recruits. Mayne was not at all happy about this, but he agreed with as good a grace as possible. To cope with instruction in demolition work, Stirling had managed to borrow Captain Bill Cumper from the Royal Engineers. He was an older man with a bouncy Cockney wit, who later joined the SAS as a full-time member. Peter Warr was in charge of the parachute course.

The raiding party was to leave by air for Jalo on 11 January, but shortly before this a bedraggled group of men arrived at the base camp. It was Bill Fraser's party, who had an amazing tale to tell of sheer endurance and the will to survive, in the very best tradition of the SAS. Their task had been to raid an enemy landing strip at Marble Arch, the British nickname for a vast triumphal arch erected by Mussolini in the middle of the desert to mark the border of Tripolitania. However, they were unaware that Lewes's party who were on their way to pick them up had been attacked, and there was confusion about the actual rendezvous point. In addition to Fraser, the party consisted of Tait, DuVivier, Phillips and Byrne. The following account is based on Byrne's memoirs.[10]

At what they supposed to be the rendezvous they sat down to wait, unaware that a relief patrol of the LRDG had been sent out to pick them up – from a different place. At the end of the third day their water was running short, as each man had only had two pints in his water bottle. On the sixth day, with the water supply exhausted and no hope of a patrol arriving, they decided to walk to the nearest British lines which they thought were 200 miles to the east. In poor physical condition they set off under the blazing sun, marching for fifty minutes and resting for ten.

We took turns to lead, every one of us setting a cracking pace, determined to match each other's resolution. Weary beyond belief, we kept tramping on, stamping our feet into the soft desert sand and lifting them up again like automata, every step an effort. . . . The sun burned into our eyes from high overhead and was reflected up again from the sand. There was no escape from it and we longed for the luxury of sun glasses or a peaked cap. At dusk we dug holes in the sand, curled up in our blankets and tried to sleep.

They carried on in this fashion for another day and a half, travelling at night to conserve energy. Then they came to an area of salt lakes. They tried to drink the water, which made them sick, and had a go at their own urine until that too simply ran out. The next day they lay up in a cave and managed to distil a small quantity of water which tasted vile. While this was being done, Byrne and Phillips went off on a recce down to the road. There they managed to capture two Germans who had stopped their lorry for a rest, and obtained a jerrycan full of water. They turned their captives loose and, with their bottles full once again, the patrol set off, marching for a further two days. Again short of water, they found themselves after a brief sandstorm in the middle of a group of Italian vehicles. Creeping up on one, all they managed to steal was some food. There was no water – even the radiator tap was rusted up. Marching on that night, suffering terribly from thirst, they came on a track that was not marked on their maps but was used by vehicles.

Letting the first one pass they decided to hijack the next one. Pretending to be an Arab, Phillips stood in the middle of the track with a blanket over his head.

Sure enough along came a vehicle with its headlights on, a small open staff car with two Germans in it, who stopped to investigate the gesticulating 'Arab'. The patrol pounced and grabbed the surprised Germans, only to discover that they also had no water with them. But at least they had the car and, forcing one of the Germans to drive, they set off along the coast road towards Mersa Brega. Traffic began to peter out and they found themselves in the middle of extensive minefields. Attempting to make a detour, the car got bogged down in a salt lake and was abandoned. Still walking east, the party were aware that they were almost at the front line and had to proceed with caution. They heard firing from time to time and at one point were challenged. Some Arabs in a tent gave them a little water and then the exhausted men finally stumbled into an outpost of the King's Dragoon Guards.

That was the first of several epic desert walks carried out by both groups and individuals from the SAS who had become cut off during the campaign in North Africa. The desert was an unforgiving place, but their training had equipped them to cope, when at any time they could have taken the easy way out and walked down to the coast road to surrender. As it was, it took them two weeks to get back to Kabrit, to a great welcome from their astonished comrades, who had given them up for lost.

Back in Jalo, Stirling organized his raiders for their trip. He took a relatively large party with him, including Cooper and Seekings. A newcomer was Flight Lieutenant Rawnsley who had attached himself to L Detachment and went on several of their raids. A further addition were two men of the Special Boat Section (SBS), Captain Duncan and Corporal Barr. They had a folding canoe (folboat) and limpet mines for blowing up any shipping that was in the harbour.

The SBS was another of the 'private armies' that owed its parentage to the Commandos. Lieutenant Roger Courtney joined No. 8 Commando at the same time as Stirling, and during the training period in the latter part of 1940 he organized a small group to train in the Scottish lochs with folding canoes. Most of them ended up in the Middle East with Layforce, and when that was broken up they attached themselves to Combined Operations in Alexandria. They landed agents from submarines and carried out a number of successful demolition raids along the Italian coast. It was this expertise that Stirling intended to harness on his trip to Bouerat.

They set off on 17 January, carried by Captain Hunter's LRDG patrol and navigated once again by Mike Sadler. With them they had a radio truck. Information from aerial photographs would be signalled to Stirling *en route* to give him up-to-date knowledge of the target. The outward journey was quite uneventful as far as the Wadi Tamit, a steep defile leading down the escarpment on to the coastal plain. They were travelling over familiar territory and life on the march had slipped into a routine.

Most of the time we were loaded to do the complete journey which was why we needed well-run-in trucks. Everything was grossly overloaded. We'd carry food, water and petrol. . . . We also carried ammunition. We needed lots of that. . . . And we fed well. We got on to the LRDG ration scale which was different from the rest of the army. They had tinned fruit. They were really twenty-four-hour jobs, those patrols. You were covering as many miles a day as you possibly could, depending on the going. . . . We were continually mending punctures . . . It was really rough going on those jobs. Good fun.[11]

At all times someone was on watch for aircraft, and the nearer the coast they were, the slower they tended to travel, to cut down the dust plume. Stops for meals and for the navigator to fix their position were a welcome break from the jolting ride. A mess tin of McConachie's meat and vegetable stew cooked over a petrol fire was a staple for a bunch of hungry men. When they stopped to sleep, the whole column had to be as well hidden as possible. If there was no natural cover, camouflage nets were slung over the trucks, while the men tended to disperse themselves some distance away, preferably in the lee of a rock. A wise precaution was to send out a party equipped with bundles of brushwood to sweep away the tracks leading to the encampment.

Searing heat during the day and bitter cold at night had to be contended with, and thus regulation dress went by the board. Photographs of the period show groups of men in a motley collection of semi-uniform. Many sported Arab headdress, and sheepskin-lined jerkins were popular at night. In the desert, rank tended to be forgotten as officers were addressed by their Christian names – but back at base it was 'sir' and a smart salute.

Navigation was very much a specialist skill and the maps of the desert were more or less blank. Only the coast, the oases, ridges of hills and the main roads were marked. For the rest, the terrain was mainly featureless sand with the dunes constantly moving.

You had to travel in straight lines and know in what direction you were going. You had to be able to fix your position just like a ship at sea, with sextant and star charts. For plotting a course you had to have an accurate speedometer. You travelled in a series of zigs and zags, keeping a record of it all in a notebook – the bearing on which you were travelling, the time of the start and end of each leg. .... At lunchtime, when everyone was brewing up, the navigator plotted all those little legs on to a map.[12]

On arrival at the Wadi Tamit where Captain Hunter had decided the party would lie up during daylight, the real hard work began. The trucks themselves had to be manhandled down the steep rock-strewn defile and as the men were sweating away at this in the hot sun an Italian aircraft picked them up. Knowing that it would call up the fighter bombers, the convoy scattered into whatever cover could be found. For the rest of the day there were almost continuous air attacks, but as dusk crept over the scene it was discovered that no damage had been done to the LRDG patrol. The wireless truck and its crew, however, had totally disappeared, never to be seen again. Stirling would have to do without up-to-the-minute intelligence of the target area.

The whole patrol drove to a position within about sixty miles of Bouerat, and there the raiding party all piled on to one truck which was to be driven close to the port by Hunter himself. Sixteen SAS and SBS members and four men of the LRDG managed to squeeze on board with the fragile canoe wedged between them. They set off quite cheerily, but when they were within a few miles of the tarmac coast road, the truck hit a gully and gave a sickening lurch. With a loud splintering crack the canoe broke, ending all hopes of damaging enemy shipping. But, optimistic as ever, Stirling realized that there were other tempting targets around. He suggested that the two SBS men should attack the harbour wireless station instead while his men would concentrate on the actual port installations.

Sadler navigated the party to within a mile of the town, and splitting into groups the men headed off into the darkness laden with their bombs. Moving cautiously in among the buildings by the waterfront, they discovered that there were no guards whatsoever. Warehouses were soon liberally festooned with bombs, and on the way out a number of parked fuel-tanker lorries were attended to. Everyone made it back to the rendezvous where they laid up for the day, returning in the evening to pick up the SBS group which had managed to deal with the radio station. On the way back, the patrol drove for several miles along the coast road, destroying another fuel-tanker in the process and roaring through an Italian ambush with guns blazing.

In the end the loss of the canoe had not made any difference as there was no shipping in the harbour anyway. Stirling was puzzled as to why the place was not a scene of feverish activity, but while they had been about their business Rommel was in the process of retaking Benghazi. On 21 January the Afrika Korps launched a massive counter-attack. While the SAS were returning to Jalo a battle was raging and the Eighth Army was in retreat back to the Egyptian frontier. Hearing a BBC broadcast on 30 January, both Hunter and Stirling were worried that Jalo might have been evacuated, as indeed it had. The LRDG had pulled out, leaving a small rearguard party to destroy the remaining supplies. Seeing trucks approaching, the latter made ready for battle, but luckily there was mutual recognition before any shooting started.

The patrol then headed off for Siwa, another oasis 200 miles to the east. This had long been the LRDG's main base with clear water and even a few European houses. It is chiefly remembered by the SAS because they could swim in 'Cleopatra's Pool', a large basin supplied by a spring. From there the SAS returned to Kabrit, where Stirling found much that was not to his liking. Mayne, who had retired to bed when they left, still mourning McGonigal, had contributed little to the training programme. Sergeant-Major Riley was put in charge, and after an altercation with Mayne, Stirling was forced to admit that the Ulsterman's strengths lay in fighting the enemy rather than in dealing with paperwork. The Free French group, however, had been making excellent progress and were well on the way to becoming operational.

Back in Cairo, Stirling found headquarters sunk in despondency, having lost all the gains they had made in December. As the next moonless period was in early March, there was some time for reorganization, and with the Eighth Army dug in defensively along the Gazala line there was no major offensive in the offing. It was therefore decided to mount a series of raids on the airfields in the Benghazi area. Stirling also had a pet project up his sleeve. After the successful penetration of Bouerat, he wanted to explore Benghazi harbour, once again taking some SBS men with him. This was, however, a target of a completely different order, as Benghazi was a large town which would be well guarded and had a civilian population still in occupation. Stirling had little patience with the planning staffs' obsession with large set-piece armoured battles in the desert. He clearly saw that the extended nature of Rommel's supply lines made them extremely vulnerable to attack and that destruction of port facilities would severely limit his ability to wage war. Stirling envisaged a much larger force of raiders with a permanent base deep in the desert, supplied by air, which could descend at will on the coastal lifeline of the Axis forces.

In the background, the fight for control of L Detachment was still rumbling on. On 25 December, Brigadier Whitely, Deputy Director of Operations at MEHQ, had issued a lengthy secret memorandum concerning the amalgamation of the various small clandestine units under one commander. He was referring to the remainder of Layforce which had been formed into the Middle East Commando, the Folboat Section (SBS) and the 'parachute personnel'. His reasoning was that GHQ could not deal with such a large number of small units. His recommendation was that a commanding officer be appointed with an administrative staff. Such a man 'of a certain experience was required for general disciplinary purposes ... some unit commanders such as Stirling want to be absolutely independent and directly under GHQ. Our experience in the past has proved this very unsatisfactory.'[13]

Had this proposal been implemented, it would have had a disastrous effect on the morale and effectiveness of L Detachment. A martinet of a staff officer in charge at Kabrit would have led to the collapse of Stirling's force and the end of any form of free independent spirit. The problem remained, however, that they were still only a tiny remnant of the original unit, which severely limited their ability to carry out large-scale operations. Obviously Stirling had been lobbying hard for new blood. An unsigned internal letter dated 13 February to the operations staff at MEHQ states that Stirling was making arrangements with the Eighth Army for further raids.

It is strongly recommended that after this operation the unit should be allowed to reform up to strength and be retrained as a parachute unit, and it should not be required to operate again before May.

Proposed additions to the war establishment of L Detachment S.A.S. Brigade will be before the W.E. committee on 20 February. It is intended that the unit should consist of two troops each of thirty all ranks, with first reinforcements equivalent to one troop.

This W.E. should allow two troops to be kept permanently up to strength for operations.[14]

This must have been agreed, as on 22 February, Major-General Galloway of MEHQ wrote to Eighth Army Headquarters to inform them that after the next series of operations, L Detachment would be withdrawn to re-form up to strength and be retrained as a parachute unit. It was expected to be ready for operations by 1 May with a strength of two troops. It was also noted that the Free French would be ready to operate by 1 March.[15]

It is clear from the above that higher headquarters placed great emphasis on L Detachment remaining essentially as a parachute unit, and this was in keeping with Stirling's doctrine that his men should be able to arrive at a target by whatever means were most suitable. Although parachutes were not used again by the SAS in North Africa, training in their use continued right up to the end of the campaign.

The whole detachment set off on 15 March from Siwa in the trucks of John Olivey's Rhodesian patrol, heading for the Jebel mountains to the south of Benghazi, a journey of 400 miles. There were some new faces in the party, including Captain Allot and Lieutenant Sutherland from the SBS. In Cairo, Stirling had recruited Bob Melot, a Belgian who had been in business in Egypt before the war. He had become involved with British intelligence and spoke fluent Arabic. At his suggestion, two soldiers from the Senussi tribe, a local Libyan people some of whom served as auxiliaries to the British Army, were included who could act as guides. Lastly, there was Gordon Alston who had previously been in Benghazi when the town had been under British control. Stirling himself was driving a hybrid vehicle that he had obtained in Cairo which became known as the 'Blitz Buggy'. This was a basic Ford shooting-brake which had had the windows and roof removed to turn it into an open truck. It had twin Vickers K aircraft machine guns mounted at the rear and a single one in front. Further modifications for desert travel included a water condenser, a sun compass and a large extra fuel tank. It was painted a drab olive grey to look like a German staff car and even had the monthly enemy air recognition panel painted on the bonnet. The SBS men had a genuine captured staff car with them.

All went well until the patrol reached the area of the Trig al Ab, the old camel track leading into the desert from the coast road where L Detachment had made their rendezvous after the first operation. The track had been extensively mined by the Italians and the captured German staff car ran over one, injuring Lieutenant Sutherland who had to be taken back to Siwa. From there they proceeded to the Jebel mountains and made camp in a pleasant area of trees and plentiful water. The local Senussi tribesmen were bitterly anti-Italian and provided a sheep to roast as a gesture of welcome. The two Senussi soldiers were sent off on a recce and reported back the following day that there was no checkpoint on the road leading into the town.

That night Stirling set off in the 'Blitz Buggy' with his usual crew of Cooper and Seekings, Ken Allot plus two corporals from the SBS with a folding canoe, and Gordon Alston. They simply drove into Benghazi, headlamps blazing, and parked down near the waterfront. The actual port area was wired in and guarded, but the plan was to assemble the canoe outside. However, the water was extremely rough and quite unsuitable for such a fragile craft. They decided to unpack it anyway in case the wind dropped. In order to avoid the hitches of the last trip, they had carried it in its bag, but when unpacked it was discovered that one of the parts was damaged. With regret Stirling realized that he would have to abandon offensive action that night and decided to withdraw without placing any bombs, so as not to jeopardize a future visit.

In addition to Benghazi, a series of raids on the airfields in the vicinity had been planned, but these proved to be a disappointment. Stirling went twice to Benina and found it deserted. Fraser managed to deal with one aircraft and some trucks at Barce, Slonta was too heavily defended and Alston never managed to find Berka Main. As usual it was Paddy Mayne who achieved the best bag, a total of fifteen aircraft at Berka Satellite airfield. The only consolation was that a series of valuable recces had been carried out in an area they had not previously visited.

Back at Kabrit there was time for the planned reorganization. While the unit had been away in the field, the usual correspondence was being exchanged between the various staffs involved, almost certainly without Stirling's knowledge. On 10 March, Lieutenant-General Arthur Smith, Chief of Staff at MEHQ, wrote to General Ritchie at Eighth Army Headquarters. The latter had evidently enquired as to whose command Stirling's detachment came under and Smith informed him that it was his, but that L Detachment would revert to GHQ control on completion of their current tasks. The letter goes on:

It is hoped that this will not be later than approximately 8 April by which time they are wanted back here to get on with parachute training. I have heard that Stirling is planning an operation against shipping in Benghazi. I don't know the details of the plan as it is of course an Eighth Army operation, but I would like to stress the point that Stirling's chief value is that of commanding a parachute force. We are, therefore, anxious that he should not be thrown away in some other role and I hope that any plan he has made will be carefully examined so as to ensure that as far as possible he does not do something foolhardy.

Handwritten at the bottom is a postscript. 'He needs restraining and we can't afford to throw him away.'[16] In the same series of correspondence, General Smith wrote to General Ritchie suggesting that if he had an operation in mind he should consider using the Free French troop as there was a danger of them becoming stale after their period of intensive training.

It is clear that the higher echelons at headquarters regarded Stirling and his men as very valuable, but were also alive to his impetuous nature. Treated as a wayward child who at the same time was exceedingly precocious, he was considerably indulged as long as he continued to sow confusion in Rommel's back yard. The problem of recruiting remained, however, and fighting units were unwilling to give up their most enterprising officers and men. Stirling continued to trawl among acquaintances and friends for likely candidates. One friend was Randolph Churchill, who had come out to Cairo originally with Layforce and had then been given a job of liaison with the press. A large, ungainly and abrasive man, he was not the sort of material to make the grade in the SAS in the normal way, but Stirling obviously had his reasons for taking him on. In spite of his strict interpretation of the principles governing selection, Stirling, as we shall see, was not entirely above using politics to serve his own long-term aims.

A group of recruits was, however, gathered in time to start the formation of a second troop. Most prominent was Captain the Earl Jellicoe, son of the First World War admiral. Other officers included Lieutenants Sandy Scratchley, a well-known amateur jockey, Stephen Hastings and Carol Mather. The expansion also meant a round of promotions for the stalwarts who had been in from the beginning. Reg Seekings, Bob Bennett and Johnny Cooper were all promoted to sergeant and Pat Riley became regimental sergeant-major. Cooper has vivid memories of his introduction to the rituals of the sergeants' mess.

Once you were promoted you had to go to the bar on first entering the mess and drink a pint of whatever drink you designated without taking your lips from the glass. One Saturday morning, Reg and I entered the mess tent and were welcomed by Pat Riley. To me he said, 'Well, young Cooper, I know you don't drink alcohol, so you had better have a non-alcoholic drink.' 'Yes, serjeant major,' I replied, somewhat overawed by the whole occasion. Pat continued, 'We have a drink here which is definitely non-alcoholic – it's called cherry brandy.' A tankard was filled with red liquid and handed to me. At first it was quite sweet and enjoyable, but then I found it sickly and thick. I only just managed to get it down before bolting from the tent just in time to get rid of the contents of my stomach.[7]

The opportunity was taken to get in some leave. Several of the men always stayed in a small hotel in Cairo in Suleiman Pasha Street run by a character they called the 'Honest Greek'. He used to keep their pay packets in his safe and only dole out enough money on a daily basis to see them through, to save them from getting robbed. Stirling himself took over his brother's flat again where the floor would be littered with maps and bits of equipment. At that time there was evidence that the strain of running the unit more or less single-handed was beginning to tell. He was suffering from frequent migraine attacks and had persistent desert sores which refused to heal.

His restless mind had returned to the unfinished business of Benghazi and the possibility of destroying shipping which he had so far signally failed to achieve. This second expedition to Benghazi is not mentioned in any official documents and it has all the hallmarks of a David Stirling private-enterprise job, especially in view of the personnel who were to be involved. The first thing was to get hold of more reliable boats than the fragile collapsible canoes that were capable of withstanding a desert journey. Fitzroy Maclean and Bill Cumper, the engineer, managed to obtain a pair of small black inflatables, with the intention that the team would operate them rather than using SBS personnel. Bill Cumper provided the necessary training in the use of limpet mines and two crews were formed, Stirling with Seekings and Maclean with Cooper. Hours were spent paddling around in the dark on the Suez Canal until they believed they had mastered handling of the inflatables.

Stirling then dreamed up the idea of a true-to-life rehearsal against shipping at Port Suez, without bothering to inform the Navy. The four drove to Suez with the boats and some dummy limpet mines, infiltrated the heavily guarded dock area and launched themselves into the water. They paddled out into the middle of a large convoy that was anchored there, attached the mines and returned to Kabrit for breakfast. There was uproar when the Navy discovered the mines and Stirling had to own up, only to be told that they often dropped small depth charges at random into the harbour and if they saw anything suspicious sprayed the area with machine guns. When told this, Johnny Cooper was not amused. 'We could all have been killed on this exercise. David calmly pointed out that the scheme would have been pointless if the "enemy" had known of our intentions. Reg and I were most vitriolic about the risk to which we had been exposed and hoped that the Germans would be just as inefficient.'[18]

This was typical of Stirling, who was always prepared to bear the risk himself. However, it is only fair to comment that he did place the lives of two of his most valuable NCOs in jeopardy as well as that of an officer whom he could ill afford to lose. One of Stirling's problems was that he was not content to let others do the raiding from time to time, though he had proved his own courage and nobody would have thought the worse of him had he decided to concentrate on sorting out the many administrative problems that beset L Detachment. Taking off on this second trip to Benghazi removed him from Cairo at a time when his influence there was needed.

At the last minute Reg Seekings had to drop out as he had injured his hand when a detonator exploded prematurely. Somehow or other Randolph Churchill managed to wheedle his way into the party, which otherwise consisted of Stirling, Fitzroy Maclean, Gordon Alston, Cooper and Rose. They set out from Siwa in mid-May, travelling in the 'Blitz Buggy' in convoy with an LRDG patrol led by Robin Gurdon. The aim was to raid shipping in Benghazi harbour on the night of 21 May. All went well on the long trip to the Jebel mountains and from there the intrepid raiding party set off for their target. From then on an element of tragi-comedy gripped the entire enterprise. The story of the trip is well known, but certainly bears repeating.

They got down the escarpment on to the coastal plain without mishap and drove along a dirt track beside Benina airfield. Coming to a barrier across the road manned by a pair of bored Italian sentries, Fitzroy Maclean shouted out that they were German staff officers. Then, with headlamps full on, they joined the main tarmacadam coast road. Stirling accelerated and immediately a loud screaming noise came from the front of the vehicle. Something was badly out of alignment which only became apparent at speed. They pressed on, with the noise getting worse, and drove into the outskirts of the town. Alston knew his way around and had therefore taken over the navigation. David Stirling, who was driving, noticed the lights of a car coming towards them. As it passed, he realized that it had slowed down, turned around and was starting to give chase. The faster Stirling drove, the faster the car behind tried to catch up. Directed by Alston, the screaming 'Blitz Buggy' turned off and shot down through the narrow side streets of the Arab quarter.

They parked up among some bombed-out ruins, assuming that they had been rumbled. David gave orders for the food and water to be unloaded and for bombs to be placed on their vehicle. There was nothing for it but to try to make their way on foot out of the town and walk back to the rendezvous with Robin Gurdon. Imagine the scene: the Prime Minister's son, a Member of Parliament and the officer commanding a specialist raiding unit together with their companions, in the middle of the night in a town several hundred miles behind the enemy lines. At this juncture the peace of the night was rent by the sudden wail of air-raid sirens, and as they started to walk off they bumped into some Italian soldiers. Fitzroy Maclean spoke to them and discovered that they were not at all suspicious. Immediately David Stirling ordered Johnny Cooper to rescue their car from imminent destruction. He had to run back in the dark and make safe the Lewes bomb. This entailed replacing the safety pin in the ten-minute time pencil and extracting the detonator, which he managed with only seconds to spare.

Casting around they discovered a deserted building with a garage attached. The car was backed inside and Randolph Churchill and Corporal Rose were left to guard it. The rest managed to walk into the docks through an unguarded gate carrying one of the dinghys. Arriving at the edge of the quay, Fitzroy Maclean attempted to inflate it, only to discover that it had a puncture. The wheezing noise of the bellows had by this time excited the interest of some sentries on a large freighter moored nearby, but Maclean shouted out that they should mind their own business. He and Cooper then set off to get the other boat, which they discovered to their fury was also defective. By this time Stirling had disappeared and they needed to find him as there was only half an hour of darkness left. They bumped into him as they went back through the wire and held a whispered council of war. It was too late to do any worthwhile damage and with some regret they came to the conclusion that it was best not to place any bombs.

They all then went back to collect the boats and their explosives, having an altercation on the way with a black sentry from Somaliland who did not appear to speak much Italian. Gathering up their equipment they marched off again, only to find that two Italian sentries had fallen in behind them. Maclean realized that their only chance was to bluff their way out of the situation, so they set off for the main gate. All had several days' growth of beard and were dressed in a motley collection of civilian clothing. At the main gate they came across a sentry who was upbraided by Maclean for his slovenly appearance and ordered to call the guard commander. A sergeant then appeared pulling on his trousers. He received a dressing down for not keeping a proper guard. What if they had been English saboteurs, Maclean demanded. That fantastic proposal was greeted with a smirk.

With a final torrent of abuse, Maclean dismissed the man and they simply walked out of the main gate into the town. Back in the deserted house, which Randolph Churchill had christened No. 10 Downing Street, they made themselves as comfortable as possible for the day. Corporal Rose had tried to fix the car but discovered a bent track rod end which was beyond his capabilities. As the day wore on, more and more people came out into the streets. Looking cautiously out, the intruders found that they had holed up directly opposite the main German headquarters.

In the afternoon, feeling bored, Stirling decided to go for a walk. Wearing dark glasses and dressed in a polo-neck sweater, corduroy trousers and desert boots, with a towel round his neck, he simply strolled out of the house and down towards the harbour. There he saw a pair of motor torpedo boats tied up at one of the quays and decided to attack. As dusk fell they all piled back into the 'Blitz Buggy' and, with the track rod end still giving forth its loud protesting wail, drove down to where the torpedo boats were moored. The aim was to toss bombs into them as they drove past, but when they got there they discovered that the sentries were being changed. An attack would have been tantamount to committing suicide, so reluctantly Stirling gave orders to leave the town and head back for the rendezvous with the LRDG. A few days later they were all back at Siwa, somewhat disappointed. On the plus side, the expedition had proved once again that it was not difficult to penetrate an enemy-held town and carry out a reconnaissance. However, it was obvious that if they wished to attack moored shipping, they had to find suitable boats from which to do so. Stirling nevertheless felt that the trip had been English saboteurs, Maclean demanded. That fantastic proposal was greeted with a smirk.

3
Expansion and Regimental Status

After his arrival back from Siwa, Stirling was driving from Alexandria to Cairo when he was involved in a serious road accident. Overtaking a convoy of lorries he struck one of them and his car landed in the ditch. A journalist who had hitched a lift was killed, Fitzroy Maclean ended up in hospital for three months and Randolph Churchill had to be invalided back to England with a back injury. Luckily for the future of the SAS, Stirling himself escaped with a damaged wrist – which had the virtue of stopping him from driving for while. Anyone who knew him will gladly testify that he was a disaster behind a steering wheel. Nevertheless he had no time to nurse his injury as he was pitched once again into the struggle to recruit more men and to retain the independence of his unit.

Before departing on the expedition to Benghazi, he had written a memorandum addressed to the Director of Military Training at MEHQ on the future of L Detachment.[1] It had been proposed to form two parachute battalions recruited from Indian personnel serving in the Middle East. Stirling's stated purpose in writing the memo was to suggest that recruiting his unit up to strength should take precedence over the equipping of these new battalions. He pointed out that on 3 March 1942, his original recruits were down to three officers and thirteen men, and if brought up to strength they could be far better employed as a raiding force than as instructors for the proposed Indian units. From this it is clear that the idea of breaking up L Detachment had been floated at headquarters, using the excuse of a shortage of manpower. Stirling sensibly argued that it was illogical to form two new battalions when the few men he required were being denied him.

He went on to propose that he be allowed to recruit five men from each infantry and motorized battalion in the Middle East as had been previously agreed by the Adjutant General's branch. In addition he suggested that he could obtain further men from the SBS and the Middle East Commando, and that the Free French be permitted to expand to the same size as L Detachment. In this way he could form three detachments, controlled through a slightly expanded headquarters staff.

This excellent piece of reasoning then went into their future operational role. Stirling naturally stressed, as he had all along, that the SAS must remain outside any airborne brigade, otherwise they ran the risk of falling into the operational vacuum which lay between the small specialist raid and the larger tactical operation. Here he was stressing forcibly his original principle that his unit should never be used tactically, only strategically. He claimed that an expanded L Detachment could on the same night simultaneously attack the ten most important aerodromes in Libya and Cyrenaica, the bulk storage points on the enemy lines of communication and the main airfields in Crete, Rhodes, Greece and possibly Sicily. This would entail at least 30 targets to be attacked by between 120 and 160 men.

Stirling finished by saying that this would be the maximum expansion he envisaged, as any further growth would lead to a lowering of standards. If the above conditions were not acceptable, then those officers who had recently joined should be allowed to return to their original units as the terms on which they had volunteered no longer applied.

The background to the above was set out in a letter from the Operations branch at MEHQ dated 22 February, in which they proposed the use of L Detachment as parachutists in a tactical role, for seizing and holding ground in co-operation with other forces landing by sea or advancing across the desert.[2] This went directly against Stirling's concept of the role of his men, which had still not been clearly understood or even accepted at headquarters. Operational planners viewed L Detachment as a parachute force pure and simple, which should be available to them for short-term aims. When they got their way, disaster ensued.

The rump of Layforce had been formed into the Middle East Commando, which later became known as I Special Service Regiment. This included a number of parachute-trained personnel whom Stirling was naturally keen to recruit. He sent an extract from his memo to the officer commanding the Middle East Commando on 10 May, requesting

45

the transfer of Captain Schott and the trained men. Schott was attached to the Raiding Forces Staff G(R) at headquarters, which at the time was led by Colonel Pembroke. This request was obviously not well received, for at the bottom of the letter is the hand-written comment: 'At first sight it certainly appears a bad case of body snatching, but I assume this is not so.'[3]

A few days later, Colonel Airey of Middle East Commando wrote angrily to the Operations branch at MEHQ concerning the above. 'While we are anxious to assist L Detachment in any reasonable way, we feel you will agree that the suggestions contained in the attached letter are unreasonable and cannot be entertained.' He went on to say that they had been at great pains to build up an efficient fifth-column unit and should not be expected to give up their best men as soon as they were trained. All that could be agreed would be to loan trained men for a specific operation. The last paragraph reads: 'We should be grateful if the suggestions contained in the attached letter could be firmly suppressed. We also consider that requests for assistance should come through the Deputy Director Operations as arranged and not be dealt with in a haphazard way between unit commanders who are presumably not in the full operational picture.'[4]

One can of course see Colonel Airey's point, although the fact remains that his Commando was unemployed at the time and Stirling was about to be required to undertake an important series of raids. All Stirling could obtain was the loan of one officer and twelve other ranks. When he had departed for Benghazi he had left Lord Jellicoe in charge at Kabrit, and on 20 May Jellicoe wrote to MEHQ asking for an order to be issued to the Commando to release the men. This was granted subject to the firm understanding that 'they remain a sub-unit and are not absorbed into L Detachment and lose their identity'.[5]

So much for David Stirling's attempts at body-snatching. He did, however, obtain the services of another small unit of extraordinary provenance, the Special Interrogation Group (SIG). This had been formed by Captain Buck and consisted of a dozen Jewish immigrants to Palestine, all of whom spoke fluent German. They had volunteered and were prepared to masquerade in German uniform, knowing full well the risks they ran if caught. To make sure that their knowledge of enemy military procedure was correct and up to date, Buck had also recruited a couple of Afrika Korps men who had been taken prisoner. In early March the SIG moved to Kabrit and were put through a hard training programme to fit them to operate in the desert alongside the SAS.

In May 1942, the Eighth Army was dug in along the Gazala line on the defensive. Churchill had been egging Auchinleck on to attack, and so relieve the pressure on the beleaguered island of Malta which was threatened with starvation unless convoys could get through. The further west Allied aircraft could be stationed, the easier it would be for them to protect the sea lanes which were vulnerable to enemy air power based in Sicily and Crete. Malta was the key to the Mediterranean and the only hindrance to Rommel's supply lines which stretched back to Italy. If the island fell the Germans would have a free hand throughout the area. Auchinleck claimed that he was not ready to attack, but was ordered by Churchill to do so, to coincide with the running of two convoys to Malta in the moonless period in June. One was to start from Alexandria and the other from Gibraltar.

Headquarters was fully aware of the need to provide as much protection as possible and Stirling submitted a plan to mount a whole series of raids on airfields on the night of 13 June, mainly making use of the Free French who were longing to get to grips with the enemy. Only a few stalwarts of the original L Detachment were included, together with Stirling himself and Paddy Mayne. A subsidiary raid on Crete was to be carried out by Commandant Bergé, Lord Jellicoe and three Free French NCOs.

The various groups who were to carry out raids along the North African coast gathered at Siwa at the beginning of June, aiming to leave for their targets between the 6th and the 8th of the month escorted by LRDG patrols. Stirling, Mayne, Lieutenant Zirnheld and a Free French group left with Robin Gurdon for their familiar base in the Jebel mountains overlooking Benghazi. Stirling was accompanied by Seekings and Cooper as usual, and planned to drive to his target in the 'Blitz Buggy'. Unfortunately this was damaged on the way when they ran over a mine and had to be abandoned. As it happened, on 2 June the following was issued by MEHQ: 'It has been decided that Major Stirling, L Detachment S.A.S. Brigade, will not take part in active operations with his unit until further notice. The reason for this decision is to enable Major Stirling to train other officers who will be available to take his place should he become a casualty.' Yet the same day another signal stated, 'This letter is cancelled.'[6]

Paddy Mayne had Lilley, Warburton and Storey with him. The three raiding parties laid up in the mountains during the day to observe their targets and descended on to the coastal plain as darkness fell. Stirling, Cooper and Seekings headed for Benina which they knew from past experience was a major repair base. They got on to the field without difficulty in the middle of a bombing raid by the RAF on Benghazi, and sat there while their leader gave them a lecture on deer-stalking in the Highlands. There was no reason for not talking, and the two young soldiers listened to the tall quietly spoken officer as he explained the skills of silent movement. Once the commotion had died down, he told them to break the time pencils and get to work. They placed bombs on two isolated aircraft and then headed for the hangars where they expected to find some worthwhile booty. Creeping around from hangar to hangar and dodging patrolling sentries they successfully ensured the destruction of several more aircraft, brand-new crated engines and machinery. As a final gesture they came upon the guardroom. Stirling kicked open the door and threw in a grenade, apparently saying 'Here, catch.' As the bombs in the hangars started to go off they beat a hasty retreat across the field.

Scramblimg up the escarpment leading into the mountain ridge of the Jebel, David was forced to call a halt, saying that he was feeling unwell. The three of them sat down and watched the fantastic firework display on the airfield that they had caused. The ammunition in the burning aircraft went off, weaving patterns of coloured tracer against the massive fires caused by burning fuel stores. Then the anti-aircraft guns opened up, firing into the air against an imagined air raid. Tiny figures in the distance, silhouetted against the flames, rushed about trying to exting-uish the blazing hangars. Johnny Cooper thought it almost impossible that three men carrying only sixty small bombs between them had created such havoc and destruction.

It was at this stage that Reg and I realised that David Stirling was suffering from one of his frequent migraine attacks. ... Reg and I each took one of his hands and we led him, staggering and half blind, to the top of the ridge. There we crawled into a well camouflaged position and Reg managed to find a disused well which was covered by a wooden lid with metal hinges. Reg tore this apart and produced wonderful cool refreshing water which revived us all.[7]

Back at the rendezvous Stirling felt better after the usual tea laced with rum and was pleased that at last his team had managed to destroy some aircraft. Paddy Mayne, however, had not had such good luck. He had headed for Berka Satellite field, whose commandant had obviously taken the lesson of previous raids to heart. As they headed for the first aircraft they were fired on by a sentry. Then others opened up and a miniature battle ensued. Mayne and his group crept away, leaving the guards to fight it out between themselves. By then Stirling's bombs had started to go off and Zirnheld was involved in a battle on the nearby Berka Main aerodrome. All this activity alerted the Germans and they sent out patrols to locate the SAS. Mayne's party spent the rest of the night dodging the enemy and, as dawn broke, they discovered that they were in the middle of a large military camp. They split up and simply walked through in broad daylight. All of them made it back to the rendezvous where they also met up with Zirnheld's group who had managed to account for eleven aircraft.

What happened next was a classic example of foolhardy daring which very nearly came badly unstuck. When together, Stirling and Mayne had an urge to compete; now the former started to rag the latter about his success. They decided to drive down to view the destruction and shoot up anything worthwhile along the road to Benghazi. The transport problem was solved by the silver-tongued Stirling who persuaded Robin Gurdon to lend him one of the LRDG Chevrolets, swearing that it would be returned intact. Mayne drove with Stirling beside him in the passenger seat. Crammed in the back were Cooper, Seekings, Lilley, Storey and Karl Kahane. The latter was one of Captain Buck's SIG men, a Palestinian Jew who had served for several years in the German army. His job was to talk them through any roadblocks.

At nightfall they set off down the escarpment and in holiday mood were soon bowling merrily along the coast road. Just as they got to Benina airfield, Lilley shouted out that there was trouble ahead – a string of red lights across the road. They came to a halt at a barrier, assuming it was manned by a few nervous Italians. The reality was a group of at least a dozen efficient-looking Germans armed with machine pistols. An NCO clutching a grenade marched up to the barrier and Kahane told him that they were coming back from the front and were in a hurry. In the back, the rest of the group clutched their tommy-guns and eased pins out of grenades. The German NCO demanded the password. Kahane gave him the one for the previous month, explaining that they had been out in the desert for six weeks. He even embellished the story in a flood of fluent German, explaining that they had captured the British truck and had had a hard time of it at the front. Then, just as the sentry was starting to relax, Mayne cocked his Colt .45 automatic. This was followed by a series of similar clicks from the back. The sentry, faced with the prospect of instant death, ordered the barrier to be opened, and the Chevrolet drove through.

A few miles further down the road they came on a group of Italians with rifles waving at them to stop, obviously having been alerted by the German post. Mayne put his foot down and Seekings dispersed the enemy with a burst from the Vickers machine gun in the back. It was clear that they were in a trap but still they went on until they reached a roadside filling station and café. Men leaped from the back and swiftly placed bombs among the enemy transport parked there. Then as they roared away they machine-gunned the buildings. Lights were already showing back down the road along which they had come, and in the distance there was the sound of shots being fired. It was time to depart.

They decided to cut across the coastal plain and head for a wadi that would provide a route back to the top of the escarpment. Driving fast, their truck jolted and lurched over the uneven desert towards safety. Dodging a motorized patrol sent out to cut them off, they made the crossing point and, as dawn broke, managed to shove and coax the truck up the steep track. Just as they reached the top and comparative safety, Lilley yelled for everyone to bale out. He had smelt burning and realized that the time pencil in one of their bombs had activated. They had twenty seconds. Johnny Cooper still has vivid memories of that frightening moment. 'I have never left a vehicle more quickly in my life. I flew over Paddy's shoulders, bounced off the bonnet and rushed away like a madman. The explosion, seconds later, bowled us all over. The truck was blown to kingdom come. Miraculously nobody was hurt. Once again, Allah had been generous.'[8]

It was said afterwards that the remains of the truck could have been packed into a kitbag. Somewhat bruised, the raiding party made their way back to their rendezvous on foot, with David Stirling wondering how he was going to explain away the loss of the truck.

They set off for Siwa, arriving on 21 June only to discover that the LRDG was in the process of abandoning the place. Tobruk had fallen and Rommel's troops were surging towards Egypt. The Eighth Army had suffered a crushing defeat and was digging in along the Alamein line, only sixty miles to the west of the Nile.

At Siwa they met up with Lieutenant Jaquier, one of the Free French, and his patrol, who had managed to blow up ammunition dumps at Barce, and a solitary Lieutenant Jordan accompanied by Captain Buck. Their party had set off to raid the Derna and Martuba airfields in a convoy of four German vehicles driven by SIG men with the French hidden in the back under tarpaulins. They got to their target area without any great difficulty, the false 'Germans' being apparently accepted at checkpoints. On the night of the attack, Jordan and Corporal Bourmont each with four men set off to raid the two airfields at Derna. They travelled in a truck driven by a German called Brueckner, one of the ex-Afrika Korps men, who was accompanied by two of the Palestinian Jews. Once on the first aerodrome, Brueckner stopped and made some excuse about engine problems, saying that he had to try to get a key for the toolbox. He went off and shortly afterwards the truck was surrounded by German troops. It was clear to Jordan that they had been betrayed. He was grabbed by one of the enemy as he looked out to see what was happening, and then one of his men threw a grenade. As it exploded, Jordan managed to free himself and escape.

He reached the rendezvous safely where he met up with Captain Buck. Realizing the extent of the betrayal, it was clear to both of them that they could not hang around so close to the target area hoping for survivors. Both men left hurriedly for their meeting place with the LRDG where they waited in vain for a week for stragglers to come in. Jordan later discovered that two of his party had managed to get away and had made for the rendezvous point which the group aiming for Martuba was to use. This too had been given away by Brueckner and was surrounded by a German patrol.

Bergé and Jellicoe had mixed fortunes on their expedition to Crete. Their party consisted of three French soldiers, a Greek guide and another young Greek who had volunteered. A submarine took them to the island and the party made a successful landing in rubber boats. After an arduous approach march they reached Heraklion airfield, but found that it was well guarded. While trying to get through the perimeter they were discovered by a German patrol, but in a flash of pure genius, one of the Frenchmen feigned a drunken snore. The patrol marched on and the raiders slipped on to the airfield where they managed to place bombs on the twenty-one aircraft, some vehicles and a fuel dump. At dawn they were well hidden in a cave and the following night they were able to march to within a few miles of the beach where they were to be picked up. The next day, Jellicoe and the guide went off to a nearby village, arranging to meet Bergé and his men on the beach. As the Frenchmen left their hiding place to head down to the shore they ran into several German patrols and, after giving a good account of themselves, were captured when they ran out of ammunition. Lord Jellicoe and the guide made a successful rendezvous with the submarine and returned safely to Alexandria.

Stirling sent his men from Siwa back to Kabrit and he himself made for Cairo, where he arrived in the midst of what became known as 'The Flap'. The air was full of the smell of burning documents, and in some quarters there was talk that the Germans would be on the Nile within a matter of days. Based at his brother's flat as usual, Stirling launched himself into a feverish round of activity. He realized that Rommel's lines of communication had become so stretched that they would be even more vulnerable to attack, and every man detached to guard them would be one less to face the Eighth Army at Alamein. The Luftwaffe was in possession of the former RAF forward airfields in the Mersa Matruh and Fuka area. It was agreed that the SAS would carry out a series of raids on these airfields in early July, leaving only a week to prepare for departure. Yet in spite of the rush, all the officers found time to attend the wedding of their engineer, the cheerful Bill Cumper.

The beginning of July 1942 marked a radical change in the operational style of the SAS. Previously the policy had been to raid during the moonless period of each month, transported by the LRDG and returning to base in between to reorganize. David Stirling felt that this was a waste of time and resources and that it should be possible for a large group to maintain itself in the desert for a period of several weeks. His idea was to set up a self-contained base inland from the coastal plain from which they could raid on an almost nightly basis. To do this, however, they would need their own transport. During his week in Cairo he managed to lay his hands on a number of newly arrived jeeps, known at the time as Willy's Bantams, and some 3-ton Ford trucks. He also managed to secure the transfer of Mike Sadler from the LRDG to act as chief navigator.

L Detachment at the time consisted of around one hundred men, most of whom had been through the basic training course. Stirling reasoned that if the Germans did continue their attack and captured Cairo, the whole unit could retreat south from its desert base, thus avoiding capture. Everyone worked with a will to equip the expedition and load up with enough food, petrol, water and ammunition for three to four weeks in the field. The fitters laboured to modify the jeeps for desert travel and to a completely novel specification. In its final version, the SAS jeep must surely have been the most cost-effective fighting vehicle ever developed.

The basic armament consisted of twin Vickers K machine guns mounted front and rear. Some versions substituted for the front pair a .5 Browning heavy machine gun, and some jeeps had a single Vickers fitted in such a way that the driver could operate it. A water condenser was fitted to the front of the radiator, an extra fuel tank was added and the suspension strengthened. The entire vehicle was festooned with a bewildering array of kit. Steel sand channels for getting out of soft ground, water containers, jerrycans, spare drums of Vickers ammunition, camouflage nets and the crew's personal kit and weapons had to be stowed. Normally three men travelled in the jeep although it was more comfortable with only two. The jeep's firepower was quite staggering, as the Vickers had a rate of fire of over 1,000 rounds per minute. The ammunition drums were loaded with a mixture of incendiary, explosive and tracer rounds, which proved to be a lethal cocktail when used against aircraft and road transport.

The convoy of thirty-five heavily laden vehicles left Kabrit on 3 July and drove to Cairo. For the first time they had a doctor with them, Malcolm Pleydell, who had been posted to L Detachment and had completed his parachute training. His book, written in 1945 when memories were fresh, gives some wonderful descriptions of life with the SAS. He said that the departure from Kabrit was a delightfully vague affair with nobody really having any clear idea of how long they were going to be away for, and not giving two hoots anyway. 'The men were going to see some action, or "have some fun" as they put it, and that was quite enough to render them light-hearted and care-free.'[9]

He went on to describe the drivers swearing as they got snarled up in the midday Cairo traffic.

> The men were in great form, however, singing and shouting; and you could not help laughing as you watched them remove certain attractive articles from the stalls of the street vendors. For you would see the jeep in front of you proceeding along the Egyptian highway in a very dignified manner, when all of a sudden it would swing in to the side of the road near a fruit-barrow, a large brown hand would shoot out, and a succulent water-melon would disappear as the jeep accelerated away again.

The whole convoy parked in the side streets near Peter Stirling's flat where they were to meet their leader. The place was in its usual chaotic state with people coming and going, discussing racing form or poring over maps. Outside the men whiled away the time brewing tea on the pavement. They then drove north to Alexandria for a final briefing at Eighth Army Headquarters, with the Germans only forty miles away.

Stirling was told that the army was about to launch an attack and that the destruction of aircraft on the forward landing fields was vital. It was also arranged that he would be given accurate intelligence by radio on a regular basis.

To get to their proposed operational area the convoy had to take a difficult route. The so-called Alamein position ran from the sea southwards to the edge of the Qattara Depression, a deep chasm 150 miles long and with very steep sides. Robin Gurdon, who met them at army headquarters, was to guide the party through the southernmost part of the British lines as they hoped that by skirting the edge of the depression, they would avoid any main concentrations of German troops. The first problem occurred when they left the road and moved off into the open desert. The sand proved so soft that the overloaded lorries repeatedly bogged down. Sadly, Stirling gave orders for much of the equipment to be offloaded and sent back to Kabrit. After that they made better progress and managed to slip undetected out into the emptiness. Three days after leaving Alexandria the whole column met up with Timpson's LRDG patrol, which was waiting for them. They parked the vehicles and camouflaged themselves for the night, before settling down to cook. Then Stirling called everyone together to explain his plans.

He intended to carry out six raids the following night, to coincide with the proposed Eighth Army offensive. Four patrols would head for the coast between Bagush and Fuka, led by Stirling and Mayne. Jellicoe and Zirnheld were to go to El Daba, and the sixth group led by Captains Warr and Schott would aim for Sidi Barrani. The last two officers were both parachute instructors and were on their first operation. Each party would be accompanied by an experienced LRDG officer to act as guide to the target area.

The next day the whole unit moved to a forward rendezvous point about sixty miles inland from the coast. From there the various groups would split up and make their way individually. The largest section under David Stirling, who had with him the repaired 'Blitz Buggy', headed for the escarpment above Fuka. There he proposed to leave a radio truck for communications with the rear. They drove through the dreadful remains of a recent battle, the desert littered with burned-out vehicles and smashed equipment. Then to David Stirling's fury they saw a convoy of light armoured vehicles moving across their line of advance. It appeared to be British and was probably one of the highly mobile units known as 'Jock' columns which were used to carry out harassing attacks on the German flanks. Stirling had not been told that such a unit was operating in the target area, despite the fact that its presence might stir up the enemy.

Once on the escarpment, a message was received that the El Daba airfield was not being used, so Stirling redirected Jellicoe and Zirnheld to strafe the road instead. Stirling and Mayne then separated from the others. They were only about forty miles behind the German lines and were thus much closer to the front line than was usual on their operations. Accounts differ as to who was present and how many vehicles they had, so what follows is an approximation of what actually happened.

They travelled in three or four vehicles, Stirling in the 'Blitz Buggy' and Paddy Mayne's crew in one or two jeeps. In Virginia Cowles' account they also had a 3-tonner with supplies and extra men inside. Once down on the road they headed for Bagoush, which ironically was the airfield from which they had taken off for their first disastrous operation the previous year. According to Cowles, the plan was that Stirling and his crew would set up an ambush on the road, which intelligence had informed him was being used by a stream of enemy traffic. Mayne's party was to attack the airfield on foot.[10]

Two large boulders were rolled on to the road and they sat down to wait, guns at the ready. Not a single vehicle passed, but after some time they heard the roar of bombs going off at the airfield. That was music to their ears as they counted up to twenty-two explosions. The flames lit up the skyline but there was no sign of Mayne. When he did appear through the darkness, he was in a foul mood, and told them that several bombs had failed to explode. Johnny Cooper on the other hand, says that they drove straight on to the airfield.[11]

What is not in dispute is that a new method of attack was discovered that night. Like warships firing broadsides, the 'Blitz Buggy' and the jeeps roared over the airfield blazing away with their twin Vickers K guns. Several more aircraft were set ablaze, and as they drove back on to the road without a shot having been fired against them, Stirling and Mayne were cock-a-hoop. On the way back to the rendezvous the next morning, however, they suffered a sad loss. They were spotted by two Italian CR 42 aircraft which came into attack and managed to destroy the 'Blitz Buggy'. Clinging to Mayne's jeep the men made their way safely back to camp.

The other parties had met with mixed success and it was obvious that the enemy were mounting far stronger guards on their airfields. Jordan managed to destroy eight aircraft, but Fraser was forced to abandon his attack. Zirnheld succeeded in placing bombs on a few trucks, while Jellicoe sat beside the road and saw nothing. The last to come back were Schott and Warr who had had the greatest distance to travel. They had been guided down to Sidi Barrani by Lieutenant Timpson of the LRDG. Captain Schott's report of the trip, originally classified 'Most Secret', is one of the few after-action reports to have survived from the SAS in the North African campaign.[12] The following quotations illustrate some of the frustrations and misunderstandings that could hamper the best-laid plans.

The attack on the airfields was carried out as ordered on the night of 12/13 July. Capt. P. E. Warr in charge of one party, consisting of Sgt. Almonds, Priv. Meyer, Priv. Ridler – objective L.G. [landing ground] 05; and myself [Schott] with party consisting of Sgt. Brough, Corp. White, Corp. Baird, Priv. Thompson – objective L.G. 121. We were to be dropped by L.R.D.G. approx. four miles from our objective at 23.50 hours on night 11 July 1942.

Unfortunately owing to errors on maps, Warr's party found themselves some ten miles from the target and myself only two to three miles away. We had some two hours sleep that night, then proceeded to align our position before first light. Capt. Warr found an excellent observation post, but our party was not so successful. We came across an enemy patrol with a L.M.G. [light machine gun] and a dog, before we could reach a point to observe the landing ground. Owing to this unfortunate meeting and our certainty of being observed, we decided to take up an all-round defensive position and fight it out when a recce. party arrived.

They lay up all the following day, expecting to be attacked at any moment, but no enemy showed up. Aircraft landing at LG 05 were seen and a recce of LG 121 confirmed that it was only used as a decoy at night. Captain Schott's party was picked up by Timpson on the night of 13 July, but Warr's failed to arrive.

The following night a recce. party went out to see if Capt. Warr had arrived. He had not. In the meantime, Timpson and myself had planned to strafe the road at Bug Bug on the night 15/16 July. We set out to carry this out and passed through our old rendezvous on route. There we found Capt. Warr and party, all very tired and fatigued owing to lack of food and water for four days.

We set out the same night for Bug Bug, but failed to make our objective owing to the bad nature of the ground for the vehicles. We all returned to the RV and spent next day servicing vehicles etc. . . . All information re. enemy transport aircraft was wirelessed back to L.R.D.G. headquarters.

Timpson then went off to strafe the road, leaving Schott with his men, a 3-tonner and a broken-down jeep. The following day they saw a column of vehicles approaching from the wrong direction to that from which Timpson should have appeared. Schott decided to make a break for the main rendezvous point with Stirling, and set off in the 3-tonner with his men. On the way they were strafed unsuccessfully by a Messerschmitt 110. It was only later that they discovered that the mysterious column, which in the heat haze had looked like twenty-five Lancia trucks, had in fact been Timpson's patrol.

Back at the desert base, David Stirling had earlier been busy on the radio, signalling the deputy director of operations on 10 July regarding jeeps.

Experience in present operation shows potentialities of twin mounted Bantams at night to be so tremendous to justify immediate allocation of minimum fifty Bantams to L repeat L Detachment for modification to be effected immediately on my return. Fear owing to miscarriage of plan, only forty aircraft and some transport destroyed to date.

This was followed on 13 July by another, similar in vein except that the demand was somewhat scaled down.

IMMEDIATE. Willys Bantams great success. Most urgent that twenty five exactly same type be despatched for modification to fix mounts for twin Vickers guns and sun compass. All gun mountings must be welded, not brazed. We will require six new Ford three tonners, proportionate desert equipment to look after increased scale of operations. Withdrawing force from operations to collect Bantams and three tonners 16th. Operationally vital. We return here with smallest delay.[13]

Underlying his pleasure at the success of the new methods and the way in which the jeeps had proved their worth, was Stirling's anger at the lack of intelligence received from the Eighth Army. First there had been the matter of the 'Jock' column. Then there was the news that El Daba airfield was not being used, though Jellicoe had brought back a couple of German prisoners who freely volunteered the information that this was the most important of their forward airfields. Stirling sent a blistering series of signals to both the Eighth Army and MEHQ which seem to have had some effect. On 17 July, Lieutenant-General Corbett, who had replaced General Smith as Chief-of-Staff, signalled the Eighth Army:

1. The first verbal report of Major Stirling on his recent operations shows that they have been imperfectly connected with other operations of Eighth Army. First, his plan for the destruction of the bulk of the German airforce was frustrated through his being ordered not to go to Daba or Fuka, when his parties were within striking distance. Secondly, he states that he was never told that there were indications of German intentions to occupy Siwa and Giarabub. An omission which might have and may still cost him serious casualties to personnel north of the Qattara depression.
2. It is considered that his present and future operations should be more carefully coordinated and controlled both in planning and in operations by H.Q. Eighth Army with whom he should have a direct point to point wireless link. He has been given instructions to this effect.[14]

To be fair, the Eighth Army was in a state of some confusion and was having to plan the defence of the Nile Delta. The concerns of a small group of desert raiders probably came very low in the order of priorities at the time. The whole affair, however, was symptomatic of the consistent refusal of planning staffs to understand or even try to appreciate the potential of the SAS, encamped within easy striking distance of the enemy's lines of communication.

Stirling, while battling with distant headquarters, was also busy setting up his next series of raids, designed to rectify the omission of Fuka and El Daba. Five parties set out on the night of 11 July, led by Martin, Jellicoe, Jordan, Fraser and Mayne. The bag was a meagre one. Stiffened defences beat off several parties and only Mayne and Jordan managed to destroy any aircraft – twenty-two between them. Fraser, trying to emulate the success of the jeep raid, managed to drive into a trench, which alerted the enemy defences. They fired away with wild abandon, but luckily with little accuracy, and he was able to extricate himself. A tragic loss was the death of Robin Gurdon who had been out with Zirnheld and Martin's Free Frenchmen. In an air attack on the way back he had been killed while firing away at the fighters who were strafing his truck.

After two weeks out in the desert it was time to take stock. Owing to the forced abandonment of supplies on the way out, food and ammunition supplies were running low. Stirling thus decided to abandon operations for a while and send a strong party back to base to collect stores and the new vehicles he had requested. There were no aircraft available for air drops at that stage of the war in the desert, which was a pity when one bears in mind that only two years later SAS parties operated in France for anything up to two months behind enemy lines, totally reliant on parachuted stores.

The Germans had closed off the route to the north of the Qattara Depression which the convoy had taken on their outward trip, so they were forced to make a risky and difficult passage through the bottom of the Depression itself, which consisted of salt marsh. This had a solid crust generally capable only of bearing the weight of a man, but the LRDG had successfully worked out a route for vehicles. Stirling and Jellicoe went on ahead in jeeps, leaving Mayne and Scratchley to follow with the 3-tonners. It was a nightmare of a trip, the trucks constantly breaking through the crust and having to be dug out. During the day the heat at the bottom of the vast bowl was the most intense any of them had ever experienced, but the whole convoy made it back to the Delta.

The turn-round in Kabrit was a rapid one. Seekings had been left behind to supervise the equipping of the new vehicles, and by dint of bullying and gentle persuasion, had managed to get them ready for service. Eight days after leaving, the new convoy was back at the desert rendezvous, much to the relief of those who had been chosen to stay behind. They were beginning to run short of food and water, but had not been disturbed by the enemy. Their only foe had been the usual plague of flies who had to be slaughtered on a regular basis. Otherwise the men had passed the time reading and keeping an eye out for aircraft.

Stirling, who arrived back bearing gifts of tobacco and rum, had made a lightning tour of headquarters, complaining of his treatment by the Eighth Army, and had managed to extract promises of greater co-operation in future. As will be seen, this proved to be illusory. He was, however, full of enthusiasm for the resumption of operations as soon as possible and had come up with a new idea. It had been discovered that the airfield at Sidi Haneish, near Fuka, was in constant use and full of aircraft. The following night the moon would be full and he planned to take a force of eighteen jeeps directly on to the airfield in two columns and shoot up anything they found. A subsidiary raid would be carried out on Bagoush airfield to create as much of a diversion as possible.

Having seen the effect of jeep fire-power during the earlier raid, Stirling was convinced that such a massed attack would achieve spectacular results. He outlined his plans and, with only a day to prepare, the camp erupted into activity. The two column leaders were to be George Jellicoe and Paddy Mayne, each with seven jeeps behind them. Mike Sadler as navigator would travel in the centre and the whole formation would be led by Stirling himself. His job would be to identify targets and signal them to the formations by firing coloured Very lights. The columns would be about forty yards apart and would fire outwards.

The night before the raid, Stirling decided on a practice run. In the middle of the desert miles behind enemy lines, the columns of jeeps drove around in the darkness concentrating on holding formation. In the front in Stirling's jeep, Johnny Cooper fired off the Very lights, causing the whole formation to wheel right or left, and then they opened fire. The noise was certainly deafening as the coloured tracer spewed out into the darkness. The drivers had the hardest job, concentrating on holding their positions and keeping out of the way of the front and rear gunners.

The jeep force set off in the late afternoon of 26 July, with about forty miles to cover to the coastal plain. They travelled in open formation, picking their way around obstacles and frequently having to stop to mend punctures. After about four and a half hours of driving, Sadler calculated that they were one mile away from the target, although there was absolutely nothing to see. Stirling ordered the crews to take up formation and, bumping over the rough ground in the moonlight, they headed for the airfield. Then suddenly the whole scene was illuminated as the runway lights were switched on. Above them they heard the drone of engines as a German bomber swept in to land. They had not been spotted after all. Without a moment's hesitation Stirling's jeep headed for the runway, the fighting formation behind him. The guns opened up with a deafening roar, and immediately the lights were switched off. That did not matter for soon burning aircraft lit the scene as though it were daylight. On down between the lines of parked aircraft they went, like Nelson's battleships at Trafalgar, firing broadsides to left and right. The enemy opened up with machine guns, but the glare of fires made it difficult for them to aim accurately. Stirling's jeep was hit and came to a stop. Cooper leaped out and opened the bonnet, to discover that a round had penetrated the cylinder block. Sandy Scratchley's jeep came past and picked them up. His rear gunner lay sprawled dead in the back.

In the midst of all this, Stirling calmly called a halt so that he could give orders for further targets. Then they were off again wheeling around the perimeter shooting up buildings and yet more aircraft. As they finally drove away from the scene, Paddy Mayne was observed to jump out of his jeep, run across to a parked aircraft and place a bomb on the wing.

Once off the airfield, Stirling gave orders for the jeeps to split up and make for the rendezvous separately, as he was sure that the following morning the sky would be full of angry German fighters out looking for them. Casualties amounted to one man killed, a few flesh wounds and two jeeps destroyed. The SAS claimed forty aircraft, many of them Junkers 52 transporters which Rommel relied on for bringing up supplies. The raid had been a triumphant vindication of Stirling's theory that his unit could operate regardless of the phase of the moon and could get on to heavily defended targets. His only real criticism was directed at the wastage of ammunition; he felt that some of the gunners had simply blazed away instead of taking precise aim at a target. A few of the jeeps had run out of ammunition before the raid had finished, which was hardly surprising considering the high rate of fire of the Vickers K guns.

The various crews all made it back to the base camp without difficulty, but they learned that Zirnheld had been killed. Returning from the raid, the three jeeps of the Free French party had been attacked by Stukas. All three vehicles continued to function but young André Zirnheld had been hit twice. He was buried in the desert by his friend and comrade, Martin, who found the following prayer which Zirnheld had written among his possessions. It is given in translation here as a tribute to a brave man who fought under British leadership for the freedom of his country.

> I bring this prayer to you, Lord,
> For you alone can give
> What one cannot demand but from oneself.
> Give me, Lord, what you have left over,
> Give me what no one ever asks you for.
> I don't ask you for rest,
> Or quiet,

Whether of soul or of body;
I don't ask for wealth,
Nor for success, not even for health perhaps.
That sort of thing you get asked for so much
That you can't have any of it left.
Give me, Lord, what you have left over,
Give me what no one wants from you.
I want insecurity, anxiety,
I want storm and strife,
And I want you to give me these
Once and for all.
So that I can be sure of having them always,
Since I shall not always have the courage
To ask you for them.
Give me, Lord, what you have left over,
Give me what the others want nothing to do with.
But give me courage too,
And strength and faith;
For you alone can give
What one cannot demand but from oneself.[15]

Back at base, Stirling had every intention of staying out in the desert and carrying on his raiding operations. Immediate plans were for four parties to leave for the area directly behind the German lines in jeeps, to attack supply dumps and soft-skinned transport. On 31 July, he again signalled his frustrations about lack of support from the Eighth Army to the Deputy Director of Operations: 'As impossible function more than 20% of capacity under existing arrangement with army, I suggest that L detachment comes under temporary R.A.F. control. ... LG.64 confirmed suitable. Effect landing operation night 4/5.'[16]

Experience had taught Stirling that the RAF were generally much more co-operative about supplying him with reliable intelligence. Even so it is quite a rarity for the commander of an army formation voluntarily to suggest coming under the command of the RAF. The latter part of the above signal refers to a plan that Stirling had concocted with the RAF during his last brief visit to Cairo. This was to use his old friends of 216 Squadron to resupply his force by landing their Bombays in the desert.

There is a lengthy signal in existence from the officer commanding the LRDG to Brigadier Davey at MEHQ which clearly illustrates the difficulties of communication and the clash of competencies.[17] As we have seen, the SAS came under the orders of the Commander-in-Chief, but were attached to the Eighth Army for immediate operational control. Requirements for aircraft had to be dealt with by the Air Officer Commanding Western Desert, and all David Stirling's communications had to be routed via the LRDG, who ended up as piggy in the middle.

The signal is dated 1 August 1942 and states that a stream of messages had been coming in from Stirling in the desert regarding the shipment of supplies by Bombays for delivery on 4 August. As these messages were 'not always entirely clear', they were summarized. On 30 July Stirling signalled the AOC Western Desert requesting three Bombays to proceed to one of two possible landing grounds on the night of 4 August. He stated that the loading list would follow. This was received, but was addressed to Warr at Kabrit via the operations branch at MEHQ. In case it had become corrupted in transmission, it was repeated. It included the following, and the list provides an indication of requirements after a lengthy period in the desert: 400 gallons of petrol, rations, 2 tow chains, 2 tins of Lockheed brake fluid, 8 jeep spare wheels and tyres, 200 1 lb. plastic bombs and fuses, beer, cigarettes, rum and 2 crates of lime powder. The list was a lengthy one.

The summary goes on to say that Stirling had asked the Eighth Army for thirty more jeeps that had already been ordered. Then a signal for Stirling from Tactical HQ, Eighth Army, said that the RAF component there was unaware of the resupply operation, but that they would endeavour to arrange the aircraft. The final message in the saga reads:

> 1230 hours, 01.8. Stirling to Tac. Army. Supply landing operation already laid on to last detail with Mid. East before departure. Only initiation of operation to have come from Eighth Army. Feasibility dependent on recce. by R.A.F. officer accompanying me who has decided L.G. [Landing Ground] to be O.K. Will make further arrangements direct with R.A.F. as Eighth Army by error apparently not informed.

But then the blow fell. Stirling was told that a new operation was being planned and that he must bring his entire force back to base. The Bombays would fly in, carrying only enough petrol to enable the vehicles to be driven back to Kabrit, while the bulk of the men would return in the aircraft. Stirling was naturally furious as he had no idea what was in the pipeline. He protested, but MEHQ was adamant. There were major changes afoot in the nature of the war in the Middle East and, like it or not, the SAS was going to be placed under far firmer control. The four patrols planned by Stirling were sent out, but only for four days. When they returned, they discovered that the main body of men had already flown out and that a party of drivers under Scratchley was waiting for them to join the vehicle convoy south through the Great Sand Sea.

4

Last Days in North Africa

On 30 July 1942, the Prime Minister arrived in Cairo with the Chief of the Imperial General Staff, Sir Alan Brooke. Auchinleck's attacks against the German and Italian positions along the Alamein line had petered out, and Churchill determined on a change of command in the Middle East. Auchinleck departed for India, to be replaced by General Alexander. Montgomery was appointed to command the Eighth Army.

Thus the offensive, in support of which the last series of raids by the SAS had been carried out, was a failure. Stirling arrived back in Cairo feeling depressed. He had proved that he could maintain his force in the desert over a considerable length of time, which by air supply could easily be extended. Yet inefficiency in the command structure had hampered his efforts to keep up the pressure on Rommel's supply lines, and in being ordered to return to base, he felt the grip of official interference. It is easy to understand and sympathize with his predicament, but he was only a major commanding a very small force. Jealous eyes were still being cast on the SAS, and various staff departments were determined to bring its activities under far stricter control.

When Stirling found out about the plan in which his unit was to be involved, he was even more furious. He discovered that he was being hoist with his own petard. After his two trips into Benghazi, he had submitted proposals for a further expedition to destroy once and for all the harbour facilities. One of his ideas had been to take a small naval party with him who would attempt to scuttle a ship in the harbour mouth. He had discussed this with a certain Colonel Hazelden who had been operating as an agent in the Tobruk area. It would seem that it was Hazelden who sold to the planners at MEHQ the idea of delivering a

65

final knock-out blow to the two main German supply ports, Tobruk and Benghazi. This fitted in with the general view that the Eighth Army could hold Rommel at El Alamein but would not be ready to attack before November.

Comparatively large 'irregular forces' were earmarked to carry out the raids, which would be commanded by Hazelden for Tobruk and Stirling for Benghazi. Two subsidiary actions were to be included. The LRDG would raid Barce airfield as a diversion and the British-led Sudan Defence Force would be used to retake Jalo Oasis to secure a more favourable return route for the raiding parties.

The SAS was to be augmented by a number of men from 1 Special Service Regiment, who were untrained in desert raiding, and also by a naval party and even two tanks. Such an unwieldy force consisting of some 200 men was to travel to the target area in 40 jeeps accompanied by another 40 3-ton lorries carrying supplies. The entire plan violated every principle upon which the SAS had been founded, yet Stirling agreed to go along with it. When asked why, he replied, 'I was bribed.'[1] The offer from the planners was that his unit would be expanded and that he would afterwards be given a free hand to harry the German supply lines all along the coast.

The Benghazi raid will be discussed in some detail later. First though, while in Cairo, Stirling met some illustrious company. Both he and Fitzroy Maclean were bidden to dine with the Prime Minister at the British Embassy on 8 August. Among those present were the Ambassador, Sir Miles Lampson, the veteran South African politician, General Smuts, the new Commander-in-Chief, General Alexander, and Sir Alan Brooke. Why Stirling and Maclean were invited remains a bit of a mystery, but it is probable that Randolph had mentioned them to his father. After the meal, Stirling had a private conversation with the Prime Minister, and put forward his views about the future of his unit in strong terms. He also spoke critically about the Benghazi raid, in spite of having been warned not to by an officer in the Operations branch. Apparently they regarded Churchill as a poor security risk.

The following morning, Major Stirling received a note from Churchill's private secretary, which read:

I have been asked by my chief to ask you to let me have for him without further delay, the short note which he called 'on what you would advise should be done to concentrate and coordinate the work you are doing'. I have been asked to make sure this is in my hands today.²

Stirling replied under the heading Most Secret:

1. I venture to submit the following proposals in connection with the reorganisation of the Special Service in the Middle East. Special Service may be defined as an action ranging between but not including the work of the single agent on the one hand, and on the other, the full-scale combined operation. The scope of L Detachment should be extended so as to cover the functions of all existing Special Service units existing [sic] in the Middle East, as well as any other Special Service tasks which may require carrying out. Arising out of this, that all other special service units be disbanded, and selected personnel be absorbed as required by L Detachment. Control to rest with the officer commanding L Detachment and not with any outside body superimposed for the purpose of coordination, the need for which will not arise should effect be given to the present proposals. ... The planning of operations to be carried out by L Detachment remains as hitherto the prerogative of L Detachment.

2. I suggest that the proposed scheme would have the following advantages:

   a. Unified control to eliminate any danger of overlapping, for which there has already been one unfortunate instance.

   b. The allocation to L Detachment of specialists taken from Special Service units would greatly increase the scope of the units' training and thereby augment its value to men who inevitably gain versatility and resourcefulness.

   c. The planning of operations by those who are going to carry them out, obviates delay and misunderstandings which happen to be caused by intermediate stages, and makes for the speed of execution which in any operation of this kind is an incalculable asset. It also has obvious advantages from the point of view of security.³

It is not often that a major commanding such a small force gets the opportunity to present his views to the Prime Minister. Indeed that evening he was once again invited to dine at the Embassy. The background to the document has to be sought in Stirling's fear that he might be absorbed into some top-heavy bureaucracy like Combined Operations or SOE. That fear was a very real one and, in view of his connections at a high level, it is probable that he was aware of what was going on.

During July, the Chief of Staff at MEHQ wrote to Auchinleck regarding the future of 1 Special Service Regiment.[4] He defined the need for special forces in the area: first as troops for post-occupational duties in captured territories; second, as 'small raiding parties of the thug variety, for which we have L Detachment S.A.S. Brigade and the Special Boat Section'; and finally as raiding parties on a larger scale which was the original purpose in retaining the old Middle East Commando.

The Chief of Staff continued by stating that he was convinced that with a short period of special training, an ordinary infantry battalion could be employed in the Commando role. It was clear to him that 1 Special Service Regiment was unsuitable; the three operations it had carried out had all been unsuccessful. He therefore suggested that it be disbanded, and that selected volunteers be allowed to join L Detachment and the SBS.

From Stirling's point of view this would have been quite satisfactory, but he smelt danger in the following proposals. It was that a Special Forces Depot be formed at Kabrit, to be commanded by a lieutenant-colonel. The latter would have overall administrative control and would be responsible to MEHQ for advising on technical and operational matters. It was this sort of in-between authority that he could not tolerate as he felt that it would only increase the existing element of confusion. If there had to be some sort of overall commander, he naturally felt that this should be himself.

During August, life at Kabrit was full of bustle. New jeeps had to be modified for desert travel, a vast amount of stores had to be sorted out and the new recruits had to be given at least some elementary training. The remaining original members of L Detachment formed the core of the unit, all by that time promoted to NCO rank, under Pat Riley, the sergeant-major. Stirling himself flitted between Kabrit and Cairo, becoming increasingly worried about the size of the operation and the number of people who seemed to know about it. He had a premonition that the enemy might be waiting for them.

To get to Benghazi, the convoy had to travel from Kabrit into Cairo and then head south to El Kharga and Kufra. From there they would skirt the south of the Great Sand Sea and cross it at its narrowest point at Zighen. Then they would head due north, bypassing Italian-held Jalo, to the rendezvous point in the Jebel mountains. This meant travelling 1,400 miles. The actual mission was to storm into the harbour area, eliminate the garrison and destroy anything they found there. The force, as finally assembled, consisted of 231 men, 45 jeeps and an unspecified number of 3-tonners, probably around 40. The two tanks were from the 10th Hussars and their job was to force a way through any roadblocks.

The unit split up into three convoys for the long march to Kufra. Paddy Mayne's convoy left first, followed by Sandy Scratchley's and finally the group led by Bill Cumper. In the latter was the doctor, Malcolm Pleydell, travelling in a brand-new specially equipped medical jeep. He has left the most graphic description of the Benghazi raid and of some of the personalities involved, including several pages on the trip to Kufra.

I can picture the convoy now: the little navigating jeep in front, the solid three-tonners rolling along steadily, and the jeeps scampering about at the back. I can remember the long cloudless days when we drove for mile after mile over desert that stretched out around us as flatly as an unruffled sea; the way we would pull the throttle out so that the needle stood up straight at the figure forty, and then would laze back with our legs stretched out across the bonnet. . . . We were like a convoy of ships, save that our horizon was a trembling yellow band, and there was not even a wake to indicate our movement.[5]

Travelling on that journey, however, was not always so idyllic. They hit many patches of soft sand and wasted hours unloading vehicles, shoving them up to the top of dunes and reloading again. The greatest joy was to make camp for the night and savour the smell from the cooks' fires as supper was prepared.

The three convoys arrived at Kufra to find the small oasis packed with men and vehicles, as the other raiding groups had also gathered there. The Benghazi force again split into three columns and left for the Jebel at intervals from 4 September. First to go was Paddy Mayne's group which was guided by the LRDG S1 patrol commanded by Lieutenant Lazarus. All parties managed to get across the narrow neck of the Great Sand Sea and arrived at their rendezvous in the mountains on 9 and 10 September. They had escaped detection from the air, in spite of the large number of vehicles involved, but had had to abandon the tanks which had become hopelessly bogged down in the sand. A number of the 3-tonners were also lost, as a result of mechanical breakdowns and mines.[6]

On arrival, the leading group met up with Bob Melot who had been hiding in the area for several weeks gathering intelligence. Melot had recruited an Arab whom he proposed to send into the town to find out if the garrison had been alerted. When the spy returned he stated that there were roadblocks and minefields on all approaches to Benghazi. This confirmed everyone's worst fears, and Stirling radioed back for instructions. He was simply told to ignore bazaar gossip and to carry on as planned.

The raid itself was an unmitigated disaster. Melot's Arab spy was engaged to guide everyone to the Wadi Fetilia which was the only practical route down the escarpment on to the coastal plain. They set out at dusk on 13 September and soon discovered that they were in the wrong wadi. Several trucks were damaged by their sumps hitting rocks, and by the time everyone had managed to back out and find the right route, the night was slipping away. The LRDG patrol which was to carry out a diversionary raid on Benina airfield decided to turn back as there was no longer enough time to drive there and back in darkness.

The main force should have got into the town under the cover of a raid by the RAF, but by the time they were at the foot of the escarpment, this was almost over. As they picked up speed along the main tarmac road it was already 3 a.m. They had not gone far before the leading vehicle halted at a metal pole stretched across the road, and the rest of the convoy bunched up behind. There was no immediate sign of the enemy, but on either side of the barrier there were coils of barbed wire and freshly dug soil. It was then that Bill Cumper spoke his immortal lines. All those who were present agree that he got out of his jeep, lifted the pole and said in a mock solemn voice, 'Let battle commence.'

And commence it did. The enemy opened up, but their fire was inaccurate. The SAS replied with their twin Vickers and the night was lit up by tracer. Jim Almonds' jeep caught fire and several men were wounded. Silhouetted by the blaze, the jeeps frantically reversed still firing, and Stirling gave the order to withdraw. It was by then too late to make for the safety of the mountains, and the scattered groups of jeeps had to hide as best they could at the foot of the escarpment. Higher up the wadi, the doctor was already busy. A small group had gone to attack a minor fort and in the battle Melot and another officer had been injured.

When dawn broke, the jeeps and trucks were scattered over a wide area, camouflaged under bushes and in the lee of rocks. Enemy aircraft swarmed overhead, methodically searching each gully and outcrop. An ammunition lorry exploded with a roar. When darkness fell, the men drove off up the escarpment and made for the rendezvous, spreading themselves out as widely as possible. A small section was left behind to pick up stragglers, as there were still quite a number of men missing. Jim Almonds had become separated from the rest and was taken prisoner. He subsequently escaped and rejoined the SAS to fight in Europe as a commissioned officer.

The following two days were a continual nightmare of bombing and strafing. Truck after truck was set ablaze and each fire acted as a homing beacon for more enemy aircraft. Pleydell and his small group of medical orderlies carried out a number of quite complicated operations whilst crouching under bushes and being machine-gunned from the air. The plight of the injured was an unenviable one; several of them could not be moved. They had to lie on their stretchers in the back of a lorry listening to the din of battle all around them.

Finally, as dusk fell, the aircraft departed and Stirling had to take stock of the situation. He had lost twenty-five trucks and their valuable contents, plus twenty-odd jeeps. Four men had been killed. There was also a group of wounded men, some of whom would not be able to make it back to Kufra. It was a difficult decision for all concerned, but four of the most seriously injured were left with one of the medical orderlies, who was instructed to contact the Italians the following day.

The rest divided themselves up amongst the remaining transport and set off with only enough petrol to cover the 400 miles to Jalo. If the Sudan Defence Force had been unsuccessful in capturing this oasis, they would be in grave difficulty, stuck in the desert without fuel, water or rations. The trip took four days but there was no further molestation from the air – just the pangs of thirst and meagre rations each evening. On arrival at Jalo they found that the battle was still in progress, but enough petrol was obtained to get the convoy safely back to Kufra.

No blame seems to have been attached to Stirling at the time. The official report states: 'To have forced his way into Benghazi when the enemy was obviously ready for him would have achieved nothing and would have involved the loss of his force.'[7] The final tally was given as six killed, eighteen wounded and five missing. The Tobruk raid had been an even worse disaster and almost the entire force employed had been wiped out. Only the LRDG raid on Barce had paid off, with the destruction of a number of aircraft.

Who was responsible for the breach of security that alerted the garrison at Benghazi has never been established. The leak could have come from any one of a large number of sources, as far too many people knew about the plans. There was an interesting sequel to this in 1967 when a book written by Len Deighton was published and sections of it were serialized in the *Sunday Times*.[8] In the book Deighton quite openly accused David Stirling of having 'insisted upon talking about the raid during two social gatherings at the British Embassy in Cairo . . .' Stirling felt this inferred that he had loosely prattled at a cocktail party, whereas the gatherings referred to were private dinner parties. He sued the author, the publisher and the *Sunday Times*, who settled out of court. Stirling wrote his account of the affair and a refutation which was published in the regimental journal.[9]

Part of the surviving force was left at Kufra, while others were flown back to Kabrit to refit and resupply. A memo by a lieutenant-colonel on the staff (whose signature is illegible) to the Director of Military Operations at MEHQ gives an insight into what was in the pipeline for L Detachment, 'which went out on the last operation hurriedly and ill organised. An attempt is being made to provide them with some form of base organisation without which they cannot develop full effectiveness. Before further operations are undertaken, it is most advisable to reform the squadron which it is intended to use shortly.'[10] This is the first reference to what was to become A Squadron, commanded by Paddy Mayne. According to Pleydell, Mayne was allowed to choose its members and naturally selected the core of the original L Detachment veterans plus a few of the newcomers.

The memo continues by stating that if the group who were to be part of the first squadron returned by road, they would waste too much time and should therefore be flown back to collect the new vehicles and supplies needed at Kufra. 'Those who are to be returned to unit as unsuitable can come overland together with those who will be required to form a second squadron to operate in a later phase.'

Previously, L Detachment had been loosely organized into troops on a raid-by-raid basis as required, certain men attaching themselves to particular officers. There had never been enough personnel to form anything as large as a squadron. On his return to headquarters Stirling discovered there were plans afoot which would have an important impact on the future of his force. Throughout August and September, a vicious battle had been waged between the Director of Military Operations and the Director of Combined Operations at MEHQ for control of all raiding forces. The former won, which was all to the good as far as the SAS was concerned. Part of the battle was over the carcass of 1 Special Service Regiment already alluded to.

General McCreery, Alexander's Chief of Staff, wrote to his superior in late September regarding the future of special units in the Middle East.[11] In referring to L Detachment, he stated that 'it has had conspicuous success in the past and its morale is high.' His recommendation was that L Detachment, the SBS and 1 Special Service Regiment should all come under one commander.

The personality of the present commander, L Detachment S.A.S. Brigade, is such that he could be given command of the whole force with appropriate rank. In view of this I make the following suggestion. That L Detachment S.A.S. Brigade, 1 S.S. Regiment, Special Boat Section should all be amalgamated under L Detachment S.A.S. Brigade and commanded by Major D Stirling with the rank of lieutenant colonel.

The above suggestion was adopted and the additional decision was made to raise Stirling's unit to the status of a full regiment of the British Army, to be known as 1 SAS Regiment. This was officially announced in MEHQ Operational Instruction No. 14,521, dated 28 September 1942.[12] However gratifying this may have been for Stirling, one distinct step was taken to clip his wings and stop his independent lobby of senior officers. The regiment was to come under the Director of Military Operations who would exercise control through a new department to be known as G (Raiding Forces) (G(RF)). 'No other contact is permitted with the general staff at G.H.Q., the naval C-in-C Mediterranean (including his staff) or H.Q. R.A.F. M.E. unless arranged by G (Raiding Forces).'

The organization of the new regiment was somewhat confused as there were two totally different tables of establishment.[13] What emerged was an HQ squadron and four combat squadrons – A, B, the Free French (later known as C Squadron) and the Folboat Section (the SBS, which became D Squadron). Each squadron was divided into three troops, each with three sections. HQ Squadron had an administrative depot troop, an intelligence troop, a signals troop, a parachute-training troop and a light repair section. The war establishment was initially set at 29 officers and 572 other ranks.

Oddly enough, Stirling might well have ended up as a brigadier with an even larger command. On 3 October, a certain Brigadier McLean wrote to the Director of Military Operations suggesting that the 'S.A.S., L.R.D.G. and 1 L.R.S. be combined and that armour, artillery and infantry the size of a regiment should be added for seaborne operations. C.O. S.A.S. Regiment to be appointed to command.'[14]

This reorganization was all very well, but David Stirling's priority was to find enough men of sufficient calibre to fill all these vacancies. In the Eighth Army, Montgomery had wielded his axe and a fresh sense of purpose infused everyone from staff officer to private. He had fought the successful battle of Alam Halfa at the beginning of September, and planning was in full swing for a major offensive at El Alamein to take place in early November.

In charge of G (RF) was Colonel 'Shan' Hackett, later to become General Sir John, a soldier with a considerable track record in battle, and one who was sympathetic to Stirling's ideas. The immediate priority was to keep up an unrelenting pressure on the enemy supply lines. To do this, Paddy Mayne's A Squadron, largely composed of experienced raiders, would be available to start out from Kufra. He also took a few new recruits, notably three young lieutenants, Harry Poat, Tony Marsh and Johnny Wiseman, all three of whom went on to make their mark on the regiment. A second squadron, B, would be formed at Kabrit from fresh volunteers and put through a crash training programme. At the time, Stirling regarded three and a half months as necessary to train SAS personnel. One of his key officers departed at around this time. Fitzroy Maclean was sent off to Persia, and his exploits there fall outside the scope of this book, although he was employing skills learned with the SAS.

Stirling took on a number of officers and men from the disbanded Special Service Regiment and the rest were distributed elsewhere, as few of them were suitable for SAS training. He then went off to the desert to see Montgomery, accompanied by Shan Hackett, to ask permission to hand-pick volunteers from the various regiments in the Eighth Army. The name Stirling does not even feature in Monty's memoirs, but Virginia Cowles has written a fair account of what happened.[15] They were received in one of the general's famous caravans, and Stirling outlined the contribution his unit could make to the coming battle. He then said that in order to do so he needed 150 experienced men. The abrasive new general brushed aside Stirling's request and proceeded to give him a lecture. He told Stirling that he needed his best men himself and he was not going to allow them to join the SAS after the 'failure at Benghazi'. This needled Stirling and the meeting ended on a sour note. The only redeeming feature was that he and Shan Hackett had lunch in Monty's personal mess and ran up a goodly drinks bill which they charged to the teetotal general. According to Virginia Cowles they met Freddie de Guingand, Montgomery's Chief of Staff, whom they both knew, after lunch, and he let slip that an Anglo-American landing was planned in Algeria, code-named Torch. That set David thinking.

On 28 September, a planning meeting discussed the tasks that the Eighth Army required to be carried out.[16] A Squadron was to be divided into six parties, to attack targets all along the coast between Tobruk and the immediate area to the rear of the enemy front line. At the same time, the remaining members of the SBS would be landed by boat in the El Daba area to attack supply dumps and motor transport. After the main battle, A Squadron's tasks would be to harass the retreating enemy forces and signal bombing targets to the RAF. It was stressed that Colonel Stirling would not take part in these raids owing to the information he possessed.

The basic outline as agreed at the planning meeting was enshrined in an operational order, No. 146, issued by MEHQ and addressed to Stirling.[17] This laid down specific objectives for each party in A Squadron in three phases, specifying that the squadron would come under the command of the Eighth Army on 16 October. The first phase was concerned with a variety of raids against the Tobruk–Mersa Matruh railway and other lines of communication, ammunition dumps and road transport. Phase two envisaged a period to regroup and resupply, with phase three coming into force immediately the main battle started on 23 October. Then, the patrols were to concentrate on airfields and ambushing retreating traffic on the coast road. What is interesting is that for the first time individual patrols would have radio communication via jeep-mounted No. 11 radio sets, but in the event of breakdowns they would also each take two pigeons.

There were many subsequent raids, carried out by small patrols, and it is difficult to build up a comprehensive picture of exactly what took place. Mayne's squadron assembled at Kufra in dribs and drabs by the beginning of October. There they set up a rear headquarters and resupply dump. Mayne's plan was to take his fighting patrols out into the Great Sand Sea and establish a forward base, from which they could sally out and harass the enemy. Malcolm Pleydell spent most of October and November there, and described the scenery.

> Our dwelling place was clean and very isolated; for we were tucked away in a deep hollow, and all around the tumbling sand dunes encompassed us about. The soft beauty of their symmetrical curves, and the sinuous outlines, accentuated as they were at morning and evening by the glancing rays of the sun, provided an artistry one could not readily forget; and I shall long remember the delicate rosy flush, reflected for a moment from the smooth sand surfaces, as the radiance of the sunset dwindled and died like a funeral pyre.'[18]

They were well placed for taking the offensive, being 200 miles behind the enemy front line and 150 miles south of the coastal plain. During the whole time they were there, they were not bothered by aircraft. A handwritten memo in the Public Record Office says that on 30 October Mayne was ordered to leave the railway alone and concentrate on destroying petrol supplies. His achievements to date were listed: charges laid on the railway in the Tobruk area on the night of 14 October; a failed attempt to do the same near Sidi Barani which resulted in the death of the patrol commander, Lieutenant Shorten; two further breaks in the railway on 24 October; nine breaks on 29 October, and finally another attack on the track on 31 October.[19]

One of the epic stories in the history of the SAS comes from this period of raiding the coastal railway. A comparative newcomer, David Sillito, was assigned as navigator on a patrol which was sent to destroy the track near Sidi Barani. They were spotted by the enemy, who attacked, and in the ensuing mêlée, Shorten was killed and Sillito got separated from the others. He found himself totally alone, with a water bottle, a compass, a revolver and no food. He could of course have taken the easy option and given himself up, or laid up along the coast somewhere until the advancing Eighth Army caught up with him. Instead he decided to march south into the Great Sand Sea, a distance of nearly 200 miles, to rejoin his squadron.

He trudged for eight silent days, trying to rest when the sun was at its hottest and using a greatcoat as a tent. On the second day his water gave out and he resorted to drinking his own urine, until that too ceased. On the eighth day, with his feet torn and bleeding, he reached the northern edge of the Great Sand Sea and, following some jeep tracks, came across an A Squadron patrol. Taken back to Kufra to recuperate, he was fit and well again within two weeks.

The Sillito story had a strange sequel, however, as can be read in a file of signals traffic for the period.[20] On 31 October, a message was sent from Kufra to the SAS base at Kabrit: 'Regret Parachutist Sillito died in hospital at Kufra today. He was brought in by L.R.D.G. suffering from diphtheria.' On 2 November, a second signal was sent to Kabrit from Kufra: 'Sillito and Laird arriving Cairo by plane 1530 3rd November, both very ill. Please provide transport from Cairo, truck not rail.' The following day, MEHQ signalled Kufra as follows. 'Sillito arrived Cairo today by air. Do not understand your message of 31.10. reporting his death from diphtheria. Signal name and number of parachutist who died in hospital at Kufra.' The mystery was finally solved in the reply from Kufra. 'Sillito reported missing when Shorten killed. He was picked up by patrol and returned to Cairo [untrue]. Sillet died in hospital as per my casualty report at 31 October. Two different men entirely.'

While Paddy Mayne and his men were busily raiding, Stirling had finally succumbed to his desert sores and had been hospitalized in Cairo. He was not so ill, however, that he was unable to keep up with what was going on. As is well known, the Battle of El Alamein was a resounding victory and established Montgomery's reputation. As his troops advanced to the west, raiding priorities altered. Sandy Scratchley's patrol was sent out to raid petrol dumps in the El Daba area and found itself caught up in the back yard of the retreating Germans. The patrol took some prisoners and drove through the lines until they met up with a British unit, who refused to believe they were who they said they were. As there was little point in returning to the rendezvous now that the pursuit had started, they went back to Kabrit.

El Alamein was really the beginning of the end of the desert campaign. At the other end of North Africa, on 8 November, Anglo-American forces had landed in Algeria, and Rommel had retreated right back to the Agheila position, where he dug in on the defensive. Montgomery too had paused to reorganize his lines of communication, but planned a final assault to dislodge the Afrika Korps and drive them right back into Tunisia in December.

Paddy Mayne's veteran A Squadron returned from the Great Sand Sea to Kufra for a few days in mid-November, having successfully raided airfields around Gazala, familiar territory from the past. They then moved west to a new holding area at Bir Zalten, sixty miles south of the German positions at El Agheila, which had been recced by Mike Sadler who had flown up there during the first week in November. In the meantime, Stirling was back in action at Kabrit, preparing to bring up B Squadron, which was formed from the new recruits who had finished a somewhat abbreviated training course. This squadron was commanded by Major Vivian Street and included few of the experienced operatives from the old L Detachment.

By this stage of the war, Stirling, with his usual grasp of the wider strategic picture, realized that he must plan for the future of the SAS Regiment. As far as immediate operations were concerned, he and Hackett had agreed that the two squadrons plus some of the Free French would use their new desert base to harry enemy road traffic along a 400-mile stretch of the coast road. He felt that if they could make travelling at night dangerous, the enemy would be forced to move in daylight, thus becoming targets for the RAF. But his main thoughts lay elsewhere, as he realized that the desert campaign was coming to an end. Thus he had already started to make dispositions for the future. David Sutherland, much to his annoyance, had been left out of raiding activities and was put in charge of training the SBS contingent for water-borne operations in the Mediterranean. His force had recently been strengthened by a group of Greeks, who became known as the Sacred Squadron, the latest recruits to the SAS empire. In December, Sutherland took his whole party up to Beirut to continue their training in Greek caiques and other odd vessels. Stirling had also made arrangements for Paddy Mayne to take his squadron to the Lebanon for ski training, as soon as their operational commitments were ended.

Stirling had always envisaged the Free French contingent as the nucleus of a French SAS regiment which would assist in the eventual liberation of their country. It is clear even at this early date that he had his eyes on a brigade structure, because his brother William, 'Bill', was in process of raising 2 SAS Regiment in Algeria. In December, the 1st SAS had a total strength of 83 officers and 570 other ranks. It was no longer a 'private army', and was still actively recruiting. The only component that had faded from the picture was Captain Buck's Special Interrogation Group, 'owing to difficulties in recruiting'!

In spite of Shan Hackett's protestations, Stirling insisted on accompanying B Squadron to their rendezvous with Paddy Mayne's force, leaving Lord Jellicoe behind in command of the base camp. They left Kabrit on 20 November and for the first stage of the journey were able to bowl down the coast road as far as Agedabia, by then firmly in British hands. From there they headed south into the desert to Bir Zalten where they arrived on 29 November. The doctor, Malcolm Pleydell, noted that David Stirling did not look well. The months of dangerous living had taken a savage toll of his health and he had bad conjunctivitis.

On arrival, Stirling divided up the area between the two squadrons. Paddy Mayne was to concentrate on the road between Agheila and Bouerat, while B Squadron was to move to the west, raiding up as far as Tripoli. Their supply base had been moved forward to Benghazi, which by that time had been captured by the British, and it was intended to stay out for as long as two months, mounting almost nightly raids. At the same time, the LRDG would be watching the road, counting traffic and signalling the intelligence back to their base.

B Squadron then moved out to their rear base at Bir Fascia, 200 miles to the west. They had to travel over extremely bad terrain on the way but by 13 December they were in place. Stirling divided them up into eight patrols of three jeeps each, with orders to keep up the pressure. He then returned to Eighth Army Headquarters, accompanied by Mike Sadler. A Squadron certainly did keep up the pressure and achieved the desired result, mining and ambushing merrily. Paddy Mayne's veterans were remarkably successful but were soon overrun by the advancing Eighth Army.

The story of B Squadron is a sad one. Admittedly many of them were hardly trained and lacked experience, and in addition they were operating in a more populated area with often unfriendly Arabs. Within a few days most of the patrols had either been killed or captured and the enemy occupied their rendezvous at Bir Fascia. Their very presence, however, unsettled the enemy and forced their commanders to detach valuable troops to round up the raiding parties. The only officers to avoid capture were the Frenchman Martin, Gordon Alston, the recently recruited Wilfred Thesiger, and Sullivan. Of the other ranks, it was the desert veterans who made it back to the British lines, including Reg Seekings and Ted Badger, both of whom had been attached to B Squadron. Alston, Thesiger and Martin holed up in a wadi near the old rendezvous. They had a radio truck with them which enabled them to keep in contact. They were ordered by Stirling to stay put and wait for him, as he was on his way back to the desert.

What was destined to be the last series of operations of the desert war was another of Stirling's grand concepts, intended to tie in with Montgomery's attack on Tripoli and beyond into Tunisia which was to start on 15 January 1943. There were four basic objectives which were agreed with the Eighth Army. The first was for Lieutenant Harry Poat to take a jeep patrol to create as much havoc as possible to the west of Tripoli, while the main army attack went in. The other three aims were much further west and were determined by geography. Rommel had been forced to base his supply operation well to his rear, using the Tunisian ports of Sfax and Gabes. At Gabes, the coastal plain narrows down to only a few miles between the sea and a large area of salt marshes. This was a bottleneck for enemy communications and Lieutenant Jordan was to take a force of jeeps into the gap and raid convoys. Between Tripoli and Gabes, there was a fortified belt known as the Mareth line which had been built before the war by the French to hinder Italian ambitions to expand their empire into Tunisia. Montgomery wanted a reconnaissance of this stretch of bunkers and anti-tank ditches to see if it was being put into a state of defence and if it could be outflanked to the south. Finally, David Stirling intended to take a small party and penetrate right through the enemy lines to join up with the First Army, which had landed in Algeria. Once there he intend to meet up with his brother and discuss future plans for their respective SAS regiments.

After the long drive up from Egypt, the various parties assembled at Eighth Army Headquarters at Bouerat. Stirling had Johnny Cooper and Mike Sadler with him, but was minus Reg Seekings who was still out with B Squadron. It was at this time that he commissioned both Cooper and Sadler in the field, in recognition of their services, an action which was later thought to have been highly irregular. They had an uneventful journey across the desert to the rendezvous, although the territory was unfamiliar to them and the maps of the area showed little detail. They met up with Jordan and his men, plus the three officers who had remained with the radio truck, at Bir Guedaffia, where the final plans were made.

Harry Poat left on his mission and Stirling split the remaining force into two groups which would travel independently to a further rendezvous at Bir Soltane, only a few miles from the Mareth line. He had decided to leave Alston and Thesiger there with the wireless truck to observe any activity in the fortifications.

The two groups set off across the desert westwards towards Ghadames. At first the going was so firm that they could travel comfortably at 50 miles per hour, but then they had to head north and traverse what is known as the Grand Sea Erg. This area of soft rolling dunes caused no end of delay, but they managed to make contact with Jordan and join up at Bir Soltane. There, Stirling heard by radio that Tripoli had fallen on 23 January, and thus Jordan's mission was vital. He was to set out with the three French patrols, drive the hundred-odd miles to the Gabes Gap and pass through it as quickly as possible to create confusion in the enemy rear areas. Stirling had originally intended to skirt south of the salt marshes and then find a way through the mountains to Gafsa where American forces had been reported, but changed his mind. He decided instead to follow Jordan through the Gabes Gap and mount an attack in the area around Sousse, a harbour being used by the Germans to ship in supplies. He was running short of petrol and that route offered him the chance to capture replenishments along the way.

They set out on 23 January, Jordan heading straight for Gabes, and Stirling some twelve hours behind, having carried out a recce on the way. Stirling had five jeeps with him, and as dawn broke the following day they arrived at the road. In typical fashion Stirling decided on a bluff which had often helped him before. Johnny Cooper wrote:

Our party of five jeeps with accelerators pressed to the floor, raced for the Gabes Gap. We passed slap through the middle of a German armoured unit dispersed on either side of the road, savouring their first cups of coffee and stretching in the early morning sun. Many of them looked at us curiously, but we just stared back and motored on. By then we thought our bluff had succeeded and after another five miles meeting enemy units on the move, we decided that enough was enough.[21]

Looking back, it seems incredible that five desert-stained jeeps laden down with kit and crewed by ruffianly looking characters sporting beards, could get away with driving among enemy vehicles in broad daylight. But that was what the SAS was all about. What they did not know was that their legendary luck was about to run out. Jordan's patrol, passing that way the night before, had been spotted, and had then shot up some trucks. The enemy was on the alert.

Stirling's party decided to lie up for the day and, leaving the road, headed into some low hills covered with scrubby bushes. They camouflaged the vehicles in a wadi and dispersed in search of shade and some sleep. After the long drive they were understandably tired, yet for some reason Stirling failed to post sentries. Their hiding place was surrounded by a German unit which began systematically to comb the wadi. Stirling shouted that it was every man for himself. Cooper, Sadler and a Frenchman, Freddie Taxis, were nearest to the top of the wadi and ran for it. Stirling and MacDermott were trapped in a cave and rounded up, thus ending the wartime career of the man who became known to the Germans as the 'Phantom Major'. He managed to escape from his captors two nights later, only to be betrayed by an Arab and retaken by the Italians.

Johnny Cooper and his two companions dived into a small depression covered by camel thorn and lay there miraculously undetected until the Germans retired with their prisoners. After a whole series of adventures and a long walk they managed to get to Tozeur, a desert outpost held by the Free French. From there they were handed over to the Americans, who suspected them of being spies and treated them accordingly. It was only when Cairo confirmed their names and service numbers that they were given the honoured status of the first Eighth Army troops to meet up with the First Army. Mike Sadler was flown straight back to the Eighth Army and assigned the task of navigating the New Zealand Division around the south of the Mareth line, while Cooper was able to enjoy the pleasures of Constantine with an old friend, Reg Seekings, who had made his way through after the B Squadron attacks on the road.

Jordan's group in the meantime had managed to sow some confusion behind enemy lines, but all of them except Lieutenant Martin and his crew were eventually rounded up. Once through the Gabes Gap there was no longer any empty desert to escape into and they were trying to operate in a densely populated area that was quite unsuitable for SAS methods. With the wisdom of hindsight it is easy to say that they should not have tried to raid there in the first place, but success had bred a certain arrogance. If Stirling had not been captured when he was, he would hardly have survived his planned raid on Sousse, having to approach his target right through the middle of the remnants of the Axis armies who were caught in an ever-diminishing pocket. Had Stirling been more cautious, he would have followed the route taken by Cooper, Sadler and Taxis, and eventually would have met up with his brother Bill. As it was, the unit he founded was very nearly thrown to the wolves as a result of his abrupt departure from the scene.

The end of the campaign in North Africa marked the end of the 'classic' phase of SAS warfare and the beginning of a period in which Stirling's high-level contacts were to be sorely missed. The regiment would no longer be a one-man band, but would inevitably become increasingly absorbed into the mainstream of army operations, with resulting misunderstanding of what its role really was.

The surviving 'Originals' of L Detachment still meet every year, by now sadly depleted in numbers. Their gatherings are always enlivened by Bob Bennett's fine tenor, accompanied by the Revd Fraser 'Fingers' McLuskey on the piano. The latter was the padre to 1 SAS Regiment in 1944–5 but has been accorded the status of 'Honorary Original'. Bob sings their own song, a private version of Lili Marlene, the anthem of all the desert warriors.

There is a song we always used to hear,
Out in the desert, romantic soft and clear.
Over the ether came the strain, that lilting refrain,
Each night again, of poor Lili Marlene, of poor Lili Marlene.
(*Chorus*)
Then back to Cairo we would steer,
And drink our beer, with ne'er a tear,
And poor Marlene's boyfriend will never see Marlene.

Check your ammunition, see your guns are right,
Wait until a convoy comes creeping through the night.
Then you can have some fun, my son,
And know the war is almost won,
And poor Marlene's boyfriend will never see Marlene.

Drive on to an airfield, thirty planes ahead,
Belching ammunition and filling them with lead.
A flamer for you, a grave for Fritz,
Just like his planes, he's shot to bits,
And poor Marlene's boyfriend will never see Marlene.

Afrika Korps has sunk into the dust,
Gone are his Stukas, his tanks have turned to rust.
No more we'll hear the soft refrain,
That lilting strain, it's night again,
And poor Marlene's boyfriend will never see Marlene.

5

The SRS in Sicily and Italy

The end of the campaign in the Western Desert leads to a necessary split in the make-up of this book, as there were by then two SAS regiments. This chapter will be concerned with the subsequent activities of David Stirling's 1 SAS in the Sicilian and Italian campaigns, and Chapter 6 will detail the formation of 2 SAS and its operational history in Italy.

The capture of David Stirling caused both consternation and chaos. He was a leader who had always played his cards close to his chest, and most of his grand designs were carried around in his head. Nobody, literally nobody, had much of an idea as to what was happening. Stirling had failed to ensure continuity in the leadership of the SAS in the event of his capture or death, and there had been no need at all for him to go off on that last trip. He had proved himself time and time again in battle, so nobody could doubt his bravery and leadership on a raid. If he had been that desperate to see his brother, he could simply have flown up to Algiers. Paddy Mayne was always regarded as the heir apparent, but he was a fighting man rather than an administrator and lacked Stirling's social contacts. Whereas Stirling had tact and charm, Paddy was blunt, rude and awkward in company. By January 1943, 1 SAS Regiment had grown into an unwieldy formation which needed the full-time attention of a commanding officer.

As it was, the regiment was spread out all over the place. The bulk of A Squadron was with Mayne, learning to ski at Cedars of Lebanon. Those of B Squadron who had evaded capture were mostly still out in the desert, as were many of the Free French squadron. Stirling's own party was still unaccounted for and Sutherland was in Beirut with the

SBS and some of the Greeks. Back at Kabrit, Lord Jellicoe had been left in charge of the training establishment. When Harry Poat returned with his patrol from the raid on Tripoli, nobody had any idea who he was, where he had been, or even why he had been there!

To the intense frustration of anyone trying to write the history of 1 SAS Regiment, an almost total fog descends over the first four months of 1943. War diaries exist, but give little more than a day-by-day report of training activities, and the memories of participants often contradict one another. A private war diary gives at least some hard and fast dates.[1] A Squadron left their desert camp on 4 January and undertook the long drive back to Kabrit, where leave was granted. They left again for Cedars of Lebanon on 24 January, a party of seven officers and seventy-seven other ranks.

The simplified version of events given in general histories so far written is that the SBS were hived off under Jellicoe, and Paddy Mayne took over the remainder of the unit, re-named SRS (Special Raiding Squadron), with the rank of lieutenant-colonel. Yet the war diary alluded to above quite clearly states that Mayne was still a major on 4 May. In July, when he was awarded a bar to his DSO for the Sicily operation, he was also still in that rank.

What actually happened can only be pieced together around the known facts. Major Street, who had commanded B Squadron and had been captured during the raids on the coastal road, had a miraculous escape. He was put on board an Italian submarine for transfer to the mainland and it was depth-charged *en route*. Street and six other prisoners managed to get out and were picked up by a British warship. He returned to Kabrit and it seems that the command devolved on him as from 15 February 1943.[2] He was replaced in early March by a certain Lieutenant-Colonel Cator, who signed himself Officer Commanding, 1 SAS Regiment.

Some small operations were carried out during this difficult period for the regiment. Tripoli had fallen on 23 January, but after that the advance of the Eighth Army was stalled at the Mareth line. Lieutenant Jordan's wild dash through the Gabes Gap had been a terrible waste and Gabes itself was not captured until 29 March. A mixed force from the Free French and the Greek Sacred Squadron plus a few men from A Squadron commanded by Bill Fraser were sent forward from Tripoli to operate in front of the New Zealand Division on the southern flank of the Eighth Army. They arrived on 17 February and raided German positions behind the Mareth line, which Montgomery was intending to outflank by sending the New Zealanders in a wide swing behind the defences. This was the area recced by David Stirling in his last patrol, and Mike Sadler was attached to the New Zealand Headquarters as navigator.

The small SAS patrol was jeep-mounted and on 10 March found themselves with a major battle on their hands. Their lying-up place was attacked by German infantry in battalion strength, supported by aircraft and artillery. Things were not going very well, but then out of the sky came a squadron of Spitfires which rapidly dispersed the enemy aircraft. When the ground forces attacking them retreated in the evening, the SAS counted fifty vehicles that they had managed to destroy. The Free French, by dismounting their Vickers K guns from the jeeps and firing from the ground, accounted for four German aircraft. The SAS did not return to the Gabes Gap until 8 April. There they then shot up Italian transport. The patrol was recalled to Kabrit on 20 April.[3]

It was not until mid-March that the great reorganization took place. Major Jellicoe was given command of the Special Boat Squadron, which was to be based at Athlit in Palestine. This was divided into three detachments identified by the initial letters of their respective commanding officers – Captains Sutherland, Langton and Maclean. The last had returned from his mission to Persia and had brought his own recruits with him. Although the SBS retained the sand-coloured beret and SAS insignia, their subsequent gallant operations in the Aegean and Adriatic form a separate story. Both the French squadron and the Greeks returned to the control of their own respective armies.

Mayne was given command of the remaining SAS personnel, reduced in numbers to a squadron and to be known, as we have seen, as the Special Raiding Squadron. Its strength was approximately 250 men of all ranks. There were to be three troops, numbered one, two and three, commanded respectively by Major Fraser and Captains Poat and Barnby. These changes came into effect on 1 April 1943 and are enshrined in a table of organization which shows that the designation 1 SAS Regiment disappeared, to be replaced by HQ Raiding Forces as the higher command for the SRS and SBS.[4] The SRS was to move to Azzib in Northern Palestine where they were to train for the invasion of Southern Europe.

Various accounts indicate that Paddy Mayne was ordered to Cairo to be informed of this decision. When he returned to Kabrit, he called the men together to inform them. There are also several references to the fact that in Cairo he became involved in a brawl and was locked up yet again. Whether this happened on that particular trip or not is unclear, as is the date when it occurred. Mayne's father had died in January and he tried to get permission to fly home for a few days; this was refused. He later told Reg Seekings what had happened. Mayne, in common with most members of the SAS at the time, felt the greatest contempt for the various reporters who thronged the best hotels in Cairo and wrote jingoistic pieces about 'our brave lads socking it to the Hun' without ever going near the front line. He had developed a special antipathy towards Richard Dimbleby, the magisterial BBC correspondent, and after a lengthy drinking bout, decided to 'duff him up' as Seekings put it. The vast Ulsterman went on a tour of the more expensive watering holes in search of his prey, without success. The alarmed authorities caught up with him on the steps of Shepheard's Hotel, where he laid out the Provost Marshal and six redcaps (military police) before he was finally overcome. The following morning, MEHQ signalled the gaol: 'Release this officer. He is more use as an officer than as an other rank.'[5]

At their camp in Palestine, the men underwent a thorough training programme to toughen them up once again for operations. There were many newcomers to absorb and the three troops had to be welded together into efficient fighting units. Parachute-training by then had ceased to be the unit's own responsibility and was handed over to an airborne battalion in Egypt. Trainees left in groups to attend the course and qualify for their wings. Pat Riley returned from the Officer Cadet Training Unit (OCTU) as a lieutenant on 27 April, and Johnny Cooper then left for the same destination. Although he had been commissioned in the field by David Stirling, this was not recognized by the authorities and off he went to be turned into a proper officer.

The Allies had decided that their next step would be to invade Sicily in July, and participation by both the SRS and 2 SAS Regiment was envisaged. On 13 May the SRS were visited by General Dempsey, commanding the 13th Corps, under whom they would be fighting. Reg Seekings marched the men to the camp cinema for the general's talk, which got off to a bad start. Apparently Dempsey was unaware of who they were and addressed them as if they were green troops. He promised that they would 'have their D-Day and get their lion's share'. This was listened to in stony silence and then Paddy Mayne bent over and whispered in the general's ear. Dempsey was visibly shaken and then made a most handsome apology, saying: 'I've been giving you all this tripe about D-Day. You've had more D-Days than I'll ever have.' Apparently he had not been properly informed by his headquarters as to whom he would be addressing. At any rate, he stayed the night with the unit and witnessed a night firing exercise. He went on to become the favourite general of the SAS in the Italian campaign.

All that the men were told by Dempsey was that their task would be to silence a coastal battery on top of some cliffs 'somewhere', and that their task was a vital one as otherwise the battery could seriously interrupt the invasion fleet. So everyone got down to scrambling up rocky paths carrying full battle kit in the heat of a Mediterranean summer. But that was only for general fitness. In the fields around the camp, a dummy layout of the battery they were to attack was marked out. The men practised attacking it by day and night under covering fire from a troop of 3 inch mortars that had been added to the establishment. On 21 May a naval party arrived to conduct training in disembarking from landing craft on to a beach. All this was of course totally contrary to the basic principles which had governed the foundation of the SAS. It was quite clear that the authorities regarded the SRS as a glorified form of shock assault infantry and that the squadron would be employed *en masse* rather than as a set of small parties. Evidently there was still a total lack of appreciation of what the SAS could do, if given the opportunity.

On 6 June, the entire unit left Palestine by rail, bound for Suez. 'Burgess H pushed his hand through a window and severed an artery. We left him at Kantara. Several chaps got very merry and Myler pulled the communication cord and caused quite a bit of confusion.'[6] On arrival at Suez the unit boarded the *Ulster Monarch*, once the pride of the Belfast-to-Heysham ferry route, and the *Dunera*. They had been modified to carry LCAs (Landing Craft Assault) which would ferry the SRS ashore. The rest of the month was spent in training with these craft and the finale was a series of mock attacks carried out in the Gulf of Akaba. It was only right at the end of all the preparations that the destination and target were revealed. They were to assault the gun battery, consisting of three Italian 15 cm. coast guns, on top of Cape Murro di Porco, a few miles to the south of Syracuse on the island of Sicily, in the vanguard of the main invasion fleet.

The fleet sailed from Port Said on 4 July 1943, and once at sea detailed maps and air photographs were issued to the officers. Troop commanders gave their orders and the section commanders briefed their men. Every man knew exactly what he had to do. On the night of 10 July the fleet hove to off the coast. A stiff wind was blowing, in contrast to the calm conditions that had prevailed during training. In the corridors and gangways of the darkened ships the men moved to their positions for embarkation. Even for the veterans this was to be their first experience of an assault landing on an occupied coastline. Overhead they heard wave after wave of aircraft going in to attack, and distant flashes of flame could be seen coming from the dim outline of the coast.

The LCAs were lowered with difficulty in the rough sea, but everyone managed to scramble on board. By then it was just after three o'clock in the morning and pitch dark. Most of the men were violently seasick and got soaked to the skin. During the run in they discovered the water was littered with wrecked gliders that had been dropped off too short. Some of the landing craft stopped to pick up the half-frozen paratroopers, while others just sailed on to the foot of the cliffs. Scrambling ashore the sections formed up and began to climb. There seemed to be little opposition. Reg Seekings encountered someone on the cliff and nearly shot him, until he realized that the man was an officer in the airborne unit suffering from exposure.

On top the sections fanned out to find their targets. There was the inevitable confusion and at one stage they were firing at each other. The gun crews had no real stomach for a fight though, and by 5 a.m. the battery site had been cleared and the guns demolished by the attached party of engineers. The SRS then took up defensive positions in case the enemy decided to counterattack, and three green signal rockets were set off to alert the invasion force waiting offshore that the battery position had been made safe. But somebody had forgotten the sticks for the rockets, according to one of the participants, so the result was a fizzling anti-climax.

After about an hour, another previously unknown battery opened up in front of them. Paddy Mayne gave the order to advance to the attack. The unit skirmished across open ground broken up by small stone walls bordering fields. Mayne, with his usual total disregard for his own personal safety, simply strolled about the battlefield, armed only with his favourite Colt .45 automatic. They cleared the second battery and found themselves embarrassed by an ever-increasing number of prisoners, who were simply herded together and stripped of their weapons. They also released a number of British paratroopers who had earlier been captured by the Italians.

The SRS by then found themselves on the cliffs overlooking the harbour of Syracuse. They had not made contact with any of the invading force and had no clear idea of how the main battle had gone. Everyone settled down to eat some rations, while overhead the air force wheeled and dived. In the afternoon, Mayne marched his force down towards the town, collecting more prisoners on the way. The following morning they linked up with men from the 5th Division already holding the town, and handed over their bag of nearly 500 Italians. They themselves had lost only one man.

The SRS re-embarked on the *Ulster Monarch*, with all concerned feeling that they had earned a rest and a chance to clean themselves up. There was a rush for the showers and a change of clothing. But during the course of the afternoon the officers were called in for a briefing by the divisional commander. Once more maps were unrolled in cramped cabins and aerial photos scanned. The orders were that the SRS were to land and capture the town of Augusta that evening.

Their ship glided into the deserted harbour of Augusta and at around seven o'clock on the evening of 12 July, the LCAs headed for the shore. The town was strongly held and a lot of fire was directed at them. Offshore, a British cruiser and two destroyers opened up. There was no finesse about the landing. They ran straight in and the men scrambled into the water to wade ashore. The various sections fanned out and went from house to house through the seemingly deserted town. The enemy were mainly positioned on the surrounding hills and could fire down into the streets. By dusk the town was cleared of remaining snipers, but sporadic shells and small arms fire continued through the night. Harrison's section was sent up to the citadel accompanied by Alec Muirhead's mortar troop, and Johnny Wiseman's section guarded the important bridge over the causeway leading out of the town. Losses were minimal.

As dawn broke, contact was made with men from the 17th Division who had marched overland. The weary SRS trickled back into the town centre and, being without rations, started to forage for food. Small fires were lit on pavements as meals were cooked, and bottles of wine miraculously appeared. With sporadic firing still in progress an impromptu party started, the singing accompanied by a piano that was dragged out into the street. Their hunger satisfied, men fanned out again into the town in search of loot. Paddy Mayne got his explosives expert to blow a safe in the bank, but all they found were a few trinkets.

Perhaps a word about loot and the SAS would be in order at this stage. Looting has traditionally been regarded as a prerequisite of the soldier's trade and men of the SAS were no exception, led by the intrepid Paddy Mayne who was particularly fond of cameras. It has to be said, however, that their scope was usually limited by the amount of gear they had to carry into battle. Booty was normally confined to watches, pistols, jewellery, cameras, binoculars and other such small attractive items. These were all regarded as fair game and the legitimate spoils of war. Looting was officially frowned upon by the higher echelons of the British Army, but was indulged in by all units in the front line. The SAS generally got the pick as they were usually there first!

The SRS were taken off from Augusta by two destroyers and returned to their mother ship at Syracuse. For them the campaign in Sicily was at an end, although they were kept in a state of constant readiness. Two days later they were briefed to land with the Special Service Brigade (Commandos) to form a bridgehead at Cape Molinari, north of Catania, but the operation was cancelled. This reawakened old resentments from the early days of Layforce when jobs were planned and then aborted at the last moment, one of the problems that David Stirling had been determined to avoid, as it was so damaging to morale. By insisting on running his own show he had been successful, but by the summer of 1943, the SRS were simply a part of the wider army planning set-up, and Paddy Mayne had little or no say in how his unit was to be employed.

On 17 July they were transported ashore to a camp at Augusta and from there were moved about the area, spending their time in training and getting to know Sicily. It was not until 6 August that another operation was mooted, code-named Walrus. This was for two troops to capture a road bridge over the railway at Capo D'Ali and then demolish it on top of the tracks below. This would have been a proper use of the talents of the SRS, but yet again it was cancelled at the last minute.

There were a number of awards made for the Sicily campaign. Paddy Mayne received a well-earned bar to his DSO, while both Harry Poat and Johnny Wiseman were awarded the MC. Sergeant Sillito got a bar to his MM which he had been awarded in the desert for his epic march. MMs went to a further six men, including Reg Seekings who added it to his DCM. Part of Paddy Mayne's citation read:

The second operation was the capture and hold [sic] of the town Augusta. The landing was carried out in daylight – a most hazardous combined operation. By the audacity displayed, the Italians were forced from their positions and masses of valuable stores and equipment were saved from enemy demolition. In both these operations it was Major Mayne's courage, determination and superb leadership which proved the key to success. He personally led his men from landing craft in the face of heavy machine-gun fire. By this action, he succeeded in forcing his way to ground where it was possible to form up and sum up the enemy's defences.[7]

Mayne had proved that he could lead the SAS in battle.

On 3 September, Montgomery carried the war to the mainland when the Eighth Army crossed the Straits of Messina, while to the north, American and British forces landed at Salerno. The SRS were detailed to capture the small port of Bagnara just north of Montgomery's landing area in order to cut German communications and ease the advance of ground forces from Reggio. The start of the operation, code-named Baytown, was a classic case of the troubles encountered by the SAS when they had to rely on other people for transport to their target. This time it was the Navy who were to blame. The squadron embarked at Catania on 1 September in two LCIs (Landing Craft Infantry). These were larger versions of the previously employed LCAs. They got to Riposto that night and one of the craft had to stay behind as it got a cable wrapped around its propeller. The other one had managed to run aground but was subsequently refloated. On 3 September the sorry procession reached Allassio where, once again, the LCI managed to jam itself on the beach. Finally four of the smaller LCAs were brought up and half the unit had to transfer themselves and all of their carefully packed kit.[8]

Reg Seekings was justifiably scathing about the Navy's performance.

There was a big scare on with the Navy, about magnetic bombs, radio-controlled bombs, all that sort of nonsense. We transferred from one boat to another. Some said they daren't start up the engines, there were aircraft overhead – so much nonsense it wasn't true. We went in eventually; it was damned near dawn. The moon had come up bright, we were in this beautiful bay. I was in the leading boat and you could see some emplacements had been pushed up in the sand, and at one stage it looked like the glint of helmets. The naval people were getting jumpy and wanted to turn back. I stuck my tommy-gun in the officer's back and said, 'Land us'.[9]

It has to be said that the Navy's conduct was in direct contrast to that of the coxswain of the LCA that had taken the SRS into Murro di Porco. He had wanted to leave his ship and join them in the assault. The only reason that he did not was his humane decision to put back to sea to try to rescue ditched paratroopers.

The various troops were landed, several hours late, on the wrong side of the bay. Initially there was no opposition at all as the men padded into town in their rubber-soled boots. Then windows and doors suddenly opened and excited Italians poured out offering bunches of grapes. They made such a commotion that Harry Poat ordered his troop to bundle them back indoors. There was in fact little opposition in the town itself and what there was was quickly mopped up. The trouble came from Germans dug in in the surrounding hills with mortars and heavy machine guns. Paddy Mayne ordered the various sections to take up positions blocking the road into town, down which any German counter attack would have to come. The action then became a series of scraps as small parties tried to worm their way up towards the German mortars. The SRS held the town for three more days until they made contact with elements of the Green Howards advancing up from Reggio.

The unit lost five killed and seventeen wounded at Bagnara. Criticism in the after-action report was reserved for the abysmal level of communications, which was typical throughout the Second World War. The radio batteries were bad and the No. 38 wireless sets issued did not work well in hilly country. The final word in the report, however, was reserved for Paddy Mayne's favourite sport. 'On September 5th, Corporal Sorps [misprint for Corps] carried out a demolition scheme on the Post Office, but failed to open the safe.'[10] Corps was Mayne's batman.

After Bagnara, the SRS were pulled back to Sicily for a rest before their next operation, which proved to be their last in the Italian campaign and which was to cost them a severe toll in casualties. The Eighth Army was trying to break through the so-called Termoli line north of Bari and it was decided to send in the Special Service Brigade, which comprised a number of Allied Commandos, to capture Termoli. This was to ease the passage of the 78th Division heading north up the Adriatic coast by disorganizing the opposition. The SRS were to land with two Commandos and various support units, with the mission of capturing two bridges. The brigade major of the Special Service Brigade was a certain Brian Franks, who will feature very strongly in later chapters.

The squadron, 207 men strong, sailed from Manfredonia in an LCI on 2 October. They arrived off the town of Termoli early the following morning and waited until No. 3 Commando had taken the beach. Then they were signalled in, and almost inevitably the landing craft went aground. The men had to be ferried ashore in the smaller LCAs once again, and moved off through the Commando's perimeter. Early on in the battle, John Tonkin's section was cut off and most of them were captured. The other sections all tangled with the enemy who were well dispersed in the surrounding countryside, and during the morning, Bob Melot, the intelligence officer, was wounded. But by midday, leading elements of the Lancashire Fusiliers had arrived on the scene. Paddy Mayne called his troops back into town in the evening, everyone assuming that the battle was over. In spite of the loss of Tonkin and his men, Operation Devon had been successfully if expensively concluded.

Also on the scene were Roy Farran and twenty men from 2 SAS Regiment. They had driven in jeeps with the 78th Division and intended to set up a headquarters in Termoli as a base for raiding behind the German lines. This would appear to be the first occasion on which men of the two regiments came together on the battlefield. During the afternoon another group of 2 SAS arrived in the harbour in an assortment of craft including a small schooner and a caique which had been requisitioned.

The following day was relatively quiet, with only occasional outbreaks of shelling and the odd raid on the harbour by German aircraft. Troops from the 78th Division took over from the Commandos, and the SRS made ready to re-embark. On the morning of 5 October, however, all the indications were that the enemy was about to mount a strong counterattack on Termoli. Pat Riley was playing billiards in a requisitioned house with Paddy Mayne, Bill Fraser and the new doctor, Phil Gunn. Shells started to crash around the building, but Mayne showed no emotion whatsoever. In a gesture reminiscent of Drake he told the others that they should first finish the game and then go and see what was happening.[11]

It was a question of all hands to the pumps, in the face of a major attack by German paratroops. Mayne was ordered by the brigade commander to get his troops into the front line to plug gaps, and Farran's men joined in as well. Some of the units in the 78th Division were green and C section of No. 2 Troop had to be sent in to bolster some Reconnaissance Regiment personnel who had abandoned their carriers and anti-tank guns. Johnny Wiseman's section was stationed in the garden of a monastery when orders came for them to move up to the cemetery where there was the danger of an enemy breakthrough. The section sergeant, Reg Seekings, had a captured German truck in the lane outside and as he piled the men on board, Wiseman climbed in beside the driver. Seekings was just fastening the tailboard when a shell landed right in the middle of the men in the back.

We were smothered in bits of flesh. It was hanging on the 'phone wires, on the roof, a helluva mess. There was a whole family that had been doing a bit of washing for us – they were just standing there waving us off. They were dead, lying in a heap. The woman must have been split open. The man was blown apart, disembowelled, and a young boy, about twelve years old. One of my men was burning. It was the first time I had seen a body burning and I didn't realize how fast a body can burn. That was Skinner. He was dead. I was stepping over the bodies to get some water to pour on Skinner, and this young boy was lying on top. His guts were blown out like a huge balloon. He got up and ran around screaming. Terrible sight. I had to shoot him. There was absolutely no hope for him, and you couldn't let anyone suffer like that.[12]

Miraculously Johnny Wiseman also survived, although the driver beside him was killed outright. Eighteen men died on that truck, although they were not the only casualties. Captain Sandy Wilson and Lance-Corporal Scherzinger were with a small group manning an abandoned anti-tank gun in the shelter of a haystack. Mortar bombs started landing amongst them, setting the hay on fire, and several were wounded. Wilson and Scherzinger were killed when the burning stack collapsed on top of them as they were trying to drag their injured men to safety.

The battle around the cemetery and astride the railway line raged on through the night and the following day. Some Canadian Sherman tanks came up, and their supporting fire stabilized the front. Roy Farran wrote that it was the only infantry battle he had been in, and that he did not want to take part in another. What finally turned the tide was the landing of the Irish Brigade in the harbour. The fresh troops of the Royal Irish Rangers attacked up the railway line with the SRS and 2 SAS giving covering fire. At 5.30 p.m. the squadron retired to billets in the town to lick their wounds and bury their dead. Nobody was much in the mood for celebrating that night. The drinking was silent and heavy.

Termoli effectively ended the campaign of the SRS in Italy. The unit had to kick its heels in the town for several days before being moved to Molfetta, near Bari. There, boredom rapidly set in, and Paddy Mayne went in for several of his desperate drinking bouts. One welcome reinforcement, however, was John Tonkin, who had managed to escape and make his way back through the lines. The only highlight was a visit by General Dempsey, who spoke to the entire unit on parade. On that occasion he did not repeat the error he had made in Palestine. After reviewing the various operations, he went on to say, 'In all my military career, and in my time I have commanded many units, I have never yet met a unit in which I had such confidence as I have in yours. And I mean that!'

General Dempsey was one of the few senior officers at the time who really understood and appreciated just what SAS troops could do – and what they could not. Paddy Mayne was pleased at the praise, but was worried about the future. The squadron was sadly depleted in numbers and nobody in authority seemed to have any plans for their future employment. Their performance had been exemplary and the unit had carried out all the assigned tasks successfully. But by being misused as a shock infantry formation, there was a very real danger that they would either be absorbed into the Commandos or broken up to provide reinforcements.

It was a great relief that in early December, Mayne was ordered to send an advance party off to Scotland to prepare billets for the SRS and to start packing up for the move home. They were to be included in the forces gathering for the invasion of France.

6

2 SAS in Sicily and Italy

2 SAS Regiment was the creation of William ('Bill') Stirling, David Stirling's older brother. He had also started off in the Scots Guards, and in the spring of 1941 was in Cairo with Peter Fleming. They were involved with a small group known as Yak Mission, whose job it was to suborn Italian prisoners of war to work for the Allies. Their efforts were a complete failure, but the two Stirling brothers would certainly have discussed matters, at a time when David was formulating his ideas. When Bill returned to Britain he drifted into the more exotic side of the Commandos and became part of the Small Scale Raiding Force (SSRF), also known as No. 62 Commando. This had been formed for raiding in the English Channel and took part in a number of attempts to snatch prisoners from the Channel Islands. The SSRF's mentor was Brigadier Bob Laycock, then commanding a Special Service (Commando) Brigade. Bill Stirling was promoted to lieutenant-colonel and took over No. 62 Commando in September 1942.

No. 62 Commando was sent out to Algeria at the end of 1942, shortly after the 'Torch' landings, but as nobody could find much use for it, it was disbanded. It was then that Bill Stirling got permission from Allied Forces HQ in Algiers to raise a second SAS regiment for service with the First Army. The two regiments were founded on exactly the same principles, as laid down by David Stirling in the summer of 1941, and tended to attract the same sort of recruits, both officers and men. Bill, however, was different to his brother in many ways. He remains an almost unknown quantity and, although both popular and respected, no one has much to say about him as a person. His style of leadership was different. Where David had had the incurable urge to go raiding, Bill left that to his squadron commanders. He stayed back at headquarters looking after the affairs of his regiment, and was probably determined not to follow his brother into the bag. This is not to say that he lacked courage. He had already proved himself, and felt that it was his job, as commanding officer, to run his regiment rather than blow up enemy aircraft.

Bill Stirling was given a camp site at Philippeville in Algeria and set about recruiting the nucleus of his unit. He obtained many volunteers from No. 62 Commando, and Bob Laycock sent him a Frenchman, known as Captain William Lee. The latter raised a small squadron of French troops, including several from the Foreign Legion. Two experienced men from the SSRF were Major Geoffrey Appleyard and Captain Philip Pinckney. The latter had spent a few months with the SBS in Palestine before transferring back to 2 SAS. One notable accession was Major Roy Farran, who had been wounded in Crete and captured, and had then escaped. Wounded again during the retreat to the Alamein line, he had fetched up in Algeria in the Armoured Corps Transit Camp. One day he bumped into an old friend, Sandy Scratchley, who had transferred to 2 SAS from 1 SAS and who organized an interview for him. Randolph Churchill had also appeared on the scene and attached himself to Bill Stirling. In spite of his leavening of hardened veterans, the bulk of both officers and men who joined 2 SAS were lacking in battle experience and even the benefit of Commando training.

Thus the regiment had to be built up from scratch and the training was every bit as rigorous as it had been in 1 SAS at Kabrit. Sergeant Dave Kershaw had been sent by David Stirling to help out with the programme, which consisted of PT, weapons-training, demolitions and the same long marches in small groups. Parachute courses were held in Morocco. All the new recruits remember the hill, known as the Jebel, which they had to run up and then down with full packs, all the while being timed. Failure to keep within the set limit meant an automatic RTU.

The Philippeville camp was set among a grove of cork trees just above the beach, from where they practised with canoes. The only disadvantage was the presence of malarial mosquitoes, a fact which was seriously to affect operations at a later date. During the first three months of 1943, a few minor jeep raids were attempted in advance of the First Army front in Tunisia, but all failed to achieve any worthwhile results. The hilly terrain was not really suitable for jeeps and the area in which they operated was quite densely populated. Major Peniakoff, the founder of Popski's Private Army, had drifted into Bill Stirling's orbit and was involved in these raids. He came from a Russian emigré background but had been working in Egypt before the war. In his mid-forties he had managed to get himself commissioned into the British Army, and formed his 'private army' which carried out some minor raiding in the desert. He rated himself somewhat more highly than his deeds deserved, but after re-forming his force, took part in the campaign in Italy with some success.

Other early operations against Mediterranean islands were equally pointless. At the beginning of May 1943 a party was sent to Lampedusa to destroy a radar station. They travelled in three motor torpedo boats (MTBs), and off the coast, transferred into dories. On arrival at the beach, the garrison opened fire on the raiders from the cliffs, forcing them to withdraw. On 28 May, another group left on Operation Snapdragon, a reconnaissance of the island of Pantellaria. Infiltration was by means of submarine and then inflatables. The patrol managed to get ashore and grabbed a sentry whom they intended to take back as a prisoner. He proved to be extremely recalcitrant and had to be knocked senseless. In trying to get him down the cliff, the men carrying him stumbled and dropped their burden. The fall broke the man's neck, so they rifled his pockets for papers and threw the body in the sea. After that, there was nothing for it but to return to the submarine.

Lord Jellicoe, with an SBS detachment, was also at Philippeville and was planning raids on Sardinia and Sicily. He had intended to take part himself, but at the last minute was banned from going by GHQ as he knew far too much about the plans for the invasion of Sicily. In the event, the Sardinia raid (Operation Hawthorn) was commanded by John Verney. This often features in lists of SAS operations but was a purely SBS affair, although Verney later served with the SAS in north-west Europe in a staff capacity. The other venture, Operation Marigold, was a joint SAS/SBS trip to Sardinia by submarine, designed to grab a prisoner. The party left in the submarine *Safari* at the end of May, with a three-man SBS folboat team and eight SAS commanded by Captain Dudgeon. The trip out was quite uneventful, but for the passengers, slung in hammocks in the forward torpedo compartment, life was claustrophobic.

They all managed to get ashore undetected, but were running late as they had had difficulties in inflating their dinghies. Once on the beach they set out to scramble up a low cliff, and one of the party dropped his rifle. Immediately all hell broke loose as the enemy opened fire, shooting wildly. Minus the hoped-for prisoner, the party retired back to the beach and managed to regain the submarine, which brought them safely back.[1]

In the spring of 1943 2 SAS was very much a part of the Allied planning set-up at GHQ and despite all Bill Stirling's intentions it never attained the free-booting independence that David Stirling had enjoyed. The regiment came under the umbrella of the new 15th Army Group Special Operations Branch, which had wide responsibilities over a vast area. Bill Stirling was a lone voice crying in the wilderness as he tried to stress the principle that his men should be used to attack strategic targets and not be frittered away by acting directly in support of army operations. On 1 July, just before the Sicily landings, he wrote a lengthy memorandum about how he saw the role of his regiment.

> The employment of S.A.S. troops, especially in the planning stage, will be more strategical than tactical. S.A.S. activities should therefore be an integral part, however small, of the main plan, rather than a diversionary role allotted at a later stage. A general directive would greatly facilitate future planning. An S.A.S. Regiment, unorthodox, fighting irregularly, depends upon the enthusiasm of the commander by whom it is employed. While the personality of a commander is positive, so the personality of a staff is invariably negative, and when the staff gets between the commander and the S.A.S. Regiment, the latter has little prospect of useful employment.[2]

He went on to suggest that his regiment could furnish 300 men in up to 140 parties dropped all over the place to harass enemy communications as far afield as Albania and Greece. If jeep patrols were to be landed by glider, attacks could be carried out with 'explosives by the ton'. All this was true, had the necessary delivery aircraft been made available and had the planning staffs had the vision. Just then, however, their minds were concentrated on the job in hand, to invade Sicily.

Bill Stirling's regiment was to be involved in this in two completely distinct ways. A Squadron under Scratchley (Operation Narcissus) was to undertake an assault landing to seize a lighthouse where it was suspected that the enemy had placed guns which could fire on to the main beach. This was similar to the sort of role undertaken by Mayne's SRS. The second task, however, was far more in keeping with SAS philosophy. Operation Chestnut involved a number of small parties being dropped by parachute in the north of the island to disrupt communications.

Chestnut was a typical case of muddled conception and planning, and the official report, from which the following account is taken, was highly critical.[3] The objectives were as follows. 'Pink' party (Captain Philip Pinckney) was to cut roads and telephone wires on the north-east coast of the island and destroy the Catania-to-Messina railway. 'Brig' party (Captain Bridgeman-Evans) was to harass an enemy headquarters near Enna and attack convoys. It had originally been intended that the two parties, consisting of eighty men, would be infiltrated on to the north coast by submarine from Malta. On 17 June, the 15th Army Group ordered that landings could not be made until the day before the main invasion of Sicily (11 July), and on 20 June the operation was cancelled. The following day it was stated that the cancellation was not firm and that a conference would take place on 22 June. This produced another outline plan which involved parachuting detachments five or six days after the main invasion. On 6 July, the operation was rescheduled for the night of 12 July. On that day two aircraft left carrying 'Pink' and 'Brig' parties, each consisting of ten men. Major Appleyard, the squadron commander, travelled with 'Pink' to supervise the drop, which was successful. Sadly, however, the aircraft failed to return and Appleyard, an experienced officer, was lost.

Bill Stirling flew to Kairouan and took over command of the squadron, leaving Major Peniakoff (Popski) in charge of the tactical headquarters. The following night (13 July), two more aircraft left carrying reinforcements. These failed to contact either party on the ground and returned without dropping. On 15 July it was decided to commit no further forces.

Captain Pinckney and those of his men whom he had been able to assemble found themselves on the ground with most of their kit and radios either broken or lost and desperately short of food. The damaged radios meant that they could not contact the aircraft bringing in the reinforcement party the following night. Pinckney set off with three men to cut communications on the Gangi-to-Palermo road. He reported that 'he had found no communications and seen no transport. This was not surprising as he had watched the wrong road.' Feeling hungry, the party then visited a shepherd and obtained two sheep, for which they gave him a chit to be handed to a British officer to exchange for food and shoes. One wonders if the shepherd ever cashed his chit. Later, still hungry, they found a deserted farm, killed six chickens and left 1,000 lire. 'Brig' party was dropped far too near built-up areas, and as a result the alarm was given. Bridgeman-Evans was captured, but later escaped. In the event, neither of the parties achieved anything worthwhile, although most of the men managed to make their way back to Allied lines.

This was the first parachute operation carried out by 2 SAS and it is worth quoting the criticisms in the official report, because they have a bearing on all drops of that sort. Section 6 is entitled 'Lessons'.

Planning. ... The plan was changed a number of times. Not only was the date moved backwards and forwards, but the mode of transport to the operational area underwent a complete change. ...

Training. It is not surprising that under those circumstances, training for so special and technical an operation should have been somewhat sketchy. Most of the men taking part had been on a parachute course, but had no experience in landing as members of a fighting body. There had been no dress rehearsal, so it cannot be said there was any reflection on those taking part, for the fact that in many cases the party commander was out of touch, not only with his men, but also his supplies and ammunition. This was to a certain extent unavoidable on an operation carried out for the first time, but it is noteworthy that Captain Pinckney, who alone of the officers landed in Sicily had been able to benefit from previous training, was conspicuous in being able to collect the highest percentage of men and containers. The officers and to a certain extent the NCO's taking part had not been engaged in active warfare previously. ...

Dropping. The first essential to a successful drop is quick concentration of men and supplies. This is much easier if the drop can be made from a low altitude which prevents undue stretching of the stick. ... A second essential is to drop either in so remote an area that discovery of the D.Z. [dropping zone] is unlikely, or to move off immediately the same night for the operational area, having covered parachutes, containers etc or to move so far away that their discovery does not compromise the parties. The earlier the drop is made, the longer the time given for concentration and moving off before dawn.

The general criticisms blamed lack of radio communication for the inability to report back on convoy movements. 'Disorganisation of "Brig" and the reinforcement parties made it impossible to carry out tasks allotted except to a minor degree.'

To conclude, the operation was only partially successful and few of the tasks were carried out. The value of damage and disorganisation inflicted on the enemy was not proportionate to the number of men, amount of equipment and planes used. It provided valuable experience for future operations and pointed out the pitfalls which are inevitable in any operation which is the first of its kind.

The assault landing to seize the lighthouse (Operation Narcissus) was far better prepared. It was to be carried out by about forty men of Sandy Scratchley's squadron, and Roy Farran was one of the troop commanders. He took the party up the coast for a proper dress rehearsal, using the mother ship *Royal Scotsman* that would carry them on the day. They landed on an offshore island according to plan, and the only problem was that, after sending up the success signal, the Navy forgot to take them off. Several days before the operation itself was due to take place, the party moved to Sousse where the 51st Highland Division was concentrating. They set up camp and carried on training, but disaster struck in the form of a violent strain of malaria. Within days their fighting strength was down to thirteen men, yet there was no thought of giving up. Sandy Scratchley became affected and had to relinquish command to Farran on the day of departure.

Farran took his depleted force on board the day before the landing and soon was forced to take to his bunk with malaria. Dosed up with quinine he slept soundly until wakened and told that the men were ready in the assault craft. Lowered into the water they discovered just how rough the sea was as the spray washed over them. Once ashore they scrambled quickly up to the lighthouse, only to find it deserted. A later search of the immediate area brought three Italians to light, hiding in a hole. Farran fired the success signal and then received orders to return to the mother ship. The operation had been carried out exactly to plan and without losses. On the plus side, they had captured a large Italian flag and a turkey.[4]

It was not until early September that the regiment was once again back in action, charged with two completely different types of operation. The bulk of the force, divided up into its five squadrons (A, B, C and D plus the French), was to land at Taranto and carry out reconnaissance and offensive patrolling in front of the advancing Allied troops. This was a job that should really have been carried out by regular armoured car patrols, but Bill Stirling, eager to get his men into action, agreed to commit them. The second operation, code-named Speedwell, was a classic SAS one, but all that remained of Stirling's grand design for operating far behind the lines was permission to drop two sticks.

Turning first to Speedwell, the aim was to cut railway lines in the north of Italy which were being used to bring German reinforcements and supplies to the front. The lines allotted were on the face of it a tall order for such a small party – Prato–Bologna, Florence–Bolo, and Bologna–Genoa–La Spezia. Stick One was commanded by Captain Pinckney and comprised Lieutenant Tony Greville-Bell and five others. Stick Two consisted of Captain Dudgeon, Lieutenant Wedderburn and again five other ranks.[5] The two sticks travelled in Albemarle aircraft to an area near Castiglione, north of La Spezia, where they were dropped successfully on the night of 7 September.

On landing, all of Stick One except for Captain Pinckney assembled. All efforts to find him failed and he was never seen again, although there is a possible indication as to his fate in a report by an escapee, Parachutist Cook, who was captured during another operation a month later. 'About the 30th June [1944] I met a band of Italian guerrillas who told me they had been with an S.A.S. officer. They described him as a captain who they called "Pinkie"; he had left them about four weeks before I arrived.'[6]

Thus command devolved on Greville-Bell who had injured himself quite badly on landing. He decided to split the group into two parties instead of three as originally envisaged. The second party was commanded by Sergeant Robinson who took Sergeant Stokes and Parachutist Curtis with him, and their adventures alone could fill an entire book. Robinson led his men to the Bologna–Prato line. There they laid their charges and successfully derailed a train. They did so in blissful ignorance of the fact that Italy had in the meantime surrendered, and as they made their escape from the scene they made a point of avoiding contact with civilians. Thus they were soon short of food and had to resort to stealing corn cobs. It was not until 21 September, when they ran into some soldiers, that they discovered that the Italians were out of the war. All three were unwell during the long march south, Sergeant Stokes suffering from a severe hernia. He had to be left behind, but the other two reached the British lines, at Frosilone, after fifty-four days of marching, interspersed with the odd train journey.[7]

Tony Greville-Bell, meanwhile, had badly damaged his back, as well as breaking two ribs. He and his men laid up during the first day sorting out their kit, which consisted of 160 lbs. of plastic explosive, $4\frac{1}{2}$ lbs. of cheese, two tins of sardines, tea and some biscuits per party. Robinson and his men left in the evening, and Greville-Bell, unsure of whether he could carry on or not, handed over to his sergeant, 'Bebe' Daniels. The following extracts are from the official after-action report compiled by Greville-Bell. They are quoted as an example of sheer courage and absolute determination to see the job through, no matter what physical hardships had to be suffered.[8]

D.3. Walked again, but was in great pain, and was finished after two miles. Decided to have one more night's rest and if not able to keep up would send Daniels and Tomasso on without me.

D.4. Felt better and ribs beginning to knit, so decided to carry on, though every time I fell there was an unpleasant grating noise.

D.5. Head now normal, took over again from Daniels. . . . Moved south parallel with road and railway, and went on railway to recce. point for demolition. Chose tunnel which was unguarded.

D.6. Fixed charge 150 yards inside tunnel and retreated up mountain side. At 2205 we heard a fairly fast train approaching from north. It entered tunnel and set off charge causing the power lines to short circuit. We were unable to see the results, but judging by the noise, I believe the train to have crashed. No traffic on this line observed during the day. Beginning to get very hungry.

D.7. Moved off towards the next line. . . . Ribs merely hurt now, but not impossibly.

D.8. Found some potatoes and tomatoes to eke out our rations. Getting very weak through hunger.

D.10. Getting worse through lack of food. Could only make five miles this night.

D.12. Failed in this operation. Placed charge on the right hand lines for southbound train. We were told quite definitely before we left that railway traffic keeps to the right. Train came down on the left line and we blew the charge (pull switch) before we could see what happened. One line put out of action temporarily at least.

D.13. Found grapes and tomatoes. . . . Repeated charge about one mile south of previous night with fog signal. Train of twelve mixed goods carriages blew charge.

D.14. Started south.

D.15. Rations finished, very weak. Went down to house and acquired a little bread and apples.

D.18. Reached villa of Marquese Roberti at Fiesole who fed us royally, as her sister happened to be a family friend of mine.

D.21. Rain worse, wet through now for 48 hours.

D.23. . . . Put in touch with some partisans.

D.24. Decided to spend a little time trying organise these partisans. They had a great deal of armament and much ammunition.

D.26. Italians a little reluctant to do anything in the way of operations.

D.28. Bought civilian clothes and went into Florence. . . . Had an ice at the Loggia bar in Piazza Michel Angelo. Full of German officers and OR's, mostly drunk. . . . The beer in this bar is very bad.

D.29. Took Daniels and two Jugoslavs off on an operation against railway north of Incisa.

D.30. Placed charge which was blown by heavy southbound train.

D.31. . . . Decided partisans were worthless and were not going to be of any use, so decided to move on.

D.40. While marching along near village of Foursa, were caught on the road by a German truck. *Unterfeldwebel* got out and opened fire with an automatic. We opened brisk fire with carbines and two Germans surrendered.

So the report went on as Greville-Bell and his men plodded steadily south. On the sixty-first day they were high in the mountains and got lost in a blizzard. Greville-Bell and Daniels suffered from snow blindness. The former also had a touch of frostbite as there was a hole in his boot. A week later, Daniels was severely ill with dysentery.

On the seventy-third day they reached the German front line and passed through safely. Their evasion was a great feat of endurance and just the first of many such epic journeys carried out in Italy by members of 2 SAS Regiment.

Captain Dudgeon's party, Stick Two, made a safe landing in the same area and, after dividing up the stores, separated for their respective targets, having agreed a rendezvous point for six days later. Dudgeon and his men were never seen again by anyone from the regiment. It is known that Dudgeon and Parachutist Brunt ambushed a German vehicle, killed the occupants and drove off in it towards their operational area. They were captured at a roadblock and shot by firing squad the following day. Sergeant Foster and Corporal Shorthall simply disappeared and their fate remains unknown.

That left Lieutenant Wedderburn and 'Tanky' Challenor, who formed a formidable if unlikely partnership. Tanky reflected that only in an SAS unit on a secret job behind the lines could two such contrasting men have been tossed together.

In peacetime we would never have met, having little in common and coming from such different social backgrounds. But in the weeks and months which followed, linked by the common bond of danger and hunger, we became closer than brothers. In small party raids such as the one we were engaged on, where each was dependent on the other, the formality of aloofness which existed between officers and men in a normal regiment was replaced by a mutual respect. When you eat together, sleep together and perform bodily functions in sight of each other, you can't always be returning salutes.[9]

The short, studious-looking upper-middle-class Scots officer and the beefy Cockney lad set off to pay their respects to the Bologna-to-Genoa railway, which they reached without mishap. After some time spent searching for a tunnel, they discovered an eminently suitable and unguarded one. 'To blow a line we would need 3 lbs. of plastic 808, which looked as harmless as sticks of plasticine. The sticks would be taped to the rails and connected by instantaneous cordtex fuse to an ordinary fog signal detonator inserted into gun cotton primer. It was crude but effective.' The two men slipped into the dark tunnel and busied themselves laying their charges on both the up and the down lines. As they were walking out, Tanky heard the sound of a train coming. Neither wished to be buried at the scene of their triumph and they ran like athletes, hurling themselves into the stream beside the line as the train thundered into the tunnel.

They heard the roar of the explosion and the rending screech of tearing metal. With triumphant grins they started to climb up the embankment when they heard another train approaching on the other line. That one blew the second charge. Two men with 6 lbs. of plastic explosive had derailed two trains in a tunnel and completely blocked the main line.

Mission accomplished, they set off southwards at the start of what was to become an epic journey. A few days later they placed their remaining explosive on the Pontremoli-to-La Spezia line and were able to claim another train. They travelled sticking to the high ground of the Apennines and lost all account of time. Invariably the Italians they encountered were friendly and hospitable. Tanky was plagued by recurrent bouts of malaria, which turned into jaundice, and Wedderburn's feet were in a very poor state. At the onset of winter they realized that they would have to lie up for a while. Meeting some escaped British prisoners, they heard that the Allied advance was stalled along the River Sangro and at Cassino.

On Christmas Day 1943, the two men decided to split up. Shortly afterwards Wedderburn was captured and Tanky Challenor set off alone, still severely ill with malaria. Then he too was taken prisoner near Chieti. Threatened with execution as a spy and badly beaten up, he managed to escape dressed as an Italian woman and once again made his way into the hills. There he was cared for by Italians, who nursed him through pneumonia and malaria. By 1 April he felt fit enough to travel once again and finally made it to the area of the front lines, only to be captured for the second time. He escaped and made it through no man's land, arriving among British troops seven months after having left for the operation. 'All I could say over and over again was "I've done it, you bastards."'[10]

Speedwell proved Bill Stirling's thesis that small parties inserted by parachute could inflict vast amounts of damage on the enemy at comparatively little cost. It also demonstrated that those parties could operate for long periods away from base when amongst a friendly local population. The flaws in the operation were that too few parties were dropped and that they were poorly equipped. No plan was devised to bring them out, and as they were restricted to what they could carry, their food supplies were insufficient. Once winter set in and the front became bogged down, all the evaders suffered incredible hardships.

While the small Speedwell parties were making their way towards their targets hundreds of miles to the north, the rest of the regiment were embarking to capture the major Italian naval port of Taranto, in support of an airborne division. Ironically, one of its brigades was commanded by Shan Hackett, who had been in charge of raiding forces at Cairo and had given David Stirling so much support. Major Symes was the force commander of 2 SAS and had five nominal squadrons, although in terms of strength they were little more than troops. They travelled aboard an American cruiser, with a number of jeeps lashed to the deck, and while still at sea, heard of the Italian surrender. Thus the landing in Taranto was unopposed and the town was swiftly occupied by the airborne division.

The various squadrons came under the orders of the airborne force commander. Their mission was to fan out into the countryside and find out what the Germans were up to. A Squadron was jeep-mounted and headed out north of the port on patrol. B Squadron was ordered to occupy the Bari road and hold up a reported German column, which never materialized. To get into position they were forced to requisition a motley collection of local transport, and spent the following few days patrolling. C Squadron patrolled on foot and was withdrawn back to base on 20 September. D Squadron was equipped with jeeps and under its commander, Roy Farran, ranged far and wide shooting up German patrols, often in the company of Lee's Frenchmen who had commandeered a ramshackle bus.[11]

The type of mission assigned was hardly suitable for SAS troops, but nevertheless they managed to stamp their usual blend of audacity and bare-faced cheek on operations. B Squadron, commanded by Captain Power, consisted of four officers, the squadron sergeant-major and twenty-three other ranks. They spent the first four days patrolling and making friends with the Italians. Headquarters needed to know if there were any Germans in the town of Pistici, so Captain Baillie travelled there and back in the guards van of a local train, returning with 'much valuable information' and two wounded US aircrew. On 15 September they became involved for the second time with the local railway system. The French squadron had commandeered a complete train which they intended to use to travel to Metaponto where a concentration camp had been discovered. Lieutenant Alastair McGregor and his troop accompanied the French who had also enlisted an Italian colonel and a Polish officer from the airborne division. The camp was in German territory and was guarded by Italians commanded by a Fascist colonel. The train made its way to the camp without meeting any opposition and 180 internees of mixed nationality were brought back in it. Two days later the squadron stumbled on an Italian army supply train and helped themselves to 40,000 military cigarettes and a quantity of food. On 21 September, B Squadron arrived in Bari, which had been liberated by Popski's Private Army.

In the meantime, Farran and his men were having good sport. It may sound callous to use such a term, but that is how men in the wartime SAS regarded their work. Many of the officers came from the wealthier land-owning class, and to them the metaphors of the hunting field were commonplace. D Squadron ambushed a German patrol and was then ordered to move north along the coast to find out where the Germans were. On the way they shot up a convoy, but were repeatedly caught up by the armoured cars of the main force advancing up from Taranto. Unable to find a way through the German positions in the hilltop villages, Farran decided to return to Taranto for fresh orders. His squadron was told to head for Bari, where they spent several days before setting out to the north on patrol again. Their many adventures are well told in Roy Farran's book *Winged Dagger*.

We have seen in the previous chapter how Farran and his men turned up in Termoli, just in time for the battle. The background to this is to be found in the following phase of 2 SAS operations in the Italian campaign. When the Italians surrendered, considerable numbers of Allied prisoners of war found that their guards had vanished. They liberated themselves and took to the countryside before the Germans could round them all up again. The more daring spirits found their own way back through the lines, but the remainder were moving around leaderless and it was decided to mount an operation to bring off as many as possible by boat. This was to be a joint effort by the SAS and the airborne division, controlled by 'A' Force, and code-named Jonquil.

Farran arrived at Termoli on 3 October, the day of its capture by Mayne's SRS and the rest of the Commando Brigade. His orders were to secure a base for the forthcoming operation in which it was intended to use the harbour. B Squadron had in the meantime commandeered a schooner at Bari, but when they attempted to set sail they discovered that as the bottom was so foul, they could only make 3 knots.[12] On 26 September they managed to struggle as far as Molfetta, accompanied by three of the Poles whom they had liberated from the concentration camp. There they scrubbed the bottom of the schooner and repaired the engine. They joined up with some SOE men who had other local fishing vessels and the 'fleet' arrived at Termoli on the day of its capture.

The Jonquil plan called for four seaborne beach parties from B Squadron to land between Ancona and Pescara to act as rallying points for the embarkation of prisoners of war. The French squadron was also involved, acting as a protection party. The ex-prisoners were to be assembled and guided by parties dropped by parachute further inland, code-named Begonia. There were five of the latter, four from the airborne forces and the fifth consisting of Lieutenant Alastair McGregor's troop.[13]

At that stage, Murphy's Law – if it can go wrong it will go wrong – intervened and proceeded to dog the entire operation. The planning was based on a number of false assumptions: first, that there would be complete air superiority, enabling fishing boats to work in safety; second, that there would be large numbers of fishing boats operating off the enemy coast to provide cover; and third, that the Eighth Army would be in Pescara on 10 October. In fact the Germans counterattacked at Termoli on 5 October, throwing the whole timetable hopelessly out of gear. As they could not use the harbour there, those vessels that were undamaged headed back to Bari. There was no shortage of enemy aircraft in the area and the Germans had impounded local fishing boats.

The parachute parties dropped on 2 October and the seaborne parties went ashore at intervals between 4 and 6 October. There were several failures when craft did not arrive at the appointed time or when German patrols interrupted the proceedings. Hundreds of ex-prisoners were collected and brought down to the beaches, but only a handful were actually taken off. The SAS teams on the beaches all made their way back either by boat or by walking through the lines, but two men were captured. The official report under the section entitled 'Lessons' summed up the whole sorry affair quite succinctly. Errors in navigation along a virtually featureless coast were inevitable, as were failures in communication since the beach parties had no radios to contact incoming vessels and there was no radio link back to base.

The report went on to state:

The military return for the use of 61 men, which produced the repatriation of 50 ex p.o.w.'s did not justify their use, when they could have been employed on more important sabotage duties. ... The marshalling of p.o.w.'s lacking in self confidence and discipline as a result of months of incarceration and forced inactivity, is in itself, a formidable task. They were noisy in movement and showed a tendency to stampede on an alarm being given. It is no criticism of the naval forces employed to say that their keeping of R.V.'s was extremely erratic. When the boats did arrive there were no p.o.w.'s to take off, and on those nights when there were p.o.w.'s to take off, the boats did not make the R.V.'s. All this could have been avoided by an efficient system of W.T. signals. In short, this scheme failed because it was mounted by amateurs whose enthusiasm exceeded their practical experience. Amendment succeeded amendment, order followed order. Parties travelled to and fro, each bearing new instructions, and the result was that many hundreds of p.o.w.'s who had been collected at the beaches, returned to the hills disillusioned and dispirited.

The above is direct and justified criticism of those who had set up the operation, the planning of which was nothing to do with 2 SAS or the squadrons involved. They were simply the executants of an example of shoddy staff work. David Stirling had been borne out in his insistence right from the start of the SAS concept that the regiment should be responsible for its own planning and that it should not be placed under the direct control of any other formation.

But what of Alastair McGregor's troop who had dropped inland near Chieti? Their adventures were another example of the resourcefulness and adaptability of small SAS parties and are well worth recounting.[14] The actual drop proved to be quite hair-raising. They were dispatched far too early, when it was still light, and on the wrong dropping zone. On the way down McGregor thought they would land in Chieti itself on the bridge over the river, and he saw some German cars and a motor-cycle coming to meet them. In the event, the whole stick landed together, surrounded by 'hundreds of peasants, all of them friendly. Indeed they were shaking my hand before I even touched the ground.' The Italians gladly made off with the parachutes, which in those days were silk and made excellent underwear, and the containers were hidden in a ditch. Then the Germans arrived on the scene and everyone disappeared. McGregor and his men were guided to a farm where they were able to hide for two nights from the enemy patrols who were combing the area in search of them.

From then until 12 October the patrol split up into pairs and managed to pass 300 ex-prisoners down towards the beaches. As the Eighth Army was expected in Chieti by 20 October, there was no hurry to return, so McGregor then devised an overland route and sent down a further 300 escapees. But the army failed to arrive on time, and many of the ex-prisoners resigned themselves to settling down for the winter, often in comfortable billets which they had secured for themselves with Italian families. Then a new menace appeared on the scene in the form of an SS unit dedicated to recapturing the roving bands of Allied soldiers and airmen. McGregor therefore decided to divert attention by attacking the Germans with his tiny force. His original intention was to mount a mobile ambush using a truck with a machine gun mounted on the back – the poor man's substitute for an SAS jeep with twin Vickers. In the end he had to make do with an Italian Breda and a small 8-cwt. truck, 'which we commandeered from an unpopular local Fascist'. Unfortunately the truck broke down, so they had to conduct ambushes on foot on an almost daily basis. Assisted by some *carabinieri* they split into two patrols. 'The plans were simple; the carabinieri, myself and the sergeant shot the driver and then attacked the remaining passengers with Thompson sub machine-guns.'

A number of truck-loads of Germans were shot up over a period of several days, and then the patrol moved on. They obtained a rowing boat which they intended to use to send back a group of prisoners of war, but the latter proved unwilling to leave. In early November, McGregor noted that a new problem had arisen. The cold weather had arrived and many of the ex-prisoners wore only rags. He therefore decided not to use the boat himself, but to stay behind to provide the men with clothes or with money to buy them. One has to bear in mind that by this time the patrol had been more than a month behind enemy lines, acting as unofficial welfare officers and quite content to carry on doing so.

On the 20th November a bomb fell on the church at Collecorvino, and as the locals believed we had arranged this by radio we decided to move north. On the 21st November we moved across the river Fino to the area Citta S. Angello. We contacted a driver of one of the Italian King's cars who had a new Fiat 6-cylinder hidden in a house until after the war. We explained that we needed a car and took it, together with 300 gallons of petrol.

There can hardly be a finer example of British understatement. One can easily imagine how Alastair McGregor explained his need to the man, backed up by a tommy-gun. He and his men, thus equipped, set out to 'spoil' the local Fascists, many of whom were betraying prisoners of war to the Germans in return for money. Between 16 and 19 December they visited such gentry in a number of locations.

This was done in our car, which proved invaluable, by a party of six men. These operations were always done at night when we arrived in a town or village, nearly all of which had Germans billeted there. Two men with Tommy guns travelled on the running-board. A very strong Fascist and anti p.o.w. from Collecorvino was driven to the cemetery one night and shot. I shot another at S. Angello who had turned in 4 p.o.w. Another was despatched near Picciano. In this way life for the remaining p.o.w. in the area became more secure. I estimate that during this period about 300,000 lire and about fifty suits of clothes were distributed to p.o.w.

Having played Robin Hood and Father Christmas, they spent the festive season pleasantly at the house of Toni, their Italian guide. McGregor then decided that they should change into civilian clothes, split up into pairs and try to regain the Allied lines. As they had plenty of money taken from the local Fascists, a tailor was summoned and a new suit was ordered for each man. To while away the time until the clothes were ready, McGregor changed into a civilian suit taken from one of their victims and went off into town with Toni. There was quite a strong German garrison in Collecorvino which did not bother them in the slightest.

We met two sergeants from Alsace, who spoke fluent French, in the local, but they gave us little useful information although some amusing evenings. On the 30th of December we contacted a pretty blonde girl who we persuaded to spy for us. We managed a dinner party at the house of Podesta, who was a friend of ours, with three German officers, hoping that she would get something useful. The results of this we did not hear as evacuation of the area soon became essential.

By that stage the Germans were determined to capture the cheeky band operating with seeming impunity in their midst. On 5 January, McGregor, Toni, three privates (McQueen, Dellow and Arnold) and the interpreter were sitting outside a farmhouse when shots were fired at them. Thirty Germans were advancing through an olive grove and they had to run for it. They split up and made for a pre-arranged rendezvous, but Dellow went missing. The rest of the patrol (Sergeant Mitchell, Corporal Laybourne and Private Sutton) failed to arrive, but locals told McGregor that the Germans had not taken any prisoners.

McGregor, accompanied by McQueen, then made for the coast in search of a boat. They eventually found one and set off on the evening of 21 January, accompanied by several Italians. They rowed for thirteen hours and at dawn saw some troops on shore repairing a bridge. Luckily they turned out to be Canadians. Thus Alastair McGregor returned, after nearly four months as a thorn in the side of the enemy, to discover that he had been posted as missing by the regiment.

As far as 2 SAS was concerned, the Jonquil disaster marked the end of attempts to evacuate ex-prisoners of war and they were permitted to turn their hand to sabotage. Two operations were mounted at the end of October 1943 code-named Candytuft and Saxifrage. These were designed to cut the railway line that ran down the coast between Ancona and Pescara. Roy Farran and Lieutenant Grant Hibbert led four small parties and were landed by MTB on the night of 27 October. During the entire six days they were behind the lines it rained incessantly. One of the men became seriously ill with malaria and only the kindness of poor Italian farmers who sheltered them prevented the others from succumbing. They managed to demolish the railway in several places, mine the main coastal road and blow down some telegraph poles. The clothing issued at the time was quite unsuitable for such conditions and everyone complained of leaking boots. The various parties, minus two men who were recaptured, were successfully picked up by the MTB.

Sleepy Lad was an almost carbon copy of the above operation and involved a number of small parties being put ashore on the night of 8 December. A considerable amount of damage was done to road traffic and the railway was again demolished in several places. Sandy Scratchley's patrol made the rendezvous on time and waited near the beach for five nights in vain. The Navy failed to appear to pick them up and he had a man seriously ill with malaria. They therefore moved off across country and managed to secure a sailing boat by pressing 10,000 lire 'into the enraged owner's hand'. They arrived back safely in spite of having been fired on by a shore battery.[15]

On the domestic front, the regiment had moved itself during the autumn from Philippeville into quarters in the villages around Noci, north of Taranto, where they proceeded to make themselves as snug as possible for the winter. Arduous training was continued, however, as all the squadrons absorbed replacements who had done their basic course in North Africa. For relaxation, there were visits to Taranto and Bari for the men, organized sports and plenty of cheap wine. Christmas presented a good opportunity for a blow-out, as described by a recent recruit, Lieutenant Jimmy Hughes.

That year Christmas dinner (in the officers' mess) was something of an event. The menu proclaimed – Soup, pork and onions, turkey with potatoes and carrots, plum-pudding and custard, blancmange, cheese savoury and fruit with, of course, sherry and a large quantity of wine. As they ate and drank themselves into a state of stupefaction, four Italian soldiers played the accordion and sang operatic songs. It was a splendid affair. There were even Christmas decorations of a sort. These had been difficult to get so they had improvised. They had taken a quantity of army issue 'French Letters' and blown them up to resemble balloons. On the festive evening they looked fine but, two days later, when some of the locals were invited to join them for drinks in the evening, the balloons had become deflated, and their origin was all too clear.[16]

At headquarters, Bill Stirling was still smarting at his superiors' refusal to provide enough aircraft to drop his parties at the time of Speedwell. In a letter to Allied Forces Headquarters he wrote: 'I submit that examination should be made into why, aircraft and personnel being available, an effective force was not sent against German lines of communication in northern Italy, so that when similar opportunity occurs in the future, advantage may be taken of it.'[17]

In fact a similar opportunity was to occur shortly. With the Allied forces stalled along the Sangro river and from there right across Italy, faced by the immovable German position in the so-called Gothic line, something had to be undertaken to break the stalemate. It was therefore decided to land in force to the north of the German lines at Anzio, and from there to capture Rome and roll up the enemy defences from the rear. It was in connection with this that the last series of raids carried out by 2 SAS in Italy was planned.

Bill Stirling proposed that, prior to the Anzio landings, his men would be dropped to cut a number of strategic railway lines which carried enemy supplies. In addition, an attack would be made on an important railway bridge between Pesaro and Fano. These operations were to be code-named Maple and Baobab. The plan was submitted to the 15th Army Group on 10 September and permission to proceed was given on 17 December, for take-off the following day. Bad weather forced cancellation and the drops had to be postponed to the start of the next moon period in January. After several more false starts, the parties finally jumped in bright moonlight on 7 January 1944.

Maple was divided into two sub-operations, Thistledown and Drift-wood. The former consisted of four parties, each of four men, who were to attack railway lines radiating from Terni and Orvieto. The latter comprised two four-man parties which were to attack the Urbino–Fabriano and Ascona–Rimini lines. The original intention had been to send in a follow-up party to Driftwood by sea, carrying a sufficient weight of explosive to demolish the railway bridge between Fano and Pesaro. Bad weather hindered this and it was eventually carried out separately as Operation Baobab at the end of January.[18]

The four Thistledown parties landed in deep snow. Three of them reached their targets and attacked them successfully. The fourth, Lieutenant Worcester's party, discovered that their target had already been damaged by bombing, so diverted to attack the Terni–Rieti line. None of the four parties managed to exfiltrate successfully and all were captured. This was blamed on the snow which made their tracks visible, the fact that the bridgehead at Anzio was slow to expand and that the German patrols were extremely active. The exact fate of Driftwood remains a mystery. A sea evacuation rendezvous had been fixed but none of the men turned up. Captain Gunston and seven others were last heard of setting off in a rowing boat on 7 March and it has to be presumed that they either sank or were captured and shot.

Operation Baobab was finally mounted on 30 January, when Lieutenant Laws and a signaller were landed from a fishing vessel near Pesaro to form a beach reception party. In the meantime, the main party was heading up the coast in a destroyer. During the day the two men made a recce of the area. Near the bridge they discovered a house being used as *carabinieri* barracks. Just before signalling the main party to come in they jammed the door of the house with a large stone. The demolition party arrived and were guided to the target by Laws. Captain Miller attached the charges. While he was doing so, the *carabinieri* managed to free themselves. As they started to open fire, Miller set the charge with a ten-minute delay and everyone embarked safely in the dories. As they pulled out to sea, a violent explosion was witnessed and chunks of debris flew up into the air. All the men returned safely after a small, neat and economical raid.[19]

The final raid to be discussed, Operation Pomegranate, demonstrated the classic use of a small SAS party, yet oddly enough it was the only attempt to destroy aircraft on the ground during the Italian campaign. It was known that the bulk of German reconnaissance aircraft were based at San Egidio, between Bastia and Perugia. If they could be knocked out the Anzio landings would stand a far greater chance of success. Two officers, Major Widdrington and Lieutenant Hughes, were chosen, together with four other ranks, Lance-Corporal Malloy and Parachutists Cox, Todd and McCormick.[20]

The party was dropped from a Dakota on the night of 12 January to the east of Lake Trasimene. They landed well together and gathered in their stores that had been dropped in oil drums, which were easier to disguise if found. Sadly, the aircraft and crew were lost during the return flight. The party marched by night, lying up during the day, but when crossing the Tiber they were challenged by a German sentry. The party scattered and only the two officers remained together. They never saw the rest of the men again, who approached the target only to discover that it had been dealt with. All four other ranks successfully crossed back through the lines.

Widdrington and Hughes carried on alone, and on the night of 17

January managed to penetrate the airfield where they placed Lewes bombs on the only seven aircraft they could find. As they had primed all the bombs they were carrying and had some left over, the first task was to make them safe before leaving the scene. While doing this, one of Major Widdrington's bombs exploded. He was killed outright and Hughes was severely wounded. When he came to he discovered that he was blind, that his trousers had been blown off and that his legs were covered in blood.

Hughes still had his wits about him and managed to burn his maps and papers.[21] Then sentries arrived and he was taken to the airfield hospital where he was well cared for. From there he was transferred to a hospital in Perugia, where he was told that as soon as his wounds had healed, he would be handed over to the Gestapo to be shot as a saboteur. His right eye was operated on and after about two weeks his hearing returned and he regained some vision in his left eye. In the hospital he became friendly with a German doctor and a fellow-patient, a German officer who had also taken part in special operations. The latter had a friend on the staff of the German Commander-in-Chief in Italy, Kesselring, and it was arranged that Jimmy Hughes' papers would be changed to give him the status of a prisoner of war rather than a political prisoner. As he left hospital he was warned that his immunity was only temporary and that he had better escape. Accompanied by two others he jumped from a moving hospital train on the night of 10 March 1944 with his wounds still only partially healed. He finally rejoined the regiment after a series of adventures culminating in a voyage in a sailing boat which brought him to British-held territory.

On arrival he was debriefed at 15th Army Group HQ at Caserta and then by Major Eric Barkworth, intelligence officer of 2 SAS Regiment. Until then there had been rumours that the Germans were executing captured parachutists and raiding parties. All concerned were still in ignorance of Hitler's so-called 'Commando order' of 11 October 1942 which called for all captured parachutists to be handed over to the Sicherheitsdienst (SD) for disposal. Barkworth wrote a report on the Commando order in 1948 as part of his work as a war crimes investigator. In it he stated:

A memorandum on Hughes' report was produced and forwarded to HQ 1 Airborne Corps, at that time the formation controlling the S.A.S. Regiments. As a result Major Barkworth was instructed to contact P.W. Cas. Branch. . . . Hughes' case was dismissed as mere interrogation technique, and reference to other men of the Regiment who had neither returned, nor had been reported as casualties, was explained away by the fact that the enemy probably wished to keep us in the dark about the success of operations.[22]

The results of the Commando order as they were applied to members of the SAS will become all too apparent in later chapters.

After the last series of raids, 2 SAS Regiment returned to North Africa where they cooled their heels until April 1944 when they set sail for Britain. There they were to join the reconstituted 1 SAS in preparing for the invasion of France. In Italy the regiment never really got a chance to show what it was capable of. Admittedly it was a new formation and many of its members were relatively unskilled at waging clandestine warfare. However, the few operations that did take place were mainly planned by outsiders and often resulted in missed opportunities. What did emerge was the fact that when properly inserted, parties could and did reach their targets and destroy them. Compared to the numbers of men involved, their losses were heavy, but those who survived formed a highly motivated cadre for later operations in France.

7

The SAS Brigade

Their mission in Italy ended, the 200-odd men of the depleted Special Raiding Squadron set sail from Algiers on Christmas Eve 1943. Their destination was Britain where, raised once more to the dignity of a regiment, they were to re-form and prepare for the invasion of France. They were preceded by Mike Sadler and Johnny Cooper who were flown home as an advance party. The latter had just rejoined the unit as a fully fledged lieutenant, having missed the fighting in Italy while attending the Middle East OCTU. Sadler's job was to set up the basis for an intelligence section, while Cooper went off to Scotland to prepare to receive the rest of the unit. He was first sent to Mauchline in Ayrshire to get a campsite ready, but as soon as he started work he was told they were to move to Darvel, situated to the east of Kilmarnock. There the men were to be accommodated in disused spinning mills which were quite spacious, and the officers moved into an old manor house overlooking the village. On arrival, every officer and man was to have two weeks' leave, which for many was the first time they had seen their homes since embarking with Layforce in the winter of 1940.

Planning for the Second Front had started in 1943 and by the beginning of 1944, the staffs concerned and the complexity of the operation had mushroomed into the size of a city. For the SAS there was a small walk-on role allotted on the sidelines of the army corps, the armies and the army groups that were to embark for France that summer. During the latter days of the desert campaign, David Stirling had envisaged the unit he created as a brigade, made up of 1 SAS, his brother Bill's regiment and a French regiment, taking part in the campaign to liberate France. An SAS brigade was about to be formed, but Stirling was a prisoner in Colditz and his concepts were to be totally ignored by blinkered planning staffs, most of whom had probably never heard of Stirling, let alone his ideas for the employment of SAS formations. This chapter is concerned with how the command system developed and the background to SAS operations during the campaign in France. Detailed studies of actual operations will be recounted later, regiment by regiment.

Although both units had fought well in Italy, little was known about their capabilities outside the Mediterranean. The impetus for bringing them back to take part in the invasion seems to have come from Lieutenant-General Sir Frederick 'Boy' Browning, who was placed in command of 1 Airborne Corps. It was decided to form a brigade composed of the two British regiments, plus two battalions of French parachutists and the Belgian Independent Parachute Company. They would be a component part of the Airborne Corps and would wear airborne red berets but be allowed to keep their winged dagger cap badges. The red berets were the final insult for the desert veterans who continued to resent them to the end of the war, although some, notably Paddy Mayne, still wore their sand-coloured ones.

On the face of it, it seemed like a simple takeover by the airborne people and a case of empire-building by Browning. There was, however, another side to the coin, as an official report published by the War Office in 1951 summarized.

It is a debatable point whether or not the S.A.S. Brigade should have been placed under the command of the Airborne Corps. The reasons for doing so at the time were that Lt. Gen. Browning took the initiative in getting approval for their inclusion in the order of battle for the invasion of Western Europe, that no suitable H.Q. existed to look after them, and that 21st Army Group and SHAEF [Supreme Headquarters Allied Expeditionary Force] were not prepared to have them under direct command owing to the detailed work concerned.[1]

One factor that nobody seemed to understand was that the SAS were not airborne troops. Parachuting was only a comparatively small part of their training and they were capable of insertion by land, sea or air. They were not trained to fight as a large formation and only did the bare minimum of jumps to enable them to land in safety.

The mission of liberating Western Europe had been entrusted by the Joint Chiefs of Staff to General Eisenhower who presided over the unwieldy staff known as SHAEF. By the time the invasion started in June 1944, SHAEF had swollen to the size of a division and numbered 15,000 souls. The actual landings and the conduct of the battle on the ground were initially the responsibility of General Montgomery, who commanded the 21st Army Group. There is no space here to become embroiled in the post-D-Day command structure and the ensuing quarrels: many excellent books have been written on the subject. The point must be made, however, that the easy access to the Commander-in-Chief in the Middle East that David Stirling had enjoyed, in the days when Auchinleck controlled two corps at the front, no longer existed. Operation Overlord was a vast enterprise and the SAS had a very small role to play. Besides, there were others who laid claim to responsibility for waging clandestine warfare. Special Operations Executive (SOE) had been involved in the Overlord planning right from the beginning and, having a network of agents operating in enemy territory, claimed to be the fount of all wisdom. The relationship between the SAS and SOE was thus bound to be a difficult one. In addition there was Combined Operations, another hydra-like headquarters overburdened with staff but with scant responsibility. Both Combined Operations and SOE had their lobbyists busy at SHAEF.

In January 1944, authority was given to form the SAS Brigade under the command of Brigadier R. W. 'Roddy' McLeod, with Esmond Baring as brigade major. On 8 February a headquarters was set up at Sorn Castle in Ayrshire, and by the end of the month its strength was listed as ten officers and thirty other ranks.[2] Under its command were the following:

HQ French Demi-Brigade (Lieutenant-Colonel R. Durand)
20 Liaison HQ (Major Carey-Elwes)
1 SAS Regiment (Lieutenant-Colonel Mayne)
3 French Parachute Battalion (Captain Conan) (3 French Para.)
4 French Parachute Battalion (Commandant Bourgoin) (4 French Para.)
Belgian Independent Parachute Company (Captain Blondeel)

2 SAS Regiment did not arrive back from North Africa until 17 March. 20 Liaison HQ was the SAS link with the Free French authorities, known at that stage as EMFFI. Lieutenant-Colonel Ian Collins was the SAS liaison officer with Airborne Corps HQ at Moor Park, outside London. His responsibility was to oversee initial and strategic planning, staff duties and training.

The majority of members of the new brigade staff had had no previous experience of SAS operations or even of airborne methods. Many were simply posted in from the pool of qualified personnel unemployed at the time. They faced a daunting task, as the two British regiments were accustomed to operating independently and did not take kindly to being deluged with paperwork. Most of the new officers settled in and did extremely well under trying circumstances, but there were some real duds. Inevitably they had to face criticism from those whose job it was to translate plans into action. The intelligence officer of 2 SAS, the late Major Eric Barkworth, stated in a letter written in 1983: 'The staff at Moor Park was the bottom of the barrel I thought. They felt that they had a new toy to play with and did not have the background and experience to plan properly. We lost a number of men through their ineptitude.'[3] This harsh judgement was echoed at the time by others. Certainly, in the early stages, the main problem was that there was no really clear idea on the part of SHAEF as to how SAS units were to be employed.

It was not until 29 March 1944 that SHAEF laid down the broad outline of requirements, which were issued for planning purposes. The task for 1 SAS was to drop on the night before D-Day (D − 1) and delay the movement of German reinforcements in an area comprising Lisieux, Alençon and Mantes. 2 SAS or 3 French Para. were to operate east of a line running through Dieppe, Beauvais and Paris. 4 French Para. was to operate west of a line running through St Lo, Domfront, Mayenne and Angers. This was enshrined as SAS Brigade Operational Instruction No. 2,[4] and, as will be seen, was to have dangerous repercussions. It is interesting to note that initial landings were envisaged before D-Day, yet at the same time the 21st Army Group laid down four principles for employment.

1. For security reasons, no SAS troops to be landed before main landings start.
2. Main object in early stages to delay enemy reinforcements into Normandy.
3. Half strength of brigade to be held in reserve in U.K. for operations as required.
4. No diversion of troop carrying aircraft to interfere with main drops on D-Day.[5]

Thus a divergence of views was already becoming apparent, but both

SHAEF and the 21st Army Group envisaged using the SAS units to help seal off the battlefield. This, however, was tactical in nature and the operational areas envisaged were far too near the front line. They would be swarming with enemy troops, and SAS parties would find it difficult to conceal themselves satisfactorily. The most they could have hoped to achieve would have been to hold up the arrival of the panzers for a few days.

As the embryo staff grappled with such weighty problems, the troops themselves settled down to some solid training. 1 SAS had to be brought up to the full strength of a regiment and thus had to absorb a large number of recruits. Most of these men were culled from volunteers for the various parachute regiments, but some simply arrived from replacement depots. One useful source of recruits were the so-called Auxiliary Units which were being stood down at the time. These were small groups set up in 1940 to form an embryo British resistance movement in the event of a German invasion. The real problem was that the two British SAS regiments were expanded too rapidly, with the inevitable result that standards slipped. Great efforts were made to weed out unsuitable personnel, but the pressure to maintain numbers remained.

A vigorous training programme was instituted on the bleak Scottish moors, watched over by the veterans of North Africa and Italy. Each troop became a squadron with its own headquarters troop, and regimental headquarters expanded to cope with this. All men were required to undergo parachute-training, and even the veterans were given refresher courses. Lectures were held on such matters as intelligence, communications, demolitions and foreign languages. Yet nobody knew what their mission was to be, such was the vacuum in information and the obsession with security.

Paddy Mayne, DSO and Bar, commanded the regiment and appointed Major Harry Poat as his deputy. The four squadrons, A, B, C and D, were commanded respectively by Bill Fraser, Eric Lepine, Tony Marsh and Ian Fenwick. Each consisted of 12 officers and 109 other ranks. A further subdivision consisted of Squadron HQ and two troops, each troop having four sections. The French battalions were stationed nearby at Auchinleck Camp and were made to undergo an identical training course, during which they distinguished themselves by their expertise in poaching. Serge Vaculik, a Czech who had French nationality, had braved numerous adventures before arriving in Britain and had joined 4 French Para. Battalion. He went on to serve in 1 SAS and vividly described the training methods.

We learned to fall into deep pits holding our weapons over our heads, and to lie face downwards on barbed wire whilst our comrades trampled forward over us, and all along the course British machine-gunners, sharpshooters to a man, kept up a constant fire with live ammunition, whipping up the ground a few feet ahead of us and behind us. If we were sometimes too exhausted to spring to our feet and dash on, the machine-gunners would treat us to a sustained burst of fire at our feet, and that would lend us renewed strength to press on.[6]

Once the men had passed out from this so-called 'battle course', they were split into small groups and set various initiative tests. They would be sent off to penetrate a guarded area or ordered to traverse long stretches of countryside with the police and Home Guard alerted to search for them. How they achieved their tasks was left open, and the means they chose were usually highly illegal. The result was a storm of protest from the local police and military authorities which Paddy Mayne had to deal with. Anecdotes from this period are legion. Many of them have naturally improved in the telling, and represent the delightful element of mischief which characterized so many SAS operations.

Certainly the SAS left a trail of angry vehicle owners behind them. Paddy Mayne had to write to Brigade HQ about the taking of an RAF truck. 'This truck was found unattended and immobilised. The party through over-enthusiasm and considering themselves, possibly too thoroughly, to be enemy parachutists, took it. The officer concerned has been reprimanded for not returning it sooner.'[7]

Serge Vaculik and a few others were told to make their way from Scotland to Chelmsford in Essex, signing their names in registers at various places *en route* to prove that they had been there. As their only food was a course of vitamin pills and as they were given no money, anything unattended was fair game. Milk bottles left on doors were emptied, poultry was merrily poached and an airborne division truck with food in the back was stolen. They even tied up some policemen who tried to arrest them and made off in the policemen's car.[8]

1 SAS also gained a padre fully qualified in parachute dropping, Captain Fraser McLuskey of the Church of Scotland. His own description of his arrival at Darvel very early one morning, and his first encounter with Paddy Mayne, is well worth quoting.

The front door [of the mess] was open and I wondered if I were too early for breakfast. Hoping for the best, I advanced into the hall, where a confused and somewhat strange sight met my eye. Officers were passing through the hall into the dining room to the strains of a small and exceedingly wheezy gramophone playing 'Mush, Mush, sing Tooral-aye-ary'. Round the fireplace and the ashes of a dead fire, and oblivious to both the breakfast procession, and the orchestral accompaniment, sat several officers, in varying attitudes of repose. From this somnolent party a large man – a very large man – detached himself on my entry and heaved himself in my direction. If he didn't actually ask who the devil I was and what the devil I was doing there, I gathered at least that it was at the back of his mind. He seemed to be someone in authority, for I observed, even in my own bleary-eyed and breakfastless state, that he was a lieutenant colonel.[9]

One of those around the fireplace was Lieutenant Johnny Cooper, who was Air Liaison officer at the time and responsible for organizing parachute-training with the RAF. He remembered the reason for the scene. The previous evening, Mayne had set up a barrel of beer and invited all the newly recruited officers to join him for a drink. He then proceeded to interview them, one by one, about their previous service and their personal backgrounds. He had just finished with the last one when the padre arrived. 'Paddy said: "Well Johnny, bring him in. Pull him a pint of beer." McCluskey entered and I handed him his pint as ordered. Paddy then said, "It's time for breakfast, Padre", and clutching our tankards we entered the mess dining room, much to the astonishment of the staff."[10]

2 SAS, which only arrived in March, had an even more difficult time. After the men had been given leave, they were only left with about two months to absorb new recruits, build up to strength and complete their training programme. They also lost their French squadron which was absorbed into the Free French forces.

While the regiments prepared for their future and still unknown assignments, the brigade staff grappled with manifold problems. Above and beyond the actual missions, they had to build up from scratch a series of procedures to deal with such matters as communications with parties in the field and resupply by air. As we have seen, communications had constantly failed in the Italian campaign, due mainly to the unreliability and short range of the sets employed. In Italy, too, parties once dropped had been left to their own devices and few attempts had been made to resupply them with food or explosives. There was, however, a wealth of experience in Britain, for SOE had been supplying agents in the field and communicating with them for three years.

The essential problem was one of scale. In the early days in the desert, David Stirling had been able to use his charm on an RAF officer in the bar at Shepheard's and arrange to borrow the odd aircraft. His raiding parties had always been relatively small and could be resupplied by truck convoys with any items that they could not carry in their own vehicles. The SRS in Italy had operated as a composite unit of 250 men, but were carrying out assault landings and were only ashore for a few days at most before a supply system caught up with them. The SAS Brigade, on the other hand, had to reckon with up to 2,000 men behind enemy lines at any one time, spread out between Belgium and the South of France. The only way to resupply their parties would be by air drop.

A War Office report written after the war made the point that the various units in the brigade were mobilized on an equipment scale prepared at the end of 1943, before the real scope of SAS activities was known. The various tables of equipment provided for all possible options – infiltration by air, sea or jeep. 'As a result it was found that there was always a deficiency of that equipment actually required for that phase of operations, together with a surplus of other equipment.'[11] A further complication was that the brigade had no aircraft dedicated solely to its requirements. Bids had to be made daily at midday for the aircraft required for the next night but one. This was then either confirmed or rejected at midday the following morning. 'Staff therefore did not know until noon on the day of a supply operation, from which airfield supplies were to be sent.'[12] 'This left little time for the R.A.F. to allot aircraft, fix routing, brief pilots and load aircraft.' The same factors applied to HQ SAS Troops who had 'to get containers packed and transported to airfield, arrange final briefing of personnel and to send necessary signals to the field to tie up reception details.'[13]

Originally it had been proposed to use Airborne Corps dumps in the Cirencester area, but the diversity of SAS requirements for supply in the field was not fully understood. During the early planning stage, a separate supply base had to be improvised. This was at Down Ampney in Gloucestershire and became known as Station 1090. Arrangements for supply to a particular party had to be co-ordinated by 1 Airborne Corps and 38 Group RAF at Netheravon and Special Forces Headquarters (SFHQ). 38 Group operated converted Halifax and Stirling bombers from a number of airfields in Wiltshire and Oxfordshire, carrying both parachutists and stores. Other aircraft used were twin-engined Albemarles and C-47 Dakotas. Fairford, operating Stirlings, was the normal SAS airfield, but sorties were also flown by Stirlings from Keevil, and by Albemarles from Harwell and Brize Norton. Jeeps were transported in Halifaxes based at Tarrant Rushton.

To give some idea of scale, the following statistics were given in a letter dated 8 April from Lieutenant-Colonel Collins to 38 Group. The SHAEF outline Overlord plan envisaged 165 SAS parties operating in one series of drops. Three parties could be carried in a Stirling and one in an Albemarle. The motor transport required depended on the number of aircraft allotted. As an example, a sortie by 70 Albemarles and 30 Stirlings would require 100 lorries to carry 160 parties on the same trip. That force would need to be resupplied on a weekly basis with 100,000 rounds each of .30 and Thompson sub-machine gun ammunition.[14]

Communication with parties in the field was naturally vital, both for operational control and for organizing resupply. Bearing in mind the technology available at the time, this presented considerable problems. The base signals layout was established at Moor Park where HQ SAS Troops set up its tactical headquarters. This consisted of a number of 12 HP transmitters installed by the BBC, each of which could transmit to five outstations. The latter consisted of Jedburgh sets, which had a sufficient range, though low power, and which were attached to parties in the field. Instructions to individual parties were also passed on broadcast channels to officers who were issued with small MCR 100 receivers. Messages were sent using the codeword SABU followed by a number which represented the officer concerned. It was not possible to provide for communication between parties or larger groups operating in the same area. If they wished to talk to one another, one had to send a message back to base, who would then retransmit it to the other. In August there were at one time twenty-five separate parties in the field, passing about a hundred in and out messages back to base each day. Encoding and decoding naturally took time and, in addition, there was considerable traffic that had to be passed via the BBC. Finally, the age-old method of military communication, carrier pigeons, was re-sorted to, with indifferent results.

The SAS Brigade war diary records the frustrations of the period. Limited air time restricted communications with the field to the laying on of air operations, the passing of immediate intelligence reports and brief operational orders. 'Once a party was committed, little was known of its movements here and little control could be exercised over them . . .

The need for a very high standard of telegraphese and faultless ciphering was apparent. Most messages arrived either mutilated or much too long – in the case of 4 French Para., normally both.'[15]

The base stations at Moor Park were operated by Royal Signals personnel, but there were insufficient signallers available to man the sets in the field, all of whom would have to be trained to SAS standards. Therefore in April, F Squadron GHQ Liaison Regiment, 'Phantom', was attached to the brigade, commanded by Major the Hon, J. J. 'Jakie' Astor. This unit had been founded in 1940 to provide reliable communications direct from the front line back to higher formations. The various squadrons were subdivided into patrols, commanded by a captain. Two patrols each went to 1 SAS and 2 SAS. The French and Belgians had their own signals organization, but the operators were trained by 'Phantom'.

The above may seem complicated, and it was. It was to become even more complicated once the invasion got underway and operational arrangements changed, often at short notice. First, however, there was an upheaval that nearly destroyed 2 SAS Regiment and could have had a knock-on effect on the other units. As we have seen in the previous chapter, Bill Stirling had in Italy been highly critical of the use made of his formation. When he saw the outline plan referred to earlier, he realized that it was essentially unsound, as did many others. There is no record of protest from anyone at brigade level at the time, but there was certainly disquiet among the few officers in the regiment who had been initiated into the secret.

It is only possible to discover the barest outline of events based on hearsay which led to Bill Stirling making his protest. The official files covering the period make no mention of it and may well have been sanitized after the war. Stirling seems to have submitted his reservations in writing both to SAS Brigade and the Airborne Corps some time in early May – which is about the time he would have been informed of the outline plan. What is known is that General Browning, the corps commander, visited the various regiments between 16 and 18 May.[16] As he had not previously inspected 2 SAS, he was to concentrate his visit on that unit and lunch with the officers. This was to be followed by a meeting with all the regimental commanders.

The upshot was that Bill Stirling resigned his command and retired back home to Scotland. He left no diaries or memoirs of the period and, as far as can be determined, never commented on the reasons for his departure. According to Roy Farran, who was close to Bill Stirling, the latter decided to send a letter stating that he had no confidence in the command set-up, but was persuaded not to send it until the regiment's own proposals had been accepted. When it was finally sent he was asked to withdraw it but, realizing that a firm stand was necessary, he refused to apologize. Farran contemplated resigning; had he gone, he would have been followed by others.[17]

It is significant that on 17 May a signal from Brigade HQ was sent to all regiments, which read: 'Operational Instruction No. 2 cancelled. All copies held to be destroyed.'[18] Lieutenant-Colonel Brian Franks, who had been the brigade major of the Commando Brigade at Termoli, took over as commanding officer of the regiment and proved to be an outstanding leader who rapidly managed to rebuild the unit's somewhat shattered morale.

A new philosophy for the employment of SAS troops emerged at the same time, which was more in keeping with their potential for causing damage to the enemy, although some elements of the old tactical thinking lingered. The new idea was to drop small advance parties deep inside France where they would link up with local Maquis groups and establish a base. Into those bases, more men, weapons and jeeps would be dropped, enabling enemy communications to be disturbed over a wide area. SHAEF laid down the priorities by area as Brittany, the Forest of Orléans, the Morvan west of Dijon and the Vienne south of Poitiers. The actual operations in France will be considered in the next two chapters, but there were wider issues common to all parties which can be discussed at this stage.

Detailed planning was frequently delayed to the last minute as information about the main battle plan took time to trickle down to Moor Park. To mount an operation, the following steps were necessary.[19] First, SHAEF had to approve the project. 'This was the most troublesome stage of all. G3 (Special Operations) Division of SHAEF, which had the last word on all our tasks, was a new-formed branch and complex liaison between it, 21st Army Group, Airborne Troops and S.A.S. Troops was needed before a task and method would be accepted as necessary and feasible.' The operational order was then issued to the unit concerned. Stage three involved the provision of intelligence. Stage four required the arrangement of reception in the field and, as we shall see, embroiled the planners in endless controversy. The fifth stage was the allotment of aircraft, which could only be confirmed on the morning of the actual drop. The final two stages were the distribution and loading of stores, and briefing.

The core of the problem lay in the relationship between the SAS and SOE which became apparent as soon as the new operating priorities were laid down. SOE regarded itself as the final authority on all matters concerning Maquis groups and the French Resistance as a whole. That was what they had been doing throughout the war and their agents had operated in civilian clothes with considerable success. As far as arming and training the Resistance was concerned, SOE was preparing to drop small liaison parties into France as soon as the invasion started. These were known as Jedburgh teams, after the radio set with which they were equipped. They would wear uniform and would organize the reception of parachuted arms. SOE was naturally not amused to learn that it was proposed to send armed and uniformed teams of SAS outside its control to do exactly the same thing.

The first SAS parties dropped on the night of D-Day, 6 June, and by 17 June, Brigadier McLeod was writing to Airborne Corps HQ in a disappointed vein.[20] He began by stating: 'I am not satisfied that the strategic employment of S.A.S. troops is being properly considered. They are military forces and should not be employed in political tasks.' McLeod reiterated that they must be able to work from a safe base, be dispersed and operate in small parties, avoiding pitched battles. His complaint was that on short notice objectives were being imposed on his parties in the field, leading to a dispersion of effort. The letter continued:

Some of these requests are undoubtedly the result of S.O.E. suggestions and I have the impression that S.A.S. troops are regarded as a military adjunct of S.O.E. to undertake those tasks that S.O.E. cannot undertake. It seems that the policy for the employment of S.A.S. troops is becoming a short-term one and is largely governed by the advice of S.O.E. There is therefore a grave danger of S.A.S. troops being employed on the advice of Special Forces H.Q. rather than on the advice of the Commanding Officer, Airborne Troops, and I am not satisfied that there is any clear policy in existence for the employment of S.A.S. troops. ... I am certain that the employment of small numbers of S.A.S. troops in tactical projects at short notice will result in a complete loss of control over S.A.S. operations as a whole and the wastage of many high class troops without a proper dividend.

Brigadier McLeod felt that he was out on a limb and that control of his units was being wrested from his grasp. Only three days after the above letter was sent, he again put pen to paper to complain to General Browning.

> I have the impression . . . that there is very little function for me since SHAEF lay down my tasks, G (S.A.S.), S.F.H.Q., C.O.H.Q. and H.Q. Airborne Tps., plan the operations, and Collins details the troops! I should be grateful if I could be brought into the discussion at an early stage in order to ensure that my views are considered before detailed planning by the combined planning staffs goes too far.[21]

One cannot help but feel sorry for the unfortunate McLeod. On the one hand, his presence was resented by the two British regiments, as he was not 'one of them' and had been imposed on them. On the other hand, interference in the operational use of his brigade had reduced his position to that of a glorified camp commandant.

On 21 June SHAEF addressed a general directive for SAS operations to Airborne Corps HQ which was intended to govern long-term policy. The priority was 'to provide resistance with a hard core of disciplined troops' and to attack *coup de main* targets. The operating bases were listed in order of priority as: Brittany; Indre; Morvan; Haute Vienne – Dordogne – Cantal; Haute Savoie – Savoie – Jura – Ain; and Vosges. The bases in Brittany, Indre and the Morvan had by then been established, and the recommendation was made that a recce party should be sent to the Vosges. The final scheme ordered that planning should be undertaken for not more than six men to be inserted into the Belgian Ardennes. For this purpose, Special Forces HQ was to obtain the permission of the Belgian government.

On the face of it, the above list did lay down strategic rather than tactical objectives for the various SAS regiments as part of a long-term strategy for the campaign which at that stage was still bogged down in the Normandy peninsular. The dispute about SOE interference, though, flared up again with regard to the directive to plan an operation in Belgium. McLeod found himself forced to write to G3 SHAEF.

> It is understood that there is absolutely no objection from the Belgian Government, but the Belgian section S.O.E. is objecting. They claim that uniformed men would enflame the Resistance too soon. S.O.E. is using the Belgian Government as an excuse. The C.O. of the Belgian S.A.S. has been assured by the *Chef de Cabinet* and the War Minister that they would be very happy to have them in Belgium.[22]

An outsider might well imagine that in 1944 everyone concerned was wholeheartedly dedicated to defeating the common enemy. Sadly this was seldom the case and internal staff rivalries frequently hindered active prosecution of the war. A poor example was set by the senior commanders, with Montgomery and Eisenhower at loggerheads over the issue of command of ground forces and the strategic aims to be followed once the break-out from Normandy had been achieved. The final word regarding SOE is provided by Lieutenant-Colonel Franks in a letter written to Brigadier McLeod on 4 August. It is an indictment of the muddle and confusion that frequently obstructed the mounting of operations, and is worth quoting at some length.[23]

As you know, I have been trying to mount the initial operations of this regiment, which in each case entailed the dropping of a reconnaissance party into areas to which you have ordered me to go. Although the personnel of these parties are perfectly prepared to drop blind, it is obviously preferable that in every case they should be received by a S.F.H.Q. reception committee. The difficulties and time wasted in endeavouring to arrange these reception committees satisfactorily has been appalling to say the least of it, and have necessitated constant journeys and considerable time spent at Baker Street. On the face of it, in view of the fact that there are five, and I believe now, a sixth S.A.S. representative at S.F.H.Q., it would appear that these journeys should be entirely unnecessary.

Franks went on to back up his criticism by citing examples on an operation-by-operation basis. He started off with Operation Rupert which involved a party being sent to blow up railway lines in the Verdun–Reims–Metz area of eastern France. It was delayed so long that by the time it did take place, advancing American forces had almost reached the area anyway. Thus all pretence at achieving a distant strategic aim was swept away and the men involved found themselves far too close to the main battle area.

Rupert
I received the instructions to carry out this operation on 11 July, but the operation had been mooted for a long time prior to this date, and was held up. Eventually after considerable difficulties with S.F.H.Q. due to: a). Difficulty of finding suitable DZ's and b). the fact that S.F.H.Q. had an operation of its own in the area under Boddington,

who appeared to be much averse to having any S.A.S. personnel in his area. The arrangements for the initial recce. party were not satisfactory due to the fact that Boddington was not prepared to receive them, which he signified by making a signal that it would be 'criminally sadistic' to do so ... Finally a DZ was chosen, which having only a receiving set, confirmation that lights would be put out could not be received [by us]. The party therefore had instructions to drop on DZ if the lights were out, or to drop blind in an area about twenty miles away which had been carefully examined. The aircraft carrying this party did not return.

It is now 4 August. The replacement recce. party is due to leave tonight. In spite of every effort and considerable discussion with S.F.H.Q., the arrangements are the same as above except that the DZ is in a different area. While discussing this operation with Group Captain Hallmark at 38 Group on 31 July, I accidentally discovered that S.F.H.Q. had flown one, if not two, sorties recently to the exact area in *Rupert* to which I had always signified I wished to go, and in fact to a reception committee within fifteen kilometres of the spot to which the party may now have to drop blind.

The next operation to be analysed in Franks's letter was Loyton in the Vosges area, which had been under consideration at least since D-Day. One problem was that the earliest date that a recce party could go to the area during the hours of darkness was 3 August. The tangle and confusion that occurred during the planning stage is well set out in the letter. Colonel Franks first endeavoured to find out if someone had been in the area recently and was informed that nobody had. To make certain he then sent one of his officers to the French authorities to find out if they had anyone with local knowledge. They came up with a man who until four months before had been the Maquis leader in the area and was employed at the time at SOE HQ in Baker Street. 'Had this been left to official channels I should never have known of his existence.'

Franks also discovered that some of the six possible dropping zones notified to him by SFHQ were in fact unsuitable for dropping men and that the Maquis in the area had not been supplied with anything since D-Day. His plan had been to accompany his initial recce party with four aircraft carrying sufficient weapons and ammunition to arm the Maquis so that they could protect the dropping zones. Yet from a round-about source he discovered that SFHQ intended to drop such supplies in one of their own operations, using the DZs supplied to his own unit, which could well have become compromised as a result. He summed up the attitude of SOE to the SAS as follows.

There is a prevalent view amongst some members of the staff at S.O.E., and this view has been unfortunately successfully inculcated into some of the S.A.S. liaison staff officers at Baker Street, that uniformed troops are not welcomed by the Maquis, and further, that in known Maquis areas, it is better to supply them with arms and explosives and let them do the tasks rather than send S.A.S. to the area. This is in strict contradiction to the views of both French and British Maquis leaders who have returned recently to this country and with whom I have had the opportunity of discussing this question. . . . Their views are far more likely to represent those of the Maquis than the views of staff officers in London. . . . In spite of a great deal of work and the large numbers of officers employed, S.F.H.Q. have not provided this regiment with anything; other than extremely valuable information which did not come through official channels.

Relations with Resistance groups were to dog many of the operations carried out, and the success or failure of an individual mission often depended on the co-operation or lack of it from the Maquis on the ground. The Resistance itself was split into factions, many of which were more interested in storing weapons away for the day of political reckoning after the war than in shooting Germans. The SAS had been ordered by SHAEF to co-operate with the local Maquis formations, yet as McLeod wrote in a memo to Airborne Corps HQ on 26 June, there were many areas of France devoid of Germans where the SAS could operate. 'Wherever a well armed Maquis appeared, the enemy concentrated.' The conclusion he drew was that it was better for SAS parties to operate independently.[24] That naturally depended on the role allotted to the regiments. His thinking was correct if they were to carry out sabotage and then make themselves scarce. On the other hand, by co-operating with Maquis groups they were able to tie down large numbers of German troops who would otherwise have been fighting at the front.

The SHAEF directive caused problems of a different kind back in Britain. On 3 July, General Browning wrote to the 21st Army Group, pointing out that the original mission allotted to the SAS had called for a series of small drops not more than forty miles from the French coast, for which a weekly resupply limit of twenty-five tons had been calculated. When SHAEF changed the mission to that of assisting Resistance groups, requests for arms and ammunition for them came in over SAS wireless sets. The result was that Airborne Corps HQ became responsible for a vast increase in tonnage to be airlifted and that staff at Station 1090 had likewise to be increased. Brigadier McLeod had demanded more staff and had, in fact, requested 'a completely new war establishment'. Browning asked for a clear directive that, as had been previously agreed, SOE should bear the sole responsibility for supplying the Resistance. He finished by pointing out that if regular airborne operations recommenced, supplies to the SAS would have to be cut to the bare minimum.[25]

By early August, the unfortunate McLeod was beginning to fight a rearguard action and there is the first mention in official correspondence of the word disbandment. On 2 August the brigadier addressed a letter to Airborne Corps HQ, two days before Franks wrote the letter referred to above. At that stage in the campaign the Allied armies were in the process of breaking out of the Normandy peninsular and seemed set to race towards the Seine. McLeod stated that 'at present, under half available troops employed . . . the basic reason for this is the obstruction and difficulties caused by S.F.H.Q. . . . It appears the S.A.S. are not wanted and nothing is being done to help them in spite of the SHAEF directive.' He ended the letter by recommending either the fullest employment or immediate disbandment.[26]

Unfortunately, McLeod was stating the unvarnished truth. The majority of his group of highly trained and motivated men were still kicking their heels in England, waiting to set off on operations that were mooted and then failed to materialize. The bulk of the French units were in the field, but the British, apart from a few parties of less than a dozen men, engaged on purely tactical tasks, were disposed as follows at the beginning of August.

> Houndsworth: Saône et Loire, 1 SAS A Squadron, *circa* 150 men.
> Gain: Fontainebleau area, 1 SAS D Squadron (part), *circa* 60 men.
> Defoe: Normandy, 2 SAS, *circa* 20 men.
> Hardy: Haute Marne, 2 SAS, advance party only.
> Bulbasket: survivors in the process of being returned to Britain by
> air.

Of the above, only the first two were achieving anything in the way of worthwhile harassment of the enemy. It is true that during August the pace of operations quickened considerably, but by then the Allied advance had speeded up to such an extent that many parties were simply overrun after only a few days in the field. The SAS themselves were not lacking in fighting spirit, but were constantly being hindered from above. The point has to be made that if the British regiments had been fully deployed deep in France by mid-June, they would have been able to tie down far larger numbers of Germans, thus hindering their use in Normandy, and could have caused havoc to communications in rear areas.

By the end of August it was clear that the campaign in France was nearly over and that it was time to look to the future employment of the brigade. There were still considerable numbers of men in the field, but their tasks were ending as the Germans pulled back towards their own borders. Lieutenant-Colonel Collins wrote to McLeod on 2 September, stating that there seemed to be little further use for the SAS in France and that it was necessary to consider their future employment. The general assumption was that the war would be over in a matter of weeks as the victorious Allies would romp on over the Rhine.

Collins's first proposal was for the British regiments to be sent to Norway, to stop Germans carrying out demolitions prior to departure, to show the flag generally and to assist in the re-establishment of a legitimate government. Second, he stated that there was a need for a considerable force to operate with the advancing front-line units in Germany, to act in a counter-intelligence role – arresting war criminals and Gestapo agents. Lastly, he floated the idea that the whole brigade might be pulled out and sent to the Far East.[27]

On 4 September, McLeod wrote letters to Brian Franks and Paddy Mayne, marked Personal and Top Secret, outlining the proposals floated by Collins. He started by considering the Far East, although he admitted he had discovered privately that there were no plans to include the SAS in the order of battle there. He then asked if the two commanders wished him to endeavour to arrange for their respective regiments to be sent to the Far East. 'Signal your answer in the form "Pigtail Affirmative" or "Pigtail Negative".' The second option to be considered was post-liberation duty in Norway. In a burst of unfounded optimism, McLeod wrote that this commitment 'might be in perhaps a fortnight's time'. It was to be eight long months before the SAS landed in Norway to supervise the disarming of the German garrison. That September, McLeod considered sending a squadron from each regiment, for a month to six weeks. The regimental commanders were to signal their views as 'Shylock Affirmative' or 'Shylock Negative'. Quite what the latter worthy had to do with the situation in Norway is obscure, unless the brigadier meant the extracting of a pound of flesh from the Germans.

Third, the option of using SAS troops as arrest squads in Germany was discussed at considerable length, under the codewords 'Policeman Affirmative' or 'Policeman Negative'. McLeod stated that an organization was in the process of being set up which would be divided into groups working closely with each of the Allied armies. They would receive their orders from counter-intelligence officers, which would mean that in SAS terms, the regimental headquarters would fulfil little more than an administrative role. As the task was likely to entail a commitment for at least six months and as it was essentially a police job, McLeod felt that volunteers should be called for. He ended by pointing out that acceptance could well mean the splitting up of the regiments, but that it might be preferable to complete disbandment.

In his final paragraphs the brigade commander referred to the need for the SAS in the post-war army, stating that it was General Browning's view that the SAS should survive in one form or another, possibly reduced to one regiment. McLeod's worry was that if they accepted the policing role in Germany, it might pre-empt any decision about the future. If one regiment were to be so employed, the other might well be left to rot away in England. He therefore asked for their views on the three options, as he feared that if none were acceptable, the alternative would be disbandment.[28]

That day, after writing the above, McLeod flew to Orléans for a conference, which was attended by Paddy Mayne and the commanding officer of 4 French Para. Battalion, plus a number of liaison officers. Mayne had been dropped into occupied France in early August to take control of the various squadrons deployed, accompanied by his wind-up gramophone and Corporal Corps, his faithful batman. In the minutes of the conference it is stated that Mayne was not keen on using his regiment on police duties, as it was not a proper task for SAS troops. He preferred the Norway option, but agreed to remain in command if the police option was ordered, to keep the regiment in existence.[29]

In fact, the Allied front line became bogged down in mid-September, effectively nullifying much of the planning process for a future that had suddenly become far more distant. Several of the SAS bases remained in being until the autumn when more or less all personnel were finally transported back to Britain. The individual operational history of the various regiments in the following chapters makes for far more interesting reading than the catalogue of muddle and confusion that tended to prevail at staff level. Once the Germans were well out of the way, staff officers seemed to evince a desire to visit parties remaining in the field. A certain Major Cliffe of the Royal Marines, who was on the brigade staff, visited Paddy Mayne's headquarters near St Amand and toured the Operation Houndsworth area in late September.

His report on his visit has been preserved. It is a masterly demonstration of the blinkered attitudes of outsiders which constantly plagued the fighting units of the SAS. Accompanied by Major Verney (ex-SBS who had escaped from Italy) and Captain Jennings, Cliffe flew by Dakota to Briare on 24 September. His report was highly critical of morale and discipline.

It is extremely hard to maintain discipline and keep up morale once parties have completed their tasks behind the lines. . . . It is considered that as soon as their tasks are completed . . . they should be regrouped if possible in a barracks or other large building and should be given every facility to enable them to return to a normal army life.

What that was supposed to mean is difficult to imagine, except perhaps for parachuting in a supply of boot polish, Brasso and blanco. He went on to suggest:

that for this purpose, Brigade should have its own mobile laundry and bath unit which should be moved forward at the appropriate time to the places where the S.A.S. are being regrouped. . . . It is considered that the standard of morale and discipline in 1 S.A.S. . . . would have been much better if these facilities had been provided.

It is hardly surprising that the above provoked a riposte from Paddy Mayne, addressed to Brigadier McLeod.

It would appear to me that Major Cliffe is taxing his ability overmuch in attempting to write an appreciation of an operational area on the strength of spending five hours there, six weeks after the enemy had left. I also consider his remark that the bases are well sited is presumptuous and unnecessary, unless Major Cliffe believes he is more experienced than Major Fraser who selected the sites. . . . If, as Major Cliffe states, it is extremely difficult to maintain discipline and keep up morale, we may consider ourselves extremely fortunate. We have had, as far as my knowledge goes, no drunkenness, absence, desertion, looting or rape. A bath unit or laundry is unnecessary. It is always possible to find and heat water. I hope that I have not wasted as much paper as Major Cliffe.[30]

That a relatively senior officer could produce such arrant nonsense is amazing, when one considers that his brigade commander was extremely worried at the time as to whether or not he would be able to keep the SAS in existence at all. One wonders if the mobile bath operators would have had to be parachute-trained.

It may seem from the contents of this chapter that the SAS achieved little during the campaign in France. In terms of a contribution to the overall Allied victory, this was certainly true, though it was hardly the fault of the units involved. As far as SHAEF was concerned, the aim was to defeat the enemy armies in the field and then advance towards Germany. Liberating France was purely a spin-off, although the Free French saw matters differently. They naturally clamoured for maximum support to be given to the Resistance and wildly exaggerated the capabilities of the scattered bands. To provide such support, however, meant diverting large numbers of aircraft, which could otherwise have been bombing important targets. SHAEF was worried that if widespread insurrection erupted all over France, they would be forced into supporting it for political reasons, thus diverting resources from the main battle.

As far as the SAS were concerned, their abilities were misunderstood by the senior planning staffs, who were simply preoccupied with getting the main body of troops ashore on D-Day and keeping them there. As we have seen, the initial idea was to use the regiments to interdict the movement of enemy reinforcements into the beach-head, which would have been suicidal. Fighting tanks with small arms from behind improvised roadblocks was hardly going to worry the Germans overmuch. Ideally, small parties should have been inserted deep into France well before D-Day, but this was impossible in view of the 21st Army Group's prohibition of uniformed troops anywhere in the country before the main landings took place. Owing to a lack of aircraft in early June, only a few small advance parties were actually dropped and those became involved with local Resistance groups. As they were built up, the parties became too large and their activities naturally attracted the attention of the enemy. These squadron-size groups were too small to defend themselves against all-out attack without heavy weapons, yet

Major David Stirling
(*right*), 1941

2. SAS paratroops in
training with the
skeleton parachute, near
Kabrit

3. A group of SAS 'Originals': (*left right from back*) Jerry Ward, Sgt. Richardson, Ted Badger (*in driver's seat*), Bob Tait, Johnny Cooper, non SAS member, Pat Riley, Dave Kershaw (*squatting by back wheel*), Reg Seekings (*front*)

4. Paddy Mayne, 1942

5. Sgts. Johnny Cooper (*left*) and Reg Seekings on leave in Cairo, 1941

Patrol jeep fitted with
ngle and twin Vickers
.' and 0.5 machine gun

7. Lt.-Col. David Stirling photographed just before his capture with a patrol commanded by Lt. Edward McDonald

8. Major Pat Hart, Paddy Mayne and Roy Farran at Stavanger airport

Members of the SRS
ter the battle at Cape
urro di Porco, Sicily,
ly 1943

10. Jeep crew on
Operation Bulbasket near
Poitiers, June 1944

11. and 12. 1 SAS crossing the Rhine in a Buffalo, March 1945

13. An SAS grave at Moussey, shortly after burial by the locals

14. 2 SAS jeep patrol in Germany, April 1945

15. Paddy Mayne and 1 SAS prepare to leave for Norway, May 1945

lacked the mobility to be able to fade away, thus defeating the main purpose of irregular warfare. The SAS certainly provided a core of trained men who could arm and stiffen the Resistance, but one can argue that they should have worked independently, relying on their own resources. One essential problem was that the SAS units of 1944 were no longer the small, personally selected élite of L Detachment. To make up the numbers, many unsuitable recruits had been more or less drafted in and they were not so highly trained or motivated. Many of the new officers had no real experience of combat and they were controlled by a non-SAS staff.

It is generally accepted that the SAS Brigade numbered 2,500 men of all ranks, and that about 2,000 of them were operational. The following figures were published after the war, covering the period June to November 1944. Enemy casualties listed were based on claims made by the units concerned, but if one reads SAS after-action reports for the period, there is no evidence of extravagant statements about the damage caused. Total SAS casualties were given as 330 killed, wounded or missing. Of these, the British regiments suffered around 100 men killed, most of whom were executed by the German security authorities. The brigade claimed 7,733 enemy killed and 4,784 prisoners, with the assistance of resistance units under the direct command of SAS officers. The latter figure naturally excluded 18,000 Germans who surrendered at Issoudun to the Americans, having been surrounded by SAS and Resistance forces.

As far as physical damage was concerned, the figures list 740 assorted vehicles captured or destroyed, and 7 trains, 89 waggons and 29 locomotives totally eliminated. There were 33 derailments and lines were cut in 164 places. Perhaps more importantly, 400 bombing targets were reported back for action by the Allied air forces. To achieve these results, the RAF flew 780 sorties, of which 180 had to be aborted and in which 6 aircraft were lost.

Thus the SAS in France, however imperfect their organization and direction may have been, accounted for six times their own numbers in enemy casualties. This only had a marginal effect on the campaign as a whole, but clandestine forces have seldom influenced the outcome of the main battle. With the benefit of hindsight, however, had they been employed according to the original principles, the regiments concerned might have achieved a far greater contribution to the eventual victory.

8

1 SAS in France

The previous chapter was concerned with the formation of the SAS Brigade, the training of its component parts for war, and the difficulties faced by the brigade in planning for operations. The following chapters will look at the actual operational history of the campaign in France, starting with 1 SAS Regiment. A glance at the map on p. xviii will show that between June and November 1944 a large number of operations were carried out all over France. It is not possible within the space available to discuss all of them in great detail. It is also difficult to deal with operations chronologically, without chopping and changing rapidly from one area to another which would be most confusing. Therefore individual operations will be looked at in order of their starting dates.

Operations in France really fell into two basic categories. First there were relatively small-scale and purely tactical missions carried out for the 21st Army Group, designed to cut communications in enemy rear areas or to provide intelligence. The parties involved did not remain long in the field and generally were expected to exfiltrate back through the lines. The second type of operation was where a larger party set up a base well behind the lines and worked from it for a period of anything up to three months. The drill for forming such a base was to land an advance party accompanied by a Phantom signals section. This party then had to contact local Maquis units and discover suitable dropping zones for supplies and the reception of further parties of men and jeeps. Some drops were met by a reception laid on by SFHQ agents already in the field, while others were blind.

Those assigned to take part in the initial missions carried out by 1 SAS Regiment left Darvel and travelled to the airfield at Fairford in

Gloucestershire at the end of May 1944. At that stage they were unaware of the nature of their mission or its destination. Fairford was a completely sealed camp, surrounded by barbed wire and patrolled by sentries. Security was essential to the success of Overlord as a whole. Once inside the camp there was only one way out – in an aircraft heading for France. It was at Fairford that briefings for missions were carried out, maps and air photographs issued and the latest intelligence passed on. The necessary containers of stores and personal equipment were sent in from Station 1090, a few miles away at Down Ampney. After that, it was a question of waiting, wondering about the weather, and checking and rechecking personal weapons, until the trucks came to take the men to the waiting Stirlings.

The casual nonconformity of the desert days with respect to clothing was a thing of the past by 1944. Standard battledress was worn, covered by the airborne Dennison smock, a jumping helmet and rubber-soled boots. The parachute was worn on the back, and each man carried a kit bag strapped to his leg. This contained a Bergan rucksack with his personal kit. Once out of the aircraft, the leg bag was released so that it hung below the man on ten feet of strong cord. He also had a scabbard strapped to his right leg to hold a rifle or carbine, a webbing belt, an entrenching tool, pouches and a holstered pistol.

The drill on landing without a ground reception party was as follows. Before leaving the aircraft the stick commander, who jumped first, obtained the compass bearing of the direction of the drop from the pilot. When he was down, he had first to bury his parachute and then walk back along the compass bearing, blowing a bird-call whistle. When the other members of the stick heard this, they also blew bird calls and held luminous glass balls above their heads. In theory it was possible to assemble a stick without unnecessary shouting.

Stores containers were long cylindrical drums divided internally into cells. To simplify matters they were delivered pre-packed with code letters on the outside denoting their contents. They could contain a mixture of clothing, rations, ammunition, weapons, 'comforts' such as rum and cigarettes, medical kit, tents and sleeping bags. A Stirling aircraft, for example, could carry twenty-four such containers with a gross weight of 3.75 tons. Soft items such as clothing, sleeping bags and tentage were dropped in panniers, which tended, however, to burst open on landing. Jeeps attached to four parachutes were dropped from Halifax aircraft. The necessary petrol, gun mountings, spare wheels and tools were dropped separately in containers. In theory, a jeep could be assembled and driven off the dropping zone within twenty minutes of arrival.

The first operation of the French campaign assigned to 1 SAS was codenamed Titanic and was a left-over from the original aim of using the regiment in direct support of the Allied landings on D-Day. A number of 'Titanics' had been envisaged in an operation instruction issued on 19 May, but by the evening of 5 June, they had been whittled down to one. The idea was to drop a small party just inland from the beach-head in Normandy, equipped with a number of devices to simulate a full-scale airborne landing – which, it was assumed, would spread alarm and confusion among the Germans in the area.[1]

Two lieutenants, Poole (A Squadron) and Fowles (B Squadron), each accompanied by two privates, took off from Fairford on the night of 5 June. They were to drop at 4 a.m. on D-Day, a few miles to the south of Carentan. This was a highly important area tactically, as the road network through Carentan was vital if the two American landing beaches, Utah and Omaha, were to be linked together. The aircraft also carried dummy parachutists made from sandbags, small bombs which fired Very cartridges on landing, detonators which would explode to simulate small-arms fire and spare containers full of sandbags. The SAS party on landing were to remove the sandbags from the containers and leave the latter scattered about to fool the enemy into thinking that weapons had been landed. Having done that, all they had to do was to cause as much havoc as possible.

They were dropped two miles south of the agreed DZ. When the men assembled, both officers were found to be missing. The four privates spent some time searching in vain for the containers, but as it began to get light, they had to content themselves with setting off some Lewes bombs before finding a place to lie up. They hid in a hedge during the following day and in the evening were contacted by a Frenchman, who took them to a ruined abbey. The following day he brought in Lieutenant Poole, who had knocked himself out on leaving the aircraft and had lain unconscious on the ground. In the jargon of the SAS, he had 'rung the bell'. Albemarle aircraft had a comparatively small jumping hatch in the fuselage floor and the parachutist had to sit with his legs dangling over the edge. On being given the signal to jump he had to slip outwards and down. Unfortunately it was easy to fall forwards, causing the head to collide with the opposite rim of the hatch.

Fowles was brought in during the afternoon of 10 June, having dropped some distance from the others. The group stayed hidden for the best part of three weeks, and as they had nothing more than their personal weapons, there was little they could do in the way of creating havoc. On 28 June, a German airborne unit moved into the vicinity, and they were forced to move to another refuge. There they were joined by three US parachutists, and decided to make for the Allied lines, by then only a few miles away. On the night of 10 July they became involved in a fracas with some Germans, which resulted in three of the SAS and two of the Americans being wounded. They carried the injured to a farm where they were surrounded and forced to surrender.

The wounded were well cared for and there was never any threat that any of them would be executed. Private Hurst was taken to a hospital in Rennes where he was freed by the Americans at the end of August. The above account of Titanic is based on the statement he gave in hospital to Regimental Sergeant-Major Rose who visited him.[2]

In fact, the whole operation had been a waste of time. There was no evidence of Germans searching the area immediately after the drop or during the days following. At the same time, a large US airborne formation had been dropped in the area slightly to the west, but became so scattered in landing that there were real parachutists all over the Cherbourg peninsula for the enemy to chase.

The next two operations were totally different in concept. In the SHAEF directive of 19 May, the SAS Brigade was ordered to establish two operating bases to interfere with the movement of enemy forces in southern France which might be sent north towards the main battle zone in Normandy.[3] The first of these was Houndsworth, in the Morvan hills to the west of Dijon, and the second was Bulbasket, in the Vienne area south of Poitiers. We will examine the latter operation first.

Captain John Tonkin, aged 23, had joined the SAS during the latter stages of the North African campaign and had taken part in the landings in Sicily and Italy with the SRS. We last heard of him when he was taken prisoner at Termoli and subsequently escaped. He was told at Fairford on 30 May that he was to take his troop of four officers and thirty-nine men from B Squadron, plus a Phantom patrol, and establish a base in the Vienne. As he prepared to brief his men, however, the plan was changed. Tonkin was told that he and Lieutenant Crisp were to be dropped in advance to recce a suitable base and prepare to receive the rest of the party. In his instructions, he was told to investigate the strength and organization of the local Resistance and the strength of the Germans. The first conclusion to be drawn was whether or not the area was safe as a base and how many SAS troops could be absorbed there.

Then the advance party were to investigate suitable dropping zones and even glider landing fields. The instructions issued to him gave a whole list of questions that needed answering. Was it possible for small parties to move in daytime? Where did the River Loire start to be fordable? To what extent could jeeps be used? Was it possible to find motor cars in the area? Was money of primary importance? And so on. The railway lines in the area were listed as Lots 1 to 5.[4]

Tonkin and Crisp were given a detailed briefing in London by SOE, whose local man on the ground was Amadée Maingard, known as 'Samuel'. One veteran of operations in France advised Tonkin that when he landed, he should have a pistol in one hand and a bar of chocolate in the other.[5] Instead of departing from Fairford, he and Crisp were taken to Hazells Hall, a mansion in Bedfordshire used by SOE to look after agents before they departed from the nearby Tempsford aerodrome. Tonkin spent the afternoon of 5 June doing jigsaw puzzles with a young agent called Violette Szabo. She was later executed at Ravensbruck concentration camp.

Operation Bulbasket, with the tragedies that attended it, is one of the few SAS missions of the period that is well covered by French sources written after the war, though the accounts are often at variance with one another. There were a considerable number of Resistance groupings and Maquis units in the area, not necessarily holding the same political aims. Post-war Resistance memoirs published in France frequently tend to self-justification and denigration of their opponents, and thus have to be approached with caution. On the British side, I have had access to various reports and papers kindly made available by John Tonkin,[6] interview material, and the book, *Das Reich*, by Max Hastings.

The two SAS officers, accompanied in the aircraft by a Jedburgh team code-named Hugh, took off from Tempsford and dropped blind at 1.37 a.m. on the morning of D-Day. Shortly after landing, they were contacted by 'Samuel', who advised them to move to a safer area. On the night of 7 June, the remainder of the advance party consisting of Lieutenant Stephens and eight men dropped successfully on to a different DZ. At that stage the Jedburgh team departed on their own task and the SAS party, who had brought their own signallers with them, were taken to meet the local Resistance leaders.

The meeting took place at the Château Manès, a headquarters used by Colonel 'Bernard'. He was head of the AS (Armée Secrète) and also a loose confederation of other groups, such as the Communist FTP, known as the FFI (Forces Françaises de l'Intérieur). Inevitably there were language difficulties and differences of opinion about what should be done, but the meeting was cordial. Bernard detailed a group of ten resistants under Captain Dieudonné (Maurice) to act as guides and maintain contact with the local population.

On 11 June, Tonkin sent a message to London that there were a number of trains of petrol wagons in the sidings at Châtellerault. They were too well guarded to be attacked on foot, and a bombing raid was requested. It had been arranged that the same night the rest of the troop would be flown in, together with a Phantom patrol to improve communications. Tonkin's men and a group of Maquis made their way to the dropping zone which was close to the main Limoges – Poitiers road. To their annoyance they discovered that a German division was moving up the road with its headlights full on. Even so it was decided to risk receiving the drop and the necessary lights were put out.

The drop itself was a messy affair. For a start, only one aircraft located the place and discharged twelve men. Then, on a second pass, a number of containers were thrown out. To the horror of those waiting on the ground, coloured lights began to shine in the sky. These were caused by the malfunction of a new invention: lamps had been fitted to the containers and they were designed to switch on on impact to make them easier to find in the dark. For some reason they lit up as the loads descended. Miraculously the German convoy swept on without intervening, as the men heaved the containers on to ox carts and dragged them away to be hidden. As they left the dropping zone, they saw in the sky to the north the glow of flames caused by a massive air raid on the railway at Poitiers. The second aircraft that should have arrived was deterred by the lights of the convoy on the road and dropped its load thirty miles to the south-east. This consisted of a further eight SAS and Captain Sadoine's Phantom patrol. The latter, for some reason, had been given a rendezvous point of which Tonkin had not been informed.

Tonkin was also surprised at the smallness of the party that had joined him, and it was left to the stick commander, Sergeant Jessiman, to inform him that the rest of the troop had been dropped blind in four small parties, as a result of a last-minute change of plan. Each was to cut a section of railway and then make their way to join the main body. Tonkin was given orders to transmit new rendezvous points to London which would then be re-broadcast by the BBC to the parties' MCR 100 receivers.

Lieutenant Morris and three men were dropped within five miles of the main Poitiers–Tours railway and successfully blew both tracks over a culvert. Morris reported one of his men missing as a result of a presumed parachute malfunction, but he subsequently turned up. Lieutenant Weaver managed to derail a train on the Bordeaux–Saumur line, in spite of being dropped quite some distance away. Sergeant Holmes and two men also succeeded in their mission against the Poitiers–Tours line. The latter, known as Lot 2, was to become a firm favourite with the Bulbasket troop. The last of the detached parties commanded by Corporal Kinnevane was not so fortunate. They were dropped way off target and landed in the town square of a small place called Airvault. One trooper was captured, and the other two were forced to flee, abandoning their kit in the process. The four parties all managed to rejoin Tonkin at various intervals.

Thus far, the operation had achieved some remarkable successes. There were the three railway demolitions described above, and in addition Lieutenant Stephens cut the Limoges–Poitiers line, estimating it would be out of action for three days. Lieutenant Crisp went out to lay mines on some roads and the RAF destroyed the petrol wagons that had been reported. Quite unknown to the SAS, the Germans who had been moving along near the DZ were part of the 2nd SS Panzerdivision, Das Reich, which was heading towards the Normandy front, leaving a trail of death and destruction in its wake. The division had been intending to refuel from the trains at Châtellerault, and thus Tonkin's men had imposed a significant if slight delay on its progress. It was a unit of Das Reich that had been responsible a few days earlier for a series of summary executions at Tulle and the wholesale massacre of the population at Oradour sur Glane.[7]

Life, however, was already becoming difficult. On 12 June, Tonkin signalled base that the area was 'lousy with enemy'. His unit was constantly having to move its base, and he requested jeeps to be sent as mobility was a serious problem. The following day he reported that 400 Germans were looking for them and that he was moving once again. He was also having problems in contacting Captain Sadoine, who seemingly had no intention of joining up with him. On the night of 17 June, four jeeps and their drivers were successfully dropped, plus the necessary stores to arm them.

Tom Stephens, who spoke a little French, had been picked to go with one of the senior Resistance people to recce a suitable DZ for receiving the jeeps. Camille Olivet, known as La Chouette, was a veteran of the Spanish Civil War and a Communist who had been in the Resistance right from the beginning. The following is based on his account of the trip.[8] He decided that Stephens should wear civilian clothes and that they would travel by bicycle. Tonkin protested that wearing civvies would prejudice their status as prisoners of war, but Olivet pointed out that they could hardly ride around in daylight in uniform. So Stephens changed into an old suit borrowed from a farmer and, before setting out, was frisked by Olivet – who removed a packet of English cigarettes and some army-issue toilet paper from his pockets. Stephens was told: 'The peasants here wipe their bums with fresh grass, soaked in chlorophyl!'

The two men set out and after some miles of pleasant riding, they stopped at a café for lunch. The English officer's accent caused slight difficulties there, as the proprietor initially took him for a German. In the late afternoon they arrived at the farm nearest to where the drop was to take place, only to discover that the area which had been selected by Tonkin on a map was covered by young trees. A hasty inspection revealed a suitable field and there they prepared the necessary bonfires to signal in the aircraft. A further complication was the fact that a cow was about to calve and the assistant to the vet was present for the occasion. He was known to have Vichy sympathies and, much to his annoyance, was ordered to stay at the farm until after the drop.

Tonkin and his men turned up in a lorry at about nine o'clock, to be welcomed by the farmer with several bottles of home-distilled rough spirits, without which a *parachutage* in France was impossible. Thus fortified, everyone went outside and waited for the sound of aircraft engines.

Ten past eleven. We heard the throbbing of the aircraft in the distance. Tonkin lit the fires and transmitted the agreed recognition signal. The aircraft passed over for the first time to reply to the signal and then they turned into the wind and came back towards us. We saw them at less than 800 metres altitude – perfect. There were four, following one behind the other, slightly spread out in a line so that the jeeps would not land on top of one another. They came nearer and nearer: the throbbing was – infernal! 200 metres before arriving over us they jettisoned their loads simultaneously. It was a grandiose spectacle – the four vehicles each suspended from twelve parachutes. [In fact, jeeps were dropped with four parachutes.] The jeeps descended slowly, as if balanced in the air. The last one to land grazed the roof of the barn and landed up in a nearby vine.

At that moment, there was a silence, then all those present let loose an enthusiastic cry. . . . The vehicle assigned to Tonkin was the last one, which landed in the vine. We charged towards it. The vine was covered in parachutes which were quickly removed by the people from the farm and Anatole's men. It was the first time that I saw the type of little vehicle called a Jeep. . . . Like all the others it had landed on a metal platform which had been slightly damaged, but the jeep hadn't suffered. Its sidelights were on, probably to aid recovery in case it landed away from the dropping zone. Tonkin came over and got out the steering wheel from under one of the seat cushions, and a Vickers machine-gun from a container at the back. The machine-gun was fixed to its mounting and Tonkin loaded it with a magazine resembling a box of camembert, got behind the wheel, pulled the starter and said to me: 'La Chouette, your place is beside me, at the machine-gun.'

The following day, Tonkin reported the safe arrival of the jeeps and noted, 'Area became unhealthy and I was compelled to contact Captain Sadoine, but failed owing to Maquis jealousy and distrust.' There had also been a spot of bother as they were leaving the DZ, and Trooper O'Neill was wounded in the hand. It was obviously impossible to keep secret such a large body of British troops, and by then the Germans were becoming increasingly active.

During the following three weeks, small parties sallied forth regularly to cut the railway lines. There were considerable difficulties over supply drops, which were either cancelled because of poor weather, or failed because the aircraft could not see the lights on the DZs. Tonkin did not have the standard homing device known as a Eureka with him. The Eureka emitted a signal which could be received by incoming aircraft to guide them to the DZ, but it was notoriously unreliable. A further cause of friction was that Captain Sadoine was constantly making excuses for not joining up with the main party and seemed intent on running his own independent operation, arming the Maquis and receiving his own supply drops.

On 25 June the main party moved to a base in some woods near the small town of Verrières. This was on a gently sloping site which ran down into a valley where there was an adequate supply of fresh water from a stream. There were thirty-five SAS in the camp, an American airman who had been shot down and about ten Maquis under the command of Maurice. Very early in the morning of 3 July, the camp was surprised by a large force of Germans and nearly all its inhabitants were killed or taken prisoner. What actually happened and why is difficult to piece together. The general view is that the location was betrayed, and the SAS may well have been guilty of poor security. Various French accounts state that they received visits from local girls in the camp and that some of the men went into the town. A day or two before the attack, John Fielding was on guard beside a track leading into the woods when he saw two men with a motor-cycle combination apparently trying to repair a puncture. He challenged them and they were taken into the camp, where they produced credentials that could not be properly checked. In retrospect, Fielding wished that he had shot them outright.[9]

The night before the attack, Corporal Sam Smith, accompanied by Troopers John Fielding and Robert Smith, had set off in a jeep to demolish the main railway line yet again, and thus had a fortuitous escape. The rest settled down for the night under the trees, wrapped in their sleeping bags. There were two men on watch, but no sentries had been posted to cover the approaches. According to Max Hastings, the men were armed only with Colt .45 automatics, but that is difficult to believe.[10] SAS parties were dropped with rifles or carbines and had in the meantime been supplied by air with a large stock of weapons. Camille Olivet took issue with Hastings over this statement in a letter. Referring to Tonkin, he wrote:

He let himself be lured by false considerations which no commander had the right to ignore. And then, when the Germans attacked, there were no sentries whatsoever in place. Then, it has to be observed that the English group comprising about forty men, plus the Maquis, were armed with four Vickers K machine guns, several light machine guns, American carbines and a considerable number of grenades as well as two rocket launchers [bazookas]. Why didn't they reply? And why, on the German side, were there no wounded or killed? Mystery. It is wrong to state that the SAS were only armed with pistols. They were armed at the time of the first parachutage at Beaumartin where they received more than six tons of material![11]

Maurice remembers that he woke up and heard the noise of engines in the vicinity at about one o'clock in the morning, but ignored it and went back to sleep. 'Alas, at seven o'clock the first mortar bombs burst. ... and at the same moment I saw one of my men, Choisy, open fire. I saw the German column which was attacking. Tonkin and I opened up with the Vickers, and the battle commenced.'[12]

Most accounts agree that there was total panic and the majority of the men stampeded down the hill, where the Germans were waiting for them. Tonkin yelled for them to separate into small groups, and courageously took the time to place bombs on the three jeeps that were present. In confused fighting in the wood, Lieutenant Stephens was wounded and seven of the French were killed. Maurice and two others managed to escape in the confusion, taking refuge in a field of cabbages. Tonkin himself survived through sheer luck.

> I was only saved because I remained behind in the camp after the men had left, to destroy the code book and do other similar things. When I was finished I discovered that the German cordon had closed right around the camp site and I could not follow the others. I remained crouching behind a rock for several hours without moving, about fifty metres from the camp, and by an incredible stroke of luck, I was not seen. During the night I left on foot.[13]

It was all over quite quickly. The Germans rounded up their prisoners and sent most of them off in trucks to Poitiers, including several who were seriously wounded. They took the injured Stephens into the village of Verrières and tied him to a tree at the top of the square. Having assembled the inhabitants, the German detachment proceeded to beat him to death with their rifle butts. He lies buried in the local cemetery, where every year on the anniversary of his death the local people lay wreaths in his honour.

Those who had been taken to Poitiers, including the wounded, were loaded into trucks on the night of 6 July and driven into the forest at Saint Sauvant. There were thirty SAS men and the American airman, Lieutenant Lincoln Bundy. They were shot at dawn and buried in ditches, together with an unidentified body, probably that of a Frenchman. The executions were carried out as a result of the Commando Order and were authorized by General Gallenkamp, commanding the German corps stationed in the area. Returning from their operation on foot a few days later, Corporal Smith and his party were warned of what had happened and made their way to the alternative rendezvous. During the afternoon of 6 July, Tonkin was able to inform base via an SOE radio that he had eleven SAS fit for operations plus the five-man Phantom patrol of Sadoine. A few others returned from operations, but the attack on the camp effectively broke the back of Bulbasket. One or two minor rail demolitions were carried out, but with only one jeep left mobility was restricted. The party was able to receive drops and passed on useful intelligence, but Brigade HQ decided that the remaining men would have to be retrieved.

On the night of 28 June, Lieutenant Surrey-Dane was dropped. He had been specially trained in RAF requirements for emergency landing strips and his task was to find a suitable place and to organize an air lift. A small advance party from 3 French Para. Battalion arrived by parachute to relieve the 1 SAS party. Just after midnight on 7 August, two Hudson aircraft touched down on a specially cleared landing strip, code-named Bonbon. They disembarked a further group of French SAS and twenty minutes later they took off, carrying twenty men including 'Samuel', Tonkin and most of his men, three American airmen and the Phantom patrol. Three nights later a Dakota brought off the rest of the party and a further group of Americans.

Like many SAS operations of the period, Bulbasket was flawed from the start by the compromise between SHAEF requirements for assistance to the Maquis and the need to avoid involvement in pitched battles against superior enemy numbers. The party was far too large to remain undetected; and as it lacked transport other than four jeeps, it had to rely on the goodwill of the French for the frequent movements of campsite. Their security became lax and thus they were surprised at dawn, snug in their sleeping bags. Their very presence animated the Maquis into action, which served to inflame the local Germans, who previously had tended to stick to the towns and keep their heads down.

Major Bill Fraser's A Squadron contained quite a significant proportion of veterans from the North African period. The mission assigned to him was to establish a base, code-named Houndsworth, to the west of Dijon. This was a hilly region, densely wooded and dotted with several lakes, known as the Morvan. Instructions were as vague as they had been for Bulbasket – harassing German communications, cutting railways and assisting the Maquis. The area chosen was far less populated than the Vienne and there were correspondingly fewer Germans garrisoning the small towns.

The advance party which was to drop on the night of 5 June brought together for the first time since the desert raids two old friends, Lieutenant Johnny Cooper and Sergeant-Major Reg Seekings, who were to go in with a Phantom patrol. The intention had been to drop to a reception committee, but the weather was so foul that the pilot was unable to find the DZ and the party had to drop blind. The stick left the aircraft in blinding rain and became quite scattered on landing. Johnny Cooper hit a stone wall, knocking himself out, and came to in a ditch all tangled up in his parachute. By dawn, however, the entire stick had managed to assemble and settled down in true British style to prepare a brew. They also released their two pigeons.

We wrote our coded messages on very thin rice paper and enclosed them in the capsules which were fixed to the pigeons' legs. Each bird was given a bit of water and a small amount of corn, then, holding them above our heads we let them go. To our amazement they dropped back down to the ground and started to peck away at a ploughed field on the edge of the forest. Reg swore like hell and rushed after them, flapping his arms and shouting to get them airborne. Finally they took off and headed over the horizon towards England.[15]

In an effort to find out where they were and contact the Resistance, they approached a farmhouse, where a teenage boy offered to see what he could do. Later in the day he returned, and Seekings and Cooper were taken to a rendezvous. There they hid in a ditch until they heard the sound of an engine approaching. Getting ready to make a run for it, they were astonished to see a coach rolling up the road propelled by a *gazogène* burner on the back. The ancient conveyance was full of heavily armed men from one of the local Maquis who took the whole stick off to their camp where a vast meal with wine was served up.

The first priority was to arrange a suitable DZ to receive supplies and, eventually, further members of the squadron. The actual selection was inevitably a matter of compromise, although a standard operating procedure (SOP) laid down the criteria.[16] 'The dropping zone should not be much smaller than a square of 400 yds. wide. It will not matter if there are tracks or hedges crossing this ground but there should be no obstacles such as tall trees, telephone lines, power lines etc. The ground should be reasonably level and marshy ground should be avoided.' A further requirement was adequate cover in the immediate vicinity for hiding containers until they could be carted away, as well as for any vehicles being used.

The standard recognition signal was by means of three lights or bonfires in a line, 100 yards apart. Ten yards to the right of the upwind fire, a person was delegated to flash the recognition letter in Morse code with a torch. The pilot could then fly into the wind down the line of fires, starting to drop his containers when he was over the first one. As mentioned earlier, the Eureka device was more often than not unsatisfactory for guiding aircraft. A further technical device that also seldom worked properly was the S-Phone, via which the DZ commander could speak to the crew of the aircraft by voice link. For the French who took part in *parachutages*, the occasion was often one for great celebration, accompanied by bottles of fortifying liquor and plenty of loud chatter. An added perquisite was parachute material – in those days usually pure white silk. Thriving cottage industries grew up in Maquis areas producing ladies' undergarments and even wedding dresses. Far less popular were the camouflage ones. The author has seen an exquisite christening gown made of parachute silk which has been used by the children of several generations of a family in the Vosges.

Headquarters made the necessary arrangements with great speed and the Houndsworth advance party received their first drop the night after they had landed. Twenty-four containers were dropped and were taken away by ox carts provided by local farmers. During the following nights, the rest of the force began to assemble. Squadron Headquarters under Bill Fraser were first in and set up camp some distance away from the Maquis. It was planned that the bulk of the personnel would drop on the night of 16 June. Three aircraft took off from Fairford. The sticks commanded by Captain Wiseman and Captain Muirhead both failed to find their DZs and returned to base. The third aircraft containing Lieutenant Cairns and fourteen other men was never heard of again and it was presumed that it had crashed. The occupants are remembered on the Bayeux memorial for those who have no known grave.

Two nights later the two sticks took off again and dropped success-fully, although Sergeant 'Chalky' White ended up on a roof and injured his back. A further reinforcement of two sticks flew in on the night of 21 June, commanded by Roy Bradford. A much-respected member of the party was the padre who had wheedled his way on to operations. He was accompanied by a pannier containing hymn books, prayer books, an altar cloth and communion vessels.

The Revd Fraser McLuskey arrived in France dangling from a parachute and came down in a tree. Hanging upside down by one leg, he cut himself free by hacking through the rigging lines.

And there I ceased to take any further interest in events. What happened exactly I shall never know. Either I cut away the only strap that held me to the branch, or else my not inconsiderable weight brought the branch down. But whatever happened, I fell, and fell to some purpose. My last recollection is of crashing head first through innumerable branches. I knew of no more until I woke up on a soft grassy bank at the foot of the tree being violently sick. . . . It was nearly 3 a.m., and all was quiet. I decided that I had done enough damage for one night, and, propping myself up against my precious kit bag, I dozed off to sleep.[17]

He was in illustrious company when it came to landing in trees. Bill Fraser found himself suspended in pitch darkness and could not see the ground. Having no notion how far his fall might be, he waited patiently for the dawn, only to discover that his feet were three inches from the ground.

The following Sunday, the padre held his first service in occupied France, under the trees in the camp of Maquis Jean. During the evening, however, a German patrol attacked the Maquis in the wood. Reg Seekings led his section off to see what was going on and to lend a hand. Unfortunately he was hit by a bullet in the back of the neck which narrowly missed his spine. Without anaesthetic a Maquis doctor dug around but could not find it. Nursed by Fraser McLuskey, Reg returned to duty within a few days and the bullet was finally removed in Chelmsford hospital several months later.

The Houndsworth area was finally built up to a total of 18 officers and 126 other ranks with 9 jeeps. It was in commission for three months and the three troops under Captains Wiseman, Muirhead and Bradford succeeded in repeatedly cutting the railways around Dijon. Serious operations started when the first jeeps began to arrive, accompanied finally by two 6-pounder anti-tank guns – the first use of air-portable artillery by the SAS.

The official report of the operation is a vast file which goes into immense detail, but certain highlights and events stand out.[18] With such a large group of SAS established in the area, it was inevitable that their presence would be talked about. In addition, the Maquis were itching for a fight to try out their new weapons. The largest German garrison in the area was based at Château Chinon, and many of its men were in fact Russians – ex-prisoners of war who had 'volunteered' to serve their captors. These so-called security units were mostly employed on anti-Maquis sweeps and could expect no mercy if caught. They were often accompanied by the hated Milice who were French paramilitary police loyal to the Vichy regime.

A large unit of Russians under German officers moved into the surrounding villages in early July, taking hostages and burning houses.

In Montsauche they captured a number of Resistance sympathizers whom they intended to remove to Château Chinon for interrogation, and a decision was made to attempt a rescue. Alec Muirhead's troop, assisted by a number of Maquis, selected a site on the road leading out of Montsauche along which the enemy convoy with its prisoners would have to travel. They found a suitable incline which would slow down the trucks, with forest on one side and open fields on the other. Just past the ambush position the road bent to the right, out of sight of any vehicles climbing the hill. Round this bend, Lieutenant Ian Welstead positioned his section and strung thin wires across the road at the height of a motor-cyclist, to take out the outriders of the convoy.

On the hill itself, stacked wood on the verge beside the forest provided excellent cover for a party armed with grenades, while behind them the Maquis established a firing line. On the other side, in the fields, Muirhead, Cooper and Seekings lay in wait with brens to cover the killing ground. Through the warm summer afternoon they waited, until word was received that the enemy was just leaving the village. They had ten minutes to go to action stations.

From my position I observed the two leading motorcyclists come up the slope and disappear around the bend to be clobbered by Welstead. At the same moment the first three tonner crammed with soldiers drew level with the wood pile and over came two plastic bombs. One hit the bonnet and the other the rear of the vehicle. Pandemonium among the occupants. Many were killed by the fire from the Maquis as they fled across the road towards the open fields. Our brens opened up with devastating effect and many of the Russians retreated back to the ditch, which was in Reg's sights. It was a massacre. Three trucks were set on fire and the hostages were released unharmed from two civilian cars.[19]

Sadly though, there was a tragic price to pay. Shortly afterwards half the village of Montsauche was burned and thirteen hostages were shot, including the mayor and the parish priest. Wherever the SAS operated in France, similar reprisals were taken, to be remembered afterwards by yet another wayside memorial. It is to the eternal credit of the French that there is no lingering bitterness. Veterans from the regiment regularly pay visits to their old operating areas where they are received with honour at the local memorial ceremonies.

On 17 July, Roy Bradford's troop prepared to make one of the periodic moves of camp which were necessary because of the fear of poor Maquis security. He sent off one of the desert veterans, Sergeant DuVivier, with Trooper Ball on bicycles as an advance party. Wearing battledress, they cycled merrily along in broad daylight without anyone attempting to question them. *En route* they heard a tremendous explosion. On making enquiries, they discovered that the Maquis had blown the railway line in order to delay an expected train. DuVivier managed to get word to the French repair gang to delay matters for as long as possible, while he and his companion cycled back up the line. Finding a suitable place they laid their charges, working for two hours in the dark, constantly alert for German patrols. They later heard that they had accounted for two locomotives and a considerable number of wagons.

The bad news, however, was that Roy Bradford had been killed. He had set out in a jeep on the evening of 19 July to ambush an enemy convoy, accompanied by Sergeant Chalky White, who had recovered in a Maquis hospital from his bad landing, as front gunner. Sergeant McGinn was the driver and Craftsman Devine, attached from the REME, was the rear gunner. Also packed in the jeep was a French guide. They travelled through the night and in the early morning reached a small village called Lucy-sur-Yonne. There they found themselves suddenly confronted by two Germans who waved at them to stop, not realizing at that stage that they were British soldiers. Chalky gave them a quick burst with the Vickers and as the jeep raced on they found themselves in the middle of a German convoy parked beside the road, preparing breakfast. It was too late to turn back as the enemy were rushing for their weapons. McGinn put his foot down and Chalky blazed away, changing magazines passed to him by Bradford. Just as they cleared the end of the convoy, a machine gun in the last truck opened up. Chalky, badly wounded, continued to fire, but Devine and Bradford were killed instantly. Around a bend the engine died. McGinn leaped out and helped Chalky and the Frenchman through a hedge. There they hid during the day and then made their way painfully from the scene. Eventually they were recovered by the Maquis. McGinn was deservedly decorated with the MM for his courage in rescuing the wounded.

On 3 August, a considerable number of Germans set off to attack the Maquis in the woods near to where Bill Fraser had his headquarters. He had previously sited one of the two 6-pounders on a slight hill overlooking the direction from which the enemy were approaching, and also had 3-inch mortars available. The use of artillery caused considerable surprise to the attackers and they withdrew before even penetrating the woods.

At the same time, a number of parties set out on a variety of demolition raids, travelling either by jeep or civilian car. Information had been received that the Germans had a refinery for making synthetic petrol near the town of Autun, which was a priority target. Two jeeps set off to travel the forty miles to the target area. In one was Alec Muirhead with his mortar crew; the other one carried Cooper and Seekings. A French guide directed them to the site without difficulty, but they were told that the timing of the attack was critical. The actual plant was sited on top of a mine which produced the raw materials, and which was worked round the clock by Frenchmen who might be trapped underground. The night shift, however, came up at 2 a.m. and the next crew did not start until two hours later.

The jeeps were driven into a field overlooking, and slightly higher than, the target. The moonlight gave enough illumination to see the storage tanks and pipework towers. While Alec Muirhead and his crew set up the heavy baseplate and lined up the mortar, Cooper and Seekings primed a mixture of incendiary, smoke and high-explosive bombs. Muirhead was a mortar expert who had used his skill to great advantage with the SRS in Italy. Shortly after two o'clock, fire was opened using smoke bombs to bed in the baseplate and give a visual sighting correction. Then a mixture of incendiary and HE were stuffed down the tube in quick succession. Even before the last round had been fired, the plant was ablaze from end to end, and it was clear that the enemy had no idea where the attack had come from, as they fired into the air with an anti-aircraft gun. As stealthily as the raiders had arrived, they left, removing all traces of their presence.

While all that was in progress, a visitor had arrived at the Houndsworth base. On the night of 7 August, Paddy Mayne, accompanied by Mike Sadler, his batman Corporal Corps and a signals officer, parachuted in. He had decided to take personal charge of the dispersed operations of his regiment. It is said that Mayne had heard that Bill Fraser had had his dress kilt and glengarry flown in to impress the locals. Not to be outdone, Paddy descended to the waiting reception committee dressed in his number one uniform, Sam Browne belt and medal ribbons, with his gramophone strapped to his leg. In fact he had very nearly failed to arrive at all. The first aircraft in which they were loaded crashed on take-off, and they had to switch hurriedly to another, minus their containers. After a brief stay to confer with Bill Fraser,

Mayne drove off in a jeep to the area of Operation Gain further north.

By mid-August, the Allies had crossed the Seine and the Germans were in full retreat back towards their own borders. This made operations difficult as the roads were extremely crowded, and anyway Houndsworth was short of jeeps and very spread out. In spite of this, a number of successful ambushes were carried out on the roads with the help of Maquis patrols, who were of a higher calibre in that area than in others where the SAS operated. By the end of the month the men were getting extremely tired after, in some cases, nearly three months of constant alertness. They had often been without supplies for long periods owing to poor flying conditions, and on one occasion two aircraft on their way to the DZ had collided almost over Roy Bradford's camp. It was therefore decided to bring A Squadron out and replace it with C Squadron.

Tony Marsh's squadron arrived in jeeps at the end of August, and on 6 September A Squadron departed for home. In the village of Mazing-em they formed up into a column that Fraser McCluskey reckons was nearly half a mile long. The remaining jeeps, requisitioned civilian cars and captured German trucks were filled with men and their equipment, surrounded by villagers who had come to see them off. Reg Seekings had obtained a Ford V.8 of which he was extremely proud. With their wounded on board, several German prisoners and a horde of Maquis armed to the teeth, the convoy departed to cheers from the villagers and escorted by fighting patrols from C Squadron. They made their way by side roads to the vicinity of Orléans where they ran into their first American patrol – who just waved them through in astonishment. They flew back in a fleet of Liberators into Middle Wallop airfield in Hampshire, having managed to persuade the Americans to give them a lift. The only snag was that Middle Wallop had a grass landing strip and the four-engined Liberators had great difficulty in taking off again.

Houndsworth proved that it was possible to maintain a large group of SAS in the field over a long period. Unlike Bulbasket the individual troops spread themselves out over a considerable area and their patrols covered 6,000 square miles. In spite of the shortage of transport, 22 railway cuts were made, over 200 Germans were confirmed as killed or wounded and 30 bombing targets were reported.[20] For much of the time, patrols and individuals moved quite freely about the countryside, and all the local people knew that they were there. Fraser McCluskey, who stayed on with C Squadron after the others had left, remembers that Bill Fraser, resplendent in kilt, addressed the inhabitants of Anost from the balcony of the Mairie. The padre actually stayed overnight several times in the house of a local family, and used regularly to eat in a café. Any member of A Squadron visiting the area is still assured of a warm welcome.

Thus far we have discussed the immediate D-Day period operations mounted by 1 SAS Regiment which had only involved one troop of B Squadron and the entire personnel of A Squadron. The next operation to get underway was Gain in mid-June, targeted on the Forest of Fontainebleau to the south of Paris. This was the northernmost point of the feature known as the Orléans Gap between the forest and the River Loire. The mission was entrusted to Major Ian Fenwick's D Squadron. Before the war he had been a successful cartoonist. His advance party, commanded by Captain Jock Riding plus five others, dropped on the night of 13 June to a reception party arranged by SFHQ. Their immediate mission was to recce the base that Fenwick had selected and to arrange for his reception three nights later. At the same time, Lieutenant Watson's section dropped into a different DZ to attack railway lines and then join up with the main party.

The base selected was in woods to the west of Pithiviers and Major Fenwick plus six others arrived safely on the night of 18 June. The local Maquis were very different from those in the Houndsworth area. Watson wrote in his report:

Maquis in the Forest d'Orléans badly organized and had too many chiefs. It began to work too soon and too near its own camp, the result being that they were dealt with by the Germans and dispersed just as their best moment for action was arriving. The Maquis contained many shady characters.[21]

For the first twelve days the patrols which Fenwick sent out operated on foot against railway lines, carrying their explosives on their backs. Lieutenant Bateman made two successful attacks on the Orléans-to-Pithiviers line. Then a number of jeeps were parachuted in together with their drivers, and the base was moved south to the Forêt d'Orléans which was considered safer. Riding remained behind at the old base with his troop.

Further reinforcements were due on the night of 4 July, when a stick of twelve men under the command of Captain Garstin climbed aboard a Stirling at Keevil aerodrome. They arrived over the DZ where the fires were lit and the correct recognition letter was flashed. One by one the men baled out into the moonlit night, but as they drifted into land, the supposed reception committee opened fire. The parachutists were silhouetted like sitting ducks and four were wounded. The Germans managed to round up nine, including the injured, but three made miraculous escapes. Troopers Norman and Morrison landed in some woods and managed to get away undetected, eventually making their way back to the Allied lines. Another man, Costello, also dropped in the woods, was captured but managed to escape.

The nine were taken to Paris by their captors, where Lieutenant Weihe and Corporal Lutton were transferred to hospital. The latter died there of his wounds the following day and is buried at Clichy New Cemetery. The remaining seven were severely mishandled by the Gestapo, but on 8 August they were suddenly given civilian clothes and were told that they were to be exchanged for Germans held in Britain. That night they were loaded into a truck which drove out of Paris in a north-easterly direction until it came to some woods near Beauvais, and at dawn the men were told to climb out. Handcuffed and under guard they were marched into the wood. One of the party was Serge Vaculik, who spoke German. He and 'Ginger' Jones were supporting Garstin, who was still weak from his wounds. Vaculik asked one of the guards if they were to be shot and was told yes. The seven were lined up facing two men armed with machine pistols, while two other Gestapo officers in civilian clothes stood by. One of the latter proceeded to read the death sentence, and as he did so, Jones and Vaculik made a run for it. They were followed by a hail of bullets and Jones tripped over. Pursuing the rapidly disappearing Vaculik the Germans rushed by him, assuming him to be dead. Both Jones and Vaculik managed to escape and, after a series of adventures with the Resistance, were overtaken by the Allies and returned to duty. Behind them, five bodies were left in the clearing – those of Captain Garstin, Sergeant Varey, and Privates Barker, Walker and Young. They were later buried in the churchyard at Marissel.

Who actually betrayed the DZ was never satisfactorily established although various accounts state that a Frenchman was caught and executed by the Resistance. Management of the DZ was an SOE affair and it was said at the time that a Frenchman had been sent back to the area by parachute, in possession of the correct recognition letter.

As soon as the jeeps arrived Lieutenant Watson got busy. His section destroyed a locomotive and burned a train at Beaune, and then carried out a raid on the Malesherbes-to-Corbeil line. Fenwick was tipped off by the Resistance that there were a number of locomotives in a shed at Bellegarde and he took a patrol of three jeeps to investigate. They found only one, and as they were placing their explosives they were attacked by a company of Germans – yet another betrayal. The patrol, trained to fight at night, beat off the enemy and made their way back to the jeeps safely.

They kept up the pressure on the enemy, but at the beginning of August, the squadron was ordered to cease offensive action and concentrate on gathering intelligence. A major airborne drop was planned in the Orléans Gap and the intention was to lull the Germans into a false sense of security. Besides, Fenwick was aware by then of the air of treachery that hung over his Resistance contacts, and frequent changes of base were necessary. Again they split up into troops, with Watson moving north, Fenwick staying in the Forêt d'Orléans, and Bateman and Parsons moving away to the east of Orléans.

Watson, however, returned from time to time to the Forêt d'Orléans base. One of his most spectacular escapades was to drive into Dourdan, which had been reported clear of Germans. As the crew cruised quite openly into the central square they noticed a number of German trucks parked with a few sentries lounging around them. No notice was taken of the jeep which drove on through and out the other end of the town. There they turned round and sped back towards what they anticipated would be an easy shoot. As they drove round the corner into the square, it was obvious that, as Watson's report stated, 'we were expected'.[22] The Germans opened up with machine guns at the careering jeep that was firing its Vickers to good effect. The German trucks erupted into flames and the enemy scattered from the square. Charging on through and zigzagging to avoid the Germans' parting shots, their French guide who was perched on the back was hit. As the jeep lurched round the last bend out of the main street, he fell out. There was no way they could stop to recover him as there were signs of pursuit, but the rear gunner noticed that he had crawled behind a wall. He turned up at their camp a few days later, none the worse for wear.

It had been Paddy Mayne's original intention to parachute into France to join up with Ian Fenwick, but fate intervened and struck a bitter blow to D Squadron. Watson and Riding were at the Forêt d'Orléans camp on the afternoon of Sunday, 6 August, when without any warning of an impending attack, shells started to explode among the trees. Everyone ran to their guns, and soon German soldiers began to appear through gaps in the woods. The SAS grabbed their personal

163

weapons and escape haversacks, first setting the jeeps on fire. Then they skirmished with the enemy until the late evening when the battle died down and they were able to make their escape on foot.

That particular day, Ian Fenwick had been at the base to the east of Orléans, preparing to receive Mayne on the Monday night. It seems that he was given an exaggerated version of what had happened in the morning, and assumed that all his force had been wiped out. He signalled Mayne not to drop and then set out in a jeep to discover what had happened. He was accompanied by his driver, Corporal Duffy, Sergeant Dunkley, an NCO from 4 French Para. who was attached as interpreter, and a Maquis guide. They set off in full daylight along minor roads, and as they neared the base, a Frenchwoman waved them to stop. She told them that a German unit was waiting in ambush for them in the next village, Chambon-le-Forêt.

Instead of diverting round the place, Fenwick, his temper roused, drove on towards Chambon at high speed with the guns readied. They tore into the village and were met by a hail of fire from machine guns and cannon. Fenwick and the two Frenchmen were killed outright. Duffy was wounded and crashed the jeep. Before losing consciousness he saw Dunkley being led away – never to be heard of again and presumed murdered. Duffy had a miraculous escape as the only witness to survive the ambush. He woke up in a hospital in Fontainebleau which was German-run but had French nurses. One of the latter procured the uniform of a German doctor for him and, hobbling in ill-fitting shoes, he made his escape. After several painful days in the woods he was picked up by the Resistance who led him to the Americans. Still suffering from his injuries he was taken to a military hospital and placed in a bed in a ward. There he had the distinction of being decorated with the Purple Heart, the American medal for wounds in combat, when a general arrived and went down the row of beds sticking one on each patient.

Captain Jock Riding took over the remains of the squadron, and Paddy Mayne arrived having driven up from the Houndsworth base, a distance of nearly 150 miles. He had worn full uniform the whole way, as he disdained disguising himself. His orders were for the troops to disperse and continue road-watching patrols, radioing intelligence back to base in preparation for the planned airborne attack. During this period two more men, Privates Ion and Packman, were caught and executed. The rest, after surviving yet another German raid on a Maquis camp on 10 August, were finally overrun by the advancing Americans. In spite of the unreliability of the local Resistance and the losses they suffered, patrolling by D Squadron had been particularly vigorous under the inspired leadership of Ian Fenwick. Lieutenant Watson's report, however, contained the following acid comment. 'No success achieved in the tasks briefed before leaving England.'[22]

Operation Haggard absorbed the remainder of B Squadron under its commander, Major Lepine. Six officers and forty-six other ranks were employed, later reinforced by a jeep troop from 3 French Para. Battalion. The object was to establish a base south of the Loire between Nevers and Gien, to cut communications and harass enemy movements. According to SHAEF, the area had become 'extremely important following the destruction of the Seine bridges below Paris'. It had been originally proposed to mount the operation towards the end of July, but the planning became caught up in the controversy with SOE. They felt that the presence of uniformed troops in an area where their clandestine forces were already operating would lead to too severe reprisals.

The advance party was dropped on 10 August and, in view of the rapidly approaching American forces, they discovered that there was little traffic on the roads in the area. It was thus decided to drop the main party near Villequis to cover the two main roads leading east from Bourges. They were there for thirty days and patrolled aggressively but found few worthwhile targets. The operation report concluded that had they been dropped two weeks earlier, they would have been able to cause far more damage to the enemy. In early September they were ordered north of the Loire to link up with Captain Davis's C Squadron troop in the Kipling base.

The final 1 SAS operation to be considered is Kipling. This was assigned to Tony Marsh's C Squadron which, as we have seen, ended up relieving A Squadron in the Morvan. The operation is well described in Derrick Harrison's book, *These Men are Dangerous*, one of the best first-person accounts of SAS operations during the Second World War. The initial objective was to drop the whole squadron to the west of Auxerre to be ready to co-operate with the already mentioned airborne drop in the Orléans Gap, code-named Transfigure. The base was thus situated due east of Gain and north-east of Haggard.

Captain Harrison was assigned to command the advance party and to drop blind into the Forêt de Merrivaux, where he was to establish a base and select a suitable DZ for bringing in jeeps by glider. At the last minute his plans were changed, as Major Bob Melot, the intelligence officer of the regiment, had driven up to the area with a signaller from Houndsworth. He would provide a reception committee for Harrison's party.

Harrison and five men dropped successfully on the night of 13 August and initially set up camp with a well-organized Maquis. Over the following days they received reinforcements in men and a few jeeps, but their instructions were to lie low and not stir up the neighbourhood unnecessarily. Thus an agreement had to be made with the Maquis who, freshly armed, were raring to have a crack at the Boche. It was not until confirmation was received that the airborne operation had been cancelled that permission was given on 20 August for offensive patrolling to begin.

Road recces showed that there were not all that many Germans in the area and that it was possible to drive around with little trouble. By late August, Patton's Third US Army was racing towards Reims, leaving its southern flank wide open, patrolled by the Resistance and various SAS missions. In addition, Allied forces were advancing up from the South of France after the Anvil landings, trapping the retreating German garrisons who were moving eastwards. It was a totally fluid situation without established front lines.

Harrison's men only encountered small bands of the enemy, whose strength was habitually exaggerated by Maquis reports. They took to driving with Union Jacks on the jeeps, in the hope of avoiding ambush by trigger-happy Frenchmen, and were often welcomed in villages whose inhabitants imagined that the SAS were the vanguard of liberating forces. In fact they were not far wrong, for on the afternoon of 22 August, Harrison met an American armoured column, whose commander simply refused to believe that there were so few Germans around. They spent the night with the hospitable Americans and, loaded up with rations, departed the following morning for their base in the woods.

Back at camp, Harrison was told by one of his section commanders, Lieutenant Richardson, that he was going to the Maquis workshop at Aillant to get one of his gun mountings welded. On the spur of the moment, Harrison decided to accompany him. In the two jeeps were five men: Harrison and his driver, Lance-Corporal 'Curly' Hall, Richardson and his driver, Private Breaton, and a Frenchman known as Fauchois. Emerging from the woods, they saw smoke rising from the direction of the village of Les Ormes, and decided to investigate.

As they approached they saw a woman on a bicycle, who stopped and begged them to fetch the Maquis – hundreds of Boches were in the village. A hurried conference was held and a decision made. It would be too late by the time they could mobilize the Maquis. The patrol would attack. The following account of the battle of Les Ormes is based on Harrison's text and the official report.[23] It has to be borne in mind that Harrison himself had two fingers of his left hand splinted together as a result of an accident on landing.

Union Jacks fluttering, the two jeeps roared into the village that summer afternoon. An SS man with a pistol stepped out and Harrison shot him. 'I took in the scene in an instant. The church in the middle of the square . . . a large truck . . . two German staff cars . . . a crowd of SS men in front of the church . . .'. Firing the front pair of Vickers, Harrison raked the square and the enemy vehicles burst into flames. The surviving Germans then started to fire back and Harrison yelled at Hall to reverse. But Curly was slumped dead over the steering wheel. Still firing, Harrison found that the engine was dead – and then his guns jammed. The rear guns fired one burst and then they too jammed. That left the single gun on the driver's side. He lurched across the body of Hall and opened up with that one until it too stopped. 'A dud jeep and three jammed guns. Hell, what a mess!'

All that had only taken seconds, but Harrison found himself standing in the middle of the crossroads. He could hear the guns of Richardson's jeep hammering and the crack of a Colt. Germans were firing down from the windows of a tall building overlooking the square. He grabbed a carbine from the jeep, emptied the magazine of fifteen rounds and then tried to change it, hampered by the splintered fingers. Dragging Hall from the jeep he then staggered with the weight of the body to the centre of the square, where he had to drop it. Germans advancing through an orchard had opened up and Harrison turned to deal with them, remembering in the heat of battle that it was his wedding anniversary. 'I found myself thinking: Lord, my wife will be furious if I get myself killed, this day of all days.'

A bullet slammed into his right hand and it went numb. Using his fingertips he extracted another magazine from a pouch and reloaded. His hands slippery with blood, he took aim. Nothing happened. Two rounds were jammed in the breech. Probably about four minutes into the action, he was still standing in the middle of the square, his foot propped on the disabled jeep, trying with blood-soaked hands to get the magazine out. He heard the roaring of an engine. The other jeep had managed to reverse and he was half-dragged on board. Fauchois fired a last burst into the square from the rear Vickers and they raced out of the village.

That night, Richardson drove with a patrol back into Les Ormes, where he discovered that the SS unit had not only started to fire the buildings, but had also taken twenty men to be executed. They had shot the first two when the jeeps raced into the square. In the confusion, the other eighteen men had escaped. Curly Hall lies buried in the local cemetery in the village, his grave a reminder of an act of bravery that is difficult to quantify. Derrick Harrison mourned his loss. They had been together ever since the days of the SRS, linked by the sort of relationship that is fostered in the SAS where distinctions of rank are often blurred. The attack may have been foolhardly, but it was gallantry of the highest order, for which Harrison received the MC.

His wounds bandaged, he was sitting in camp that night when the alarm was given of an approaching column. Instead of the enemy, this proved to be the squadron commander, Major Marsh, at the head of a force of twenty jeeps and forty men. They had been flown in Dakotas to Rennes in Brittany on 19 August, and had infiltrated through the lines via Orléans three days later. Peter Davis's troop was also on the way. They crossed in landing craft to Arromanches in Normandy on 26 August and drove through the lines as a convoy of twenty jeeps. The Kipling base was handed over to Davis, while the rest were to motor on to the Morvan to relieve A Squadron.

After Bill Fraser's men had left, C Squadron settled down to active patrolling through September, but were constantly hindered by lack of petrol, as bad flying weather restricted their supply drops. They discovered that the enemy had become wise to SAS tactics and were guarding convoys with 20-mm. cannon mounted on trucks and hidden under tarpaulins. One officer, Lieutenant Goddard, was killed trying to take on a German cannon single-handed, but otherwise casualties were remarkably light. As petrol permitted, patrols ranged far and wide, joining up with the French First Army which had moved up from the landings in the South of France. Lieutenant Mycock led the French into Autun and the following day took the surrender of General Elster and 3,000 men.

At the end of the month the squadron moved back to Cosne on the Loire to refit. There they lived in hotels, repaired their jeeps and prepared to drive north to Brussels, where they were to be assigned to the 21st Army Group to act in a counter-intelligence role, as discussed in the previous chapter. The official verdict on Kipling was deservedly favourable.

> By constant harrying and cutting of communications, this operation was extremely successful in deceiving the enemy as to our line of advance and in reducing the morale of his troops which resulted in two mass surrenders. The presence of uniformed Allied troops with their armed jeeps undoubtedly had a big effect on the F.F.I.[24]

The move north of C Squadron on 26 September effectively ended the role of 1 SAS Regiment in the campaign for the liberation of France. It is difficult to quantify individual results, but it would be fair to say that the units in the field caused a vast amount of damage at comparatively little cost to themselves. As knowledge of German treatment of captured SAS men trickled through, all ranks became aware that they were not fighting a civilized war, whereas initially they had tended to believe that their uniforms would ensure them the protection of the Geneva Convention.

Paddy Mayne was awarded his third DSO. 'It was entirely due to Lt. Col. Mayne's fine leadership and example, and his utter disregard of danger, that the unit was able to achieve such striking successes.'

9

2 SAS in France

2 SAS Regiment settled down quickly under the able command of Lieutenant-Colonel Brian Franks, but owing to their late arrival in Scotland, they still had a lot of training time to make up when D-Day came. Thus the regiment was not engaged on operations during the early period of the landings. The letter from Franks to McLeod quoted in Chapter 7 gives useful insights into the frustrations of getting operations underway.

It was not until 19 July that the first small party was sent to Normandy on an intelligence-gathering mission known as Defoe. Captain McGibbon-Lewis and twenty-one men were flown to the area and reported to Second Army Headquarters. There they discovered that the Operations officer who had asked for them had left the previous day and nobody had the faintest idea what to do with them. 'Their idea was that we should cross the lines on Monday, gather information on Tuesday and return on Wednesday night.' Lieutenant Silly was sent off with five other ranks to 12th Corps and they went patrolling in armoured cars. The only patrol undertaken by McGibbon-Lewis was code-named Swan and was designed to gain information about enemy movements in the Argentan area. Penetration of the lines was difficult as there were no open flanks and the countryside was densely wooded. They also lacked communications equipment and at one stage it was suggested that they take pigeons with them.

The Swan party did, however, manage to obtain a WT set and drove off in two jeeps and a 15-cwt. truck on 15 August. They were assigned to investigate the area of Flers, Argentan and Falaise. 'While everything was going with a swing, the Americans attacked from the south, the

British from the north, and we found ourselves in the Falaise cauldron. We were shelled, mortared, bombed, and almost every lethal weapon was directed against us.' They managed to evade injury and rejoined the British lines on 18 August. A week later they returned to the SAS base, having accomplished little of any use to the war effort, though this was not the party's fault.

A few days after Defoe, Operation Rupert should have started. This was another of those missions that were envisaged before D-Day but were delayed on account of objections from SOE. The intention was to drop an advance party to contact the Resistance and set up a base from which the railways in the Metz, Reims and Verdun area could be attacked. The advance party under Major Symes departed on the night of 22 July, but the aircraft crashed, killing all eight occupants. A further group was dropped on 4 August and operations commenced. Major Rooney joined the base with reinforcements on 24 August, but by then Patton's Third US Army had more or less caught up with them. Had they been dropped a month earlier the various parties would have been able to inflict far more damage on enemy communications in a vital strategic area.

The aim of Operation Gaff was to kill or capture Field Marshal Rommel at his headquarters at La Roche Guyon, a château on the Seine. A party of six men under Captain William [often known as 'Michael'] Lee was assigned to the mission which would be dropped by parachute to the east of Chartres on 25 July. Whoever wrote the operational order was *au fait* with the culinary reputation of the French. 'You will carry four pigeons which will be delivered Fairford Camp on Tuesday 25 July. These will NOT be regarded as extra rations.'[2]

Lee himself was quite a character with an interesting past, who had commanded the French squadron of 2 SAS in Italy. He was born in France in 1920 as Raymond Couraud, of a French father and American mother. He enlisted in 1938 for five years in the Foreign Legion and was decorated for bravery in the Norwegian campaign of 1940. After the fall of France he made his way to Britain, via Gibraltar, and volunteered for service. In 1941 he was commissioned as Second Lieutenant Jack William Lee and joined the SOE. He took part in the Commando raid on St Nazaire in the spring of 1942, and later that year was dropped into the South of France on a clandestine mission. Lee returned via Spain with his cover blown, which precluded further employment with SOE, so he transferred to No. 62 Commando and thence to 2 SAS.[3]

To accompany him on his mission he picked an interesting crowd of desperadoes. Second in command was Sous-Lieutenant Raillard. Then there was an Englishman, Moore, and three ex-legionnaires, a German, Sergeant Mark, Fedossof, a Russian, and the Frenchman Durban. Such a mixture was not extraordinary in the SAS which had always tended to recruit a leavening of exotic foreigners. There were several German Jews, Poles and Russians, many of whom used assumed or anglicized names.

They dropped blind from an Albemarle on the night of 25 July, but failed to find the container with their equipment. That was naturally a severe blow but, undaunted, the party set off on foot carrying their personal weapons and rucksacks. Lee became ill during the first morning, probably with a severe attack of malaria, and had to lie up in a farmhouse for two days. There, he heard that Rommel had been killed in his staff car in Normandy, having been strafed by a fighter bomber on 28 July. So Lee and his men set out on a series of patrols in the Seine area on foot, derailing two trains and shooting up seven trucks and a staff car.

On 12 August they found themselves in the medium-sized town of Mantes, and discovered from conversations with local people that the German headquarters was in a villa on the outskirts. Lee decided to attack it that night. As soon as it got dark, he posted Moore and Fedossof with the bren-gun to give covering fire, while the rest of the party hid in the garden. Then Mark cheekily went up and knocked on the door, which was opened by an orderly. He explained in German that his vehicle had broken down and he needed help. At that moment, the orderly was shot and the men stormed inside, flinging grenades left and right into the rooms, while Lee ran from office to office stuffing papers and maps into his pockets.

The fracas brought reinforcements to the scene, but Mark shouted contrary orders to them which created such confusion that the Germans started shooting at each other. In the middle of this, the six raiders slunk away and returned to their base in some woods. They heard later from the local Resistance that twelve bodies had been taken from the villa the following morning. By then, however, Lee's party was running danger-ously short of ammunition. Dressed as a gendarme and riding a bicycle, Lee set out to contact the Americans, leaving the others in the woods. His plan was to bring back reinforcements of about twenty men, divide them up into patrols of five and cover all the main roads leading into Paris from the south. He passed through the lines and was taken to Patton's headquarters at Le Mans, where they were grateful for the intelligence he had brought, but otherwise did not want to know about him. He was stuck on an aircraft bound for Britain, and his men were overrun by the Americans a few days later.

Gaff was a classic example of the application of basic SAS principles. A determinedly led small group without vast technical back-up but speaking the local language fluently managed to operate with impunity behind enemy lines for the best part of a month. They succeeded in destroying material vastly in excess of the resources employed to put them there and all returned safely. Had a hundred or so such parties been spread all over France instead of the concentration on troop- and squadron-size fixed bases, it is tempting to suppose that the mayhem caused by the SAS would have been far greater.

The first large 2 SAS operation started life as Hardy and had the usual chequered pre-history. In May it had been proposed to set up an SAS base on the Plateau de Langres, north of Dijon, starting on D-Day. This was cancelled as the RAF could not fly such a distance in the limited hours of darkness. On 4 July a plan was submitted to the 21st Army Group to send an advance party to the area. The plan was approved and the party was finally dropped on the night of 27 July. Prior to this, on 10 July, a draft plan was submitted, code-named Nelson, for operating jeeps in the Orléans Gap in conjunction with the projected breakthrough by the Americans. This plan was never finalized but authority was given to release and modify sixty jeeps. On 8 August a further plan was submitted and approved in the light of the projected airborne operation in the Gap. Forty SAS jeeps were to be landed by glider as part of the airborne force. This was cancelled but at the last moment, on 16 August, a new plan was prepared to land the jeeps at Rennes. This was mounted in 48 hours, although it proved difficult to obtain approval as it was thought the patrols might come into conflict with advanced US forces.[4]

Of the forty jeeps referred to above, twenty belonged to C Squadron of 1 SAS which drove down to the Houndsworth base (see Chapter 8). The remainder were Major Farran's 2 SAS C Squadron and were designated as Operation Wallace which has to be considered in conjunction with Hardy. The advance party for the latter under the command of Major Grant Hibbert dropped on the night of 27 July and built up a base in troop strength in the Forêt de Châtillon, north-west of Dijon, an important strategic area. Grant Hibbert's orders were to lay in a secure supply dump and provide intelligence of enemy activities. Offensive action was to be undertaken at 'a later stage'. The Hardy base was built up to a total of nine officers and forty-seven other ranks with twelve jeeps delivered by parachute.

The interesting part of the operation was Wallace which turned into the most epic jeep drive of the campaign in France. Roy Farran's force of twenty jeeps and sixty men finally landed from Dakotas at Rennes on 19 August, having been actually loaded into gliders two nights before. Immediately on arrival they set off for Orléans. Manoeuvring around isolated pockets of Germans they made their way to the north bank of the Loire, greeted by enthusiastic French who saw them as the vanguard of the liberating forces. Farran differed from many of his fellow officers in that he had a high regard for the bellicose attitude of the Resistance whom he considered the best guerrillas in Europe.[5] He was, however, aware that most of the information he was being given by willing villagers was misleading. As chief interpreter he had the services of the ubiquitous Captain Lee whose thirst for adventure had not been dulled by his experiences on Gaff. Before he had even had time to finish his report he had been attached to Farran's squadron and sent back to France, probably over-tired and stale.

Farran's aim was to remain unnoticed until he had reached the Hardy base, and on the evening of 22 August he decided to split the squadron into three separate patrols: five jeeps under Lee as the advance, eight under Farran, and the rest commanded by Lieutenant Leigh as the rearguard. They were to set off at thirty-minute intervals and were briefed to avoid trouble wherever possible. Lee, naturally enough, found it. He must have shot his way through a German patrol, losing a jeep in the process, for when Farran arrived, he found the enemy waiting for him. Sensibly he withdrew and gathered the three columns together again that night – 100 miles behind the lines.

There were more skirmishes the following day. Lee, whose command had been reduced to two jeeps, lost both of them when he ran into veteran German troops in a village reportedly clear of the enemy. Unable to get a warning to Farran, the latter ran full tilt into the same enemy unit, who fired a 75-mm. gun at point-blank range. In a battle lasting over an hour, more vehicles were lost, and Leigh, running into the same group, was killed. Roy Farran found himself the following morning reduced to seven jeeps. A group of survivors of the above action were gathered in by Lee. Mounted on five jeeps, they again ran into trouble in a village, but managed to recover their vehicles the next morning. At that point, Lee heard on the radio that Paris was being liberated, and evinced a desire to take part. Although he had set off to find Farran in four of the remaining jeeps, he turned north and took his detachment into the capital. Lieutenant Gurney, accompanied by Tanky Challenor and Will Fyffe, drove the remaining jeep back through the American lines to the Normandy beaches and embarked for Britain. The battles in the area had cost the lives of three men and two had been captured by the Germans.

Farran set off again with his reduced force, heading east through the Côte d'Or. Machine-gunning a train which came past while they were waiting at a level crossing was some compensation, and they made the rendezvous with Grant Hibbert at the Hardy base camp in the Châtillon forest. There they were able to receive a supply drop and, on 27 August, commenced offensive patrolling in the area. That night, as part of a further *parachutage*, two more drivers were dropped. One was a Polish Jew, Private Joachim Kalkstein, whose 'chute failed to open. He was buried the following day with full honours in the local cemetery at Recey-sur-Ource, where he still lies today.

The day was also spent in shooting up convoys with great success, and in gathering information. In a chain of events that was to lead to the famous Battle of Châtillon, Grant Hibbert and Farran visited a farmhouse with a view to arranging a mortar attack on a local German headquarters. The farmer obligingly picked up the telephone and got on to the Mayor of Châtillon, who told them that the headquarters was no longer occupied, but that the garrison in the town was in the process of being relieved. There were only 150 of the enemy in the place at that moment. As Farran wrote: 'I have never heard of a more farcical way of obtaining accurate information, but it was the sort of comedy which was always being played in guerrilla warfare.'[6]

The two officers, accompanied by Lieutenant Morris, their mortar expert, then proceeded to motor into Châtillon for a thorough recce. The enemy were quartered in the old castle situated high above the town, and Grant Hibbert duly scrambled up the rocky bluff, climbed a wall and proceeded to observe what the Germans were up to. By that time the population were getting quite excited about the presence of the jeep, so they decided to withdraw. Leaving town discreetly and heading back to the forest, they noticed four enemy trucks. They attempted to head them off but were too late, and the trucks ran into a Maquis ambush. As the SAS jeep arrived on the scene, a furious gun battle was in progress, but a few bursts from the twin Vickers suddenly arriving from the rear soon put paid to the opposition.

That evening, Hibbert and Farran dined with the local Maquis leader and, as the latter admitted, they ate and drank exceedingly well. The upshot was that it was decided to attack Châtillon the following morning, with the help of the Maquis. The entire squadron was employed and a full set-piece battle developed throughout the small town on 30 August. Farran's plan was to occupy the main junction of the Montbard and Dijon roads with Captain Mackie's troop, send the mortar section to the south of the castle and the rest of the men with brens through the town to attack from the north. The latter force consisted of forty men. They occupied the area of the market square and at seven o'clock the mortar opened fire on the castle.

At about the same time a large German convoy approached Mackie's position at the crossroads, where they were engaged by Sergeant Vickers's jeep. He brewed up the first five trucks, but the survivors brought mortars into action. The garrison had also begun to react and a full-scale war was being waged around the solid stone houses. Private Bill Holland, 21 years old, was fatally wounded, and by nine o'clock Farran decided that it was time to withdraw, there being no sign of the Maquis. The various troops and sections disengaged themselves, often with difficulty, and made their way back to their base in the forest, leaving ambush parties on all the roads leading out of Châtillon. It was afterwards estimated that the squadron had accounted for at least 100 Germans, as well as destroying 9 lorries, 4 cars and a motorcycle.

In theory, the engagement at Châtillon was something that should have been avoided at all costs by a small body of lightly armed troops. The fact remains that Roy Farran dared and won, against vastly superior numbers, losing only one man killed. Sergeant Vickers was later awarded the DCM for his defence of the crossroads that morning. The people of the town have erected a fine memorial to 'their' SAS man, Bill Holland, whose body was later reburied in the war cemetery at Choloy. The afternoon after the battle, however, Farran wisely decided to move his base camp, reckoning the Germans would be out to avenge their defeat.

Reinforced by a drop of fresh jeeps that night which gave him a total of eighteen, Farran decided to split his squadron into two sections of nine jeeps each, reasoning that such dispersal would lessen the risk of detection. Grant Hibbert was to take one group and Farran himself the other, advancing on parallel lines towards the Belfort Gap. That feature is the relatively flat area between the end of the Vosges mountains and the Swiss border, towards which the bulk of the retreating Germans were heading. The remaining men who could not be accommodated on the jeeps were to move to the Caumont area north of Langres and operate on foot under the command of Lieutenant Pinci. He was a flamboyant young officer who, although educated in Britain, was equally at home on the Continent and spoke fluent French. Sadly he was killed by an Allied fighter bomber swoop when he was out patrolling in a civilian car on 11 September.

During the first week in September the general Allied advance had begun to slow down owing to a shortage of supplies, giving the Germans a breathing space to dig themselves in to the west of the Vosges. They defended the line of the Moselle in some strength, determined to keep the Americans as far away as possible from the Rhine. Farran's patrols were heading into country that was going to become increasingly unfavourable for their type of hit-and-run warfare. In addition, he was to be dogged by problems with the jeeps. The long distances travelled and lack of maintenance led to a series of clutch failures, especially on those vehicles which had been towing trailers.

The two columns set off eastwards on 2 September, in the gap between two American armies. Patton's Third Army was stalled between the Meuse and the Moselle to the north and the Seventh Army was advancing towards them from the south. The columns were thus moving amongst the mainstream of Germans trying to reach the Rhine through the Belfort Gap. Farran's troop travelled as far as possible along side roads, lying up in woods during the night and destroying any suitable targets that came their way. From time to time, sections were detached to patrol away from the main group. On 6 September, for example, Lieutenant Carpendale was sent off north towards Épinal to try to locate a crossing over the Moselle that the troop could use. He made full use of Farran's permission to attack soft targets. At one point during his three-day patrol he killed a number of the enemy whom he had caught shaving, destroyed a truck and even knocked out an anti-tank gun with small-arms fire.

In the meantime reinforcements had arrived. Lieutenant Gurney and his jeep crew, Tanky Challenor and Will Fyffe, returned, having become separated right at the beginning of the operation. The dropping zone had been manned by a group of Boy Scouts who had formed themselves into a well-run Maquis, but in the early morning when they were still collecting containers, a large force of Germans attacked. Farran had great difficulty in extracting the jeeps from the woods, and decided to lie low for a few days. From being the hunters, they had become the hunted, and instead of large forests they could only find small woods to hide in. They still kept up the pressure though, laying mines and shooting up convoys. Gurney was killed in an attack on a convoy at the village of Velorcey, when an ammunition truck blew up in front of him.

By that stage, the troop was in no man's land and had to go to ground in foxholes in some woods, occasionally shelled by the artillery of both sides. Finally, contact was made with an American patrol from the Seventh Army, and Operation Wallace officially ended. Roy Farran gathered the squadron together and in a triumphant procession they headed off to Paris for a week of celebration, dining in all the best places on the remainder of their operational money. Then the column made its way back down to Arromanches and embarked for Britain, to refit and be brought back up to strength.

The official results credited the squadron with 500 Germans killed or seriously wounded, 23 cars and 36 other vehicles destroyed, plus 1 train and 100,000 gallons of enemy petrol. This was achieved at a cost of 7 men killed, 7 wounded, 2 captured (1 of whom escaped) and 16 jeeps lost. The operation was summed up as follows.

It is maintained that this operation proves that with correct timing and in suitable country, with or without the active help of the local population, a small specially trained force can achieve results out of all proportion to its numbers. This operation must surely rank as one of the most successful operations carried out by a small harassing force behind enemy lines. The losses sustained were extremely low. Apart from morale effect, the presence of even a small force produces rumours of a fantastic nature, and even without any action being taken in a particular area, all enemy movement is considerably delayed and extra security arrangements have to be made. As was to be expected, many useful lessons have been learnt especially with reference to resupply. The specially modified S.A.S. jeeps with extra petrol tanks giving a range of six hundred to seven hundred miles, and in some cases with special armour plating, and armed with two to five Vickers K or with Bren, bazooka and 3″ mortar, have proved invaluable. Many of these modifications were improvised, and a standard modification with adjustments to fittings which proved unsatisfactory is being arranged. The parachuting of jeeps has been satisfactory with only a small percentage of jeeps being damaged on landing.[7]

There was an unfortunate sequel to Wallace which has never been satisfactorily explained, as the participants have, not unnaturally, cloaked themselves in silence. We have seen that William Lee took off for Paris with a small detachment which had become separated. In four jeeps and accompanied by some Resistance men, they hit the town, determined on a bit of a celebration. Thus the SAS can justly claim that they were the first British unit to enter Paris after the liberation. It is difficult to determine which men from the squadron had been with Lee, but certainly the party included Lieutenants Lord John Manners and Birtwhistle, and a certain Private Gosselin, from Jersey – probably a British contingent of about a dozen altogether.

Lee went off to visit the friend of his French girlfriend and discovered that this lady was married to a German, who had deserted and was in hiding at her apartment. He was naturally petrified at the thought of being caught by the Resistance, and for some reason or other, Lee decided to take him back to Britain. In the meantime, the British authorities had moved into the city and, discovering the SAS there, had ordered them to return to base immediately. According to the one account of the affair, Gosselin was persuaded to lend his uniform to the mysterious 'Freddy' who, thus disguised, was driven down to Arromanches and put on the boat for Southampton together with the rest of the detachment.

They arrived back in Britain on 10 September, and Lee made his way to London where he persuaded his wife, who worked for the Home Office, to hide the German. In wartime Britain that was a crime of great magnitude – smuggling an enemy alien into the country and then concealing him from the authorities. Lee was in disgrace anyway with his regiment, where he was accused of deserting Roy Farran. There was naturally an enquiry, and the various members of the party were interrogated during their debriefing. Somehow or other the presence of the stranger was mentioned and discreet surveillance by the security service was ordered.

Lee and the German were arrested, and Lee's wife resigned from the Civil Service. He was taken into close custody at Wellington Barracks and on 14 November 1944 faced a court martial at the Duke of York's HQ in Chelsea. He was the sole defendant and, in spite of the reading out of a laudatory letter from Bill Stirling, there was only one possible verdict – guilty. He was initially sentenced to be cashiered, which was later reduced to dismissal from the service. Bearing in mind the gravity of the crime and the fact that several other serving soldiers had obviously been accomplices, the sentence seemed extraordinarily light. His biographer hints at various mitigating factors which could not be brought openly before the court. Couraud alias Lee is dead, and therefore we may never know the full facts of the matter.[8]

There were two further minor operations carried out by detachments from 2 SAS during August. The first was Dunhill, which consisted of five parties who were dropped in eastern Brittany in early August. They were to investigate the possibility of establishing a base and to observe enemy movements in the Rennes–Laval area. The American break-out from Normandy and the swing into Brittany was so swift that four of the parties were overrun within twenty-four hours of dropping. The only success was the collection of 200 Allied aircrew. Lieutenant Johnston accompanied the operation with his Phantom troop and commented in his report that: 'the officer in command of an operation should know how to use W/T terms. Much valuable time was wasted on the air and in coding absurd messages which were of no importance to anyone.'

The other operation was Trueform. This consisted of a series of twenty-five small party drops between Normandy and the Seine, in conjunction with the Belgian SAS, to harass the enemy retreat. As was so often the case, it was mounted far too late, on 17 August, and apart from some minor ambushing, the parties were again quickly overrun. Trueform could well have paid dividends if the parties had been inserted in July and given time to establish themselves. They would then have been in position when the break-out started and could have exploited initial German confusion.

The largest 2 SAS operation in terms of numbers of men employed was Loyton, together with a group of subsidiary actions lumped together under the code-name Pistol. Like most such operations, planned for rather than by the SAS, Loyton had a chequered history similar to that of Hardy and Wallace. As mentioned in Chapter 7, the SHAEF directive at the end of May which had laid down policy for the employment of the brigade in the D-Day period had called for the establishment of a base in the Vosges mountains in north-eastern France. As was the case with Hardy, 38 Group RAF felt unable to insert the party until the longer nights in August gave adequate time for the aircraft to return in darkness. The earliest date they would consider was 3 August.

Strategically the planners had got the geography right. The Vosges mountains run roughly north to south parallel to the Rhine on the French side of the river. Relatively few roads and railways go through the chain of hills connecting France with Strasbourg and the Rhine plain. An enemy force retreating east from the Paris area would have to take the axis Châlons–Reims–Verdun–Metz and then either move up the narrow Moselle valley via Luxembourg, or cross the Vosges by the passes to reach the Rhine. Thus a blocking force established across the communication lines in the Vosges could severely hamper a German retreat with a few well-planned ambushes and railway demolitions.

SHAEF was well aware of this. On 21 June the staff again recommended sending a reconnaissance party to the Vosges, 'to provide Resistance with a hard core of disciplined troops'.[9] As far as SAS Brigade staff were concerned, the whole question then became tangled up in quarrels with SOE about who was to do what and with whom. The basic plan was laid down in Operation Instruction No. 38 which was issued by the brigade on 3 August. This stated that the intention was to co-operate with Resistance groups, initially in clandestine and later in overt offensive action against the enemy, as well as reporting back on enemy movements in the area. It was directed that an advance party should be dropped as soon as possible after 5 August, accompanied by a Jedburgh team, and that if successful, the base should be built up to squadron size. On the negative side, it was pointed out that owing to the extreme range, and uncertain weather in the mountains, resupply could well prove to be intermittent.[10]

The advance party dropped on the night of 12 August to a reception organized through SFHQ (SOE). Their operating area was in the hills around Raon l'Étape, due west of Strasbourg on the French side of the Vosges, in an area of dense forests, few roads and broken hilly country interspersed with deep ravine-like valleys. What they did not know was that they were arriving in a hornets' nest. On the face of it, the deeply wooded mountainous area should have been ideal for an SAS operation, providing excellent concealment. The snag was that by the time the operation was finally mounted the Germans had abandoned any hopes of making a stand to the east of Paris, and by the first week in September the Americans were already over the Meuse at Verdun. Thus the Germans, determined to hang on well in advance of the Rhine, planned to make their stand along the crests of the Vosges and the east bank of the Moselle. The general assumption was, however, that within three weeks or so, the Americans would have advanced far enough to liberate the area.

An added factor was that the whole area was one of divided loyalties. The inhabitants of Alsace and Lorraine had so often switched between German and French nationality that their ethnic origins had become confused. Most people spoke a German dialect and there were many among them who had no real attachment to France, hence the high degree of betrayal to which the operation was subject.

By late August the enemy had had plenty of experience of dealing with both the Resistance and the SAS, and had drafted special anti-partisan units into the area. As France was liberated, usually the first to escape from any given area were the scum who formed the whole apparatus of Nazi repression; many of the latter had reformed in the Vosges region. There were two important Gestapo headquarters in the area, at Nancy and Strasbourg, and each had mobile anti-partisan Commandos attached to them.[11]

The Loyton advance party was commanded by Captain Druce, who was a comparative latecomer to 2 SAS. Earlier in the war he had been employed in Belgium and Holland on clandestine activities by MI6 as he spoke fluent Flemish. In May 1944, on his way to Ringway for parachute-training, he met Brian Franks in a train. They got into conversation and when Druce told him that he was at a loose end, Franks recruited him. Oddly enough, he was not originally assigned to the operation at all.

I was not supposed to go on Loyton. The advance party had been set up with a troop commander whose name I can't remember and I don't want to. ... At the last moment, I understand, this chap went to Franks and said: 'I really don't feel I can do this operation. I've lost my nerve.' He was indeed a most courageous man to have the guts to turn round and say: 'I can't do it.' So he dropped out literally on the morning or the afternoon they were due to leave for Loyton, and Franks contacted me. I don't remember where I was but I came rushing like a stuck pig down to the airfield, and I was briefed there.[12]

Captain Druce, who was also known as 'Drake' and 'Docker' on the operation, dropped with a five-man Phantom patrol under Captain Hislop, a Frenchman known as Captain Goodfellow whose real name was de Lesseps, and five other SAS personnel, one of whom, Sergeant Lodge, was thought to have been a German. In addition there was a three-man Jedburgh team, 'Jacob', consisting of Captain Gough, Captain Barreaux (French) and their radio operator, Sergeant Seymour. They took with them enough arms for 200 Maquis, which Druce was to use as he thought fit.

The drop itself was successful, although Druce's leg bag slipped down and he could not release it properly. Landing on his back he concussed himself, but Goodfellow dealt with the reception committee and the removal of the containers. By the middle of the day they managed to meet up with the local Maquis who were commanded by Colonel Maximum. The latter had simply appropriated the arms and there was little Druce could do about it. The supplies were apparently regarded as the price for using their field as a DZ. The advance party were then taken to a Maquis camp run by Captain Felix, which seemed well organized, and there they were fed and had the opportunity to sleep off the exertions of the previous night.

For two days they kicked their heels waiting for the regional controller of the Resistance to turn up. It was discovered that one of the Phantom radio sets had disappeared, and as the Jedburgh operator had been injured on landing, Hislop had to lend one of his men to Captain Gough. On 16 August, the big chief of the Resistance arrived, said his piece and then left. On returning to their camp, the SAS party heard rumours that a large group of Germans had moved into the valley and were searching for them, and later discovered that their site had been 'sold' to the enemy. Druce decided that he had to abandon the camp forthwith as it was full of unarmed Frenchmen who had come in from the surrounding villages and were milling around noisily. All around them they heard the sound of gunfire in the trees, accompanied by wild rumours of the numbers of enemy involved.

Druce left a rear party under Goodfellow to cover the retreat, and he himself set off to find a way to the new campsite. From then on, the operation was to be dogged by trouble. On the way his group bumped into some Germans who were eating their lunch in the forest, and a minor scrap developed. The sound of approaching reinforcements caused Druce to order his men to disperse and make their way individually to a rendezvous, which meant abandoning Sergeant Seymour, the Jedburgh radio operator, who could not walk. Captain Felix led Druce and some of the men to a farm near the village of Moussey where they were able to sleep in the hay and have a good meal. On the way they discovered that most of the Maquis had thrown away their arms and disappeared, and when Captain Hislop came in later he had to report the loss of the remaining radio set.

With half the party already missing, the remainder hid up for two days while a large force of Germans combed the area thoroughly. On 21 August, Captain Druce wrote in his report: 'I was awakened by the sound of Germans in the back garden. We gripped our guns for a final fling, but then found that they were only putting a telephone line up.'

The following day he was finally conducted to a rendezvous with Colonel Maximum, who claimed to be in command of a large force. The interview was a prickly one, as the Frenchman was only interested in obtaining weapons. As he had the only radio in the area at the time, Druce had to use him to pass a message to London asking for seven sticks to be dropped on a DZ at Veney. He then returned to camp well after curfew, 'having only a gun as papers'.

During the next few days the rest of the party trickled in, having been dispersed during the move from the first camp. Two were missing, Sergeant Lodge and Private Davis, the first prisoners of a large group whose execution was to cast a terrible shadow over Loyton. It was also discovered that Maximum's radio had been captured but that Druce's message had been passed on via a set in Nancy. The whole operation was in difficulties as it no longer had the means of direct communication, was short of food and was being constantly harried by the enemy. Druce decided to send Captain Goodfellow through the lines, as he was unfit, but he wasted two days trying to obtain papers. On 26 August, Druce wrote: 'We were feeling very depressed and helpless, and with strong temptation of going off and shooting up what we could find.' When such a clandestine force has lost the initiative and feels cut off, its morale can sink very rapidly.

On the evening of 30 August, a message was received via a runner that a drop was expected that night. The SAS set off for the DZ followed by the Maquis who had a prisoner with them. He had been captured during the day when apparently leading a German patrol, although his excuse was that he had been looking for mushrooms. The drop, which consisted of Colonel Franks and twenty-three others, was scattered and a lot of men and containers landed in the trees. There were Germans in the vicinity and one of the containers exploded. As Druce tried to get things organized, the French set about looting the supplies, and in the middle of all this, the prisoner broke free, snatched a Sten gun and tried to escape. His guards, who were Russian and whose common language with the British was German, shouted 'Achtung', whereupon the French, thinking they were about to be attacked by the enemy, started firing wildly in all directions.

Colonel Franks and his party, newly arrived, fled into the woods, wondering what on earth was happening. When things calmed down and the prisoner was recaptured, Druce ordered him to be shot. This was carried out by Captain Barreaux on the spot by a bullet through the heart. In the background, one of the Russians was dying in agony, having eaten a lump of plastic explosive, and Druce only managed to round up fourteen of the new arrivals. They had no transport for removing stores, much of which had to be abandoned, as the group made their way to a new camp where they gathered the following morning.

In the meantime, however, another party which belonged to Loyton had been dropped twenty-five miles to the west of the advance party on the night of 27 August. Druce was completely unaware of this at the time as his message requesting reinforcements which had been passed via a French source in Nancy was confused with another one on the same day, giving two different DZs. The new party was led by Major Peter le Poer Power, commander of A Squadron, who was accompanied by Lieutenant Alastair McGregor and eight others. They dropped to a lighted DZ and were scattered in the trees on landing. When they had finally assembled they discovered an unarmed Maquis crew who were extremely surprised to see them. Then a second aircraft came over, and down came 'a twenty-stone bearded major named Brown with his Jedburgh team'.

Major Power's party spent the rest of the following three weeks dodging around from camp to camp, trying to find out where the main group was, without much success. SAS Brigade actually sent him instructions to remain where he was and operate from there, but the message was never received. However, he did get orders on 10 September to cut the railway between Lunévile and St Dié, and as there were no explosives available, had to send three men to borrow some from a Maquis unit in the vicinity. McGregor was detailed to deal with the railway job, while Power with four men left to try to make contact with Colonel Franks, which he finally achieved on 18 September.

McGregor set out on 12 September for St Dié, and the following summary is based on his account, appended to the main operational report. During the day they 'picked up a Hindu ex P.W. from Epinal; he stayed with us and did sentry duty, but he was a terrific nuisance, lousy, and came back through the lines with us; name unknown – called Rastus by us.' Three days later they reached the line and laid a charge with a pull switch to detonate it. To their annoyance, however, no trains ran that night or on any of the succeeding three nights. Not to be beaten, they then laid another charge with fog signal detonators, but a train came along and removed the signals with a sweeper attachment mounted on the front.

On 26 September, the small party holed up in a farm owned by a very brave woman. 'Germans were often passing and several times she fed us upstairs while there were six or seven Germans downstairs. She also brought us up German cigarettes and fresh information of the American front line location.' Still unable to find out the whereabouts of Colonel Franks and the main party, McGregor then set about ambushing roads by felling trees across them, and managed to kill a high-ranking enemy officer and his entourage whereby 'carbines scored a $\frac{1}{2}''$ group in the officer's head.' An attempt to contact the Americans failed, due to false information, so the party moved into the friendly farm. The problem was that the Germans had had the same idea and moved in downstairs. There was nothing for it but to take to the woods again, leaving behind Private McQueen who was seriously ill with malaria. 'October 6th. Tightened our belts and took benzedrine.' Two days later the party crossed the lines and joined the Americans, accompanied by 'fifteen noisy Frenchmen'.

Why Colonel Franks, the regimental commander, decided to take charge of a squadron-sized operation is unclear and he does not mention his reasons in his report. When Paddy Mayne dropped into France, his purpose was to gather information about several of his parties in the field and he was able to move about from base to base as well as to cross the lines. Colonel Franks arrived in a heavily wooded area overrun by Germans and without transport. Thus it would appear that he intended right from the start to take personal control of Loyton and delegated command of the regiment to Major Scratchley.

Franks met up with Colonel Maximum the following morning and he too got a frosty reception backed up by demands for arms. Druce was sent off to find a new, more secure base, and on 5 September the party moved camp, receiving a stores' drop that night. Two nights later, a reinforcement of two sticks was arranged, but only one landed, commanded by Major Reynolds. Three of his men went missing on the DZ and were later picked up and executed by the Germans, although this was unknown at the time. On 9 September, the base was attacked and the SAS party had to leave in a hurry, abandoning all their stores. This was to be a regular feature of Loyton, as the initiative remained firmly with the enemy. This is not to say that the party was rendered completely inactive. Franks sent out Lieutenant Marx and his stick to ambush soft targets and Druce was constantly out and about searching for new bases and endeavouring to find both information and food. It had simply been assumed that the Loyton party would cause mayhem for a few weeks and then be relieved by the Americans. General Patton, however, had failed to cross the Moselle in any strength and by the end of the first week in September stalemate descended on the front. It was to last until the middle of November. Freed from the threat of imminent attack, the Germans could divert forces to deal with the 'terrorists' in the forests.[13]

On 11 September, the new base was attacked and some of the Maquis bren-gunners deserted their posts. Lieutenant Black and his stick were sent to cut off the attackers while Franks and the others moved camp once again. Black's stick failed to return and joined the swelling list of eventual victims of the local Gestapo. On 15 September, Marx returned, having destroyed a number of enemy vehicles, but with the news that three of his men had become separated. A further supply drop was finally received that night, but minus the tyre bursters and grenades that had been demanded. The final blow was that Colonel Maximum's vaunted Maquis had been dispersed by the Germans with heavy losses and their commander was in hiding. It was therefore decided to move to yet another new base near the village of Moussey.

Moussey straggles for a mile or so along a typical Vosges valley, hemmed in by wooded hills. Once there was a thriving textile industry there based on cheap power provided by the rushing streams which drove the looms. The industry collapsed some years ago, and today Moussey is a sadly declining community although in 1944 it supported a population of over 1,000 souls. Yet the name of this little town will always hold an honoured place in the history of the SAS Regiment. When Colonel Franks landed, he was accompanied by Captain Christopher Sykes, who later became a well-known novelist and biographer. After the war he wrote an account of the martyrdom of Moussey in *Four Studies in Loyalty*, which in my mind must rank as probably the best account of the effect of clandestine forces on a local community in occupied France.[14] The remainder of the story of Loyton is inextricably bound up with that of Moussey.

The next stage of the actual operations involved the dropping of jeeps, the first of which were received on the night of 19 September. These were meant to give the force some mobility, but owing to the overgrown nature of the countryside, little real use could be made of them. For help in providing guides and organizing work on a DZ, a small Maquis group under the command of a man named Etienne had been recruited, who proved to be far more reliable than most. Christopher Sykes described him and his companions in graphic terms.

> He was one of the most villainous-looking men I ever saw. Cruik-
> shank's drawing of Bill Sykes in his night-cap bears a curiously close
> resemblance to him. . . . In addition to his terrible appearance, like a
> good Alsatian he spoke French with hideous Germanic gutteral
> consonants, interspersed with little flat vowels. . . . Add to this a black
> cap pulled over his brows and a simian gait, and you have some notion
> of what this ragamuffinly and courageous man looked like. He led a
> band as singular as himself and much in the same style. They were all
> elderly men for the job, the youngest not less than fifty, the oldest well
> over sixty. They came from heaven knows where, they seemed to be a
> band of old tramps and beachcombers . . . They were not a melancho-
> ly band, however. They shared a weakness for the bottle with their
> leader, and on the many occasions when we met they were all alurch
> in the highest of festal moods.[15]

Sykes also described the delights of supply drops, which became like a
festival for the local people. 'We aimed at secrecy but obtained
demonstrations.' The SAS party would receive confirmation of a drop
and issue forth to the DZ, with a few chosen Maquis helpers, by
roundabout forest tracks.

> The fun usually began towards midnight when the Groupe Etienne
> arrived, always very bright with drink and bringing some bottles of
> hideous raw spirit as protection against the cold. Their songs and
> their yells of welcome to us and their French comrades set a new tone
> for the rest of the night. There was nothing to do about it. If we had
> tried to prevent them coming they would have come just the same,
> and when I once told Etienne that the noise *must* stop forthwith, he
> cordially agreed, and, putting his hands to his mouth, fairly bellowed
> across the field: 'Silence! Tais toi! Un peu de dischipline ou je
> t'schlage.' (Silence! Shut up! A little discipline or I'll belt you one.)
> He was answered with a cheer.

By the time the aircraft were about due, the crowd had thickened,
creating a considerable hubbub with the Germans only a mile or two
away. Sykes likened the scene to a nocturnal race-meeting at Newmar-
ket where a ghostly Two Thousand Guineas was being held. 'I do not
pretend that everyone came out of altruistic patriotism: there was loot to

be had.' He went on to describe the hush as the first aircraft arrived overhead and the recognition signal was flashed. Then, as the packages descended black against the night sky, the outburst of comment. 'There are the men. It's a *containeur*, it's a "Jim" [jeep].' Reading the dry official reports of such actions it is easy to become blinded by one's annoyance at the efficiency and poor security of the French Resistance, yet in spite of the cowardice and treachery of many of their fellow countrymen, the ordinary people so often displayed an amazing will to resist.

> The excitement of the crowd was now tremendous and, as with the splintering crashes of branches, with resounding clatters on rooftops, the lurching cracks of the jeep crates, or a thump on the ground, the humans, weapons and transport landed in and a-straddle the field, dark clouds of scurrying humanity would dash to landed parachutes, while calls and shouts echoed on all hands.

> Like a horde of ants, the people laboured to drag the containers under the shelter of the trees, while others, calling out at the tops of their voices, crashed through the undergrowth looking for missing men. The crash of hammers breaking open jeep crates echoed down the sleeping valley, yet the Germans never arrived at a *parachutage*, and the local people never betrayed one.

Six jeeps in all were dropped to Loyton, but their condition proved highly unsatisfactory. They all had either no oil or too little and the guns were supplied still greased. This meant that the crews had to spend valuable time in getting the guns into working order. A further problem was that the gun mountings broke, being insufficiently strong to take the weight of the guns and the constant jolting along forest tracks. In spite of the restrictive nature of the road network in the area, the jeeps were crewed and ambushes were set up. They were not really able to achieve all that much, and once the vehicles appeared in the area, the Germans moved large forces in to patrol the few available roads. It was far too easy for the enemy to bottle up the patrols as there were so few exits from the forest, and they were never able to fan out far and wide to places where they were not expected.

Captain Druce and Lord John Manners took two jeeps out on 23 September to ambush a road, and achieved a remarkable bag. As all civilian cars had been impounded by the enemy, it was perfectly safe to assume that any vehicle travelling along a road was German. There was, however, an exception, as the local mayor had been allowed to keep his car which was an electric one. The two jeeps had just moved into position when they heard a vehicle approaching. As it came round the bend, it received a burst from eight heavy machine guns. As Christopher Sykes put it, it 'disintegrated, ceased to exist, fell in pieces'. Miraculously the mayor was not injured and managed to roll out and into the ditch. From there he waved his handkerchief and received another blast. The unfortunate man crawled from the scene on hands and knees.

A local forester, Albert Freine, who was one of the staunchest supporters of the party, came up to the camp with a very worried look on his face and told Colonel Franks what had happened. But then a messenger arrived from the mayor bearing two bottles of champagne and a note saying: 'Thank you for the salvo fired in my honour this afternoon.'[16]

There were many in and around Moussey like Freine, who provided food and shelter without question, at great personal risk to themselves and their families. As September set in the rain started, and under the dripping trees the men were soaked. It became imperative to dry clothes, and now and again to get a night in some warm straw in a barn. There were several such havens, but the community was to pay a terrible price. On 24 September a large force of Germans moved into Moussey and rounded up all the men between 16 and 60 years of age. They were herded into a factory and then marched three or four miles down the road to the Château de Belval. There they were interrogated, generally beaten up and penned into the lorries that were to take them to the concentration camps. In all, 210 were taken and only 70 were to return at the end of the war.

By that stage, morale was low at the base owing to the cold, the rain and the lack of regular food. Franks dispersed his men into temporary billets as far as possible and on 28 September he decided to send Captain Druce out through the lines to contact the Americans and hand over captured enemy documents. Druce left the following day, accompanied by Flying Officer Fiddick who had been shot down and had joined the Loyton party. They passed through safely and on the morning of 2 October, Druce reported to the brigade at Moor Park.

Franks kept up a worthwhile level of patrolling, mainly on foot, but by the first week in October, the party was getting short of food and the weather had closed in, making supply drops impossible. On 9 October, aware that the front had become static, he decided to terminate the operation and instructed his men to make their way through the lines as best they could. In the meantime, Druce had returned to the American headquarters, bearing a new radio set and crystals. He set off again on foot and recrossed the lines, where he met a Maquis leader, Captain Jean, who told him about three new German divisions in the area. Druce decided that this information was important and reported back to the Americans.

The rest of the party came out in small groups, and several more men went missing and fell into the hands of the Germans. Of the hundred or so men employed, two were known to have been killed in action and twenty-eight were missing. Their subsequent fate will be discussed in a later chapter which is concerned with the war crimes investigation set up in 1945. The official report claimed forty to fifty enemy killed, fifteen vehicles destroyed, one train derailed and two possibles. As far as Loyton was concerned the figures simply did not add up, especially when compared with other operations carried out by the two regiments in other parts of France. The plain fact was that the party had been dropped in the wrong place at the wrong time. Franks was an inspiring leader and, after David Stirling, probably the most original thinker produced by the SAS during the war. His own comments on the operation are well worth looking at in some detail, and run to nearly eight pages.[17]

Under general terms he summed up the limiting factors, such as the weather, the poor terrain and the high concentration of enemy troops. He also blamed 'the totally incompetent and unarmed Maquis, well infiltrated with informers and with no fighting spirit', and stated that the local population was terrified of the Germans. In fact, the SAS received much help from the local people who paid a dreadful price.

As far as resupply was concerned, there was indeed much to criticize: carbines that arrived solid with rust, bent Vickers ammunition which would have caused jams if not sorted by hand, training bombs sent with bazookas, jeeps with no oil, and tommy-guns with no magazines. There was quite a list and a severe inquest was held at Station 1090 on Franks's return. It seems incredible that such laxness had been allowed to creep into the organization. 'Four out of six jeep mountings were useless owing to the welding going before the guns were even fired.' In a subsequent report to Airborne Corps HQ, it was stated that on investigation it was found that the defective arms came from pre-packed Special Forces containers.

It is also an inescapable fact that by the autumn of 1944 both regiments were having difficulty in finding replacement personnel of any calibre and there was little in the way of a proper selection process.

Franks wrote that some of the men sent with the jeeps as final reinforcements were quite unsuitable. 'They arrived very nervous, and were either so scared as to be useless or so confident that they were extremely careless. Most of these men were new recruits who were clearly not of the right type and had not had sufficient training.' Sadly it is also a fact that many of those subsequently caught by the Gestapo and murdered were inexperienced men.

In his conclusion, Franks reiterated the argument that if the party had been dropped at the time of D-Day as originally envisaged, a satisfactory organization could have been built up, and if arms and instructors had been sent, the Maquis might have made a useful contribution. His final paragraph neatly sums up the frustrations felt by the regiment in being controlled by outside bodies.

The lack of appreciation in England of the situation in the area, in spite of the signals which I sent, was abundantly shown by a signal I received about the middle of September which stated that the area was now Top Priority for arms for Special Forces – what about a daylight drop? At the time of receipt of this signal, the Maquis had been entirely dispersed and the only offensive operations in the area were being carried out by us. It was difficult enough to have a night drop, and this was always under the noses of the enemy.

Loyton was not the only operation in the Vosges at the time. There was an independent drop commanded by Lieutenant Rousseau with nine men to the north. Their orders were to demolish the Nancy-to-Saarburg railway and then rejoin the main party. They were dropped on the night of 9 September, and became separated on the DZ. One group got to the line, only to discover that the Germans themselves had blown it. The whole area was alive with Germans. Another group ended up fighting with the advanced American forces, who then retreated without telling the SAS, thus leaving them to deal with the enemy who had arrived in force. Rousseau and Private Galmard were caught and shot. The rest of the party made their way in twos and threes back through the lines.

Also aimed to the north of Loyton was the last 2 SAS operation of the campaign in France, code-named Pistol. Its purpose was to disrupt rail communications running east from Metz and Nancy through the mountains to the Rhine plain. All drops were to be blind and instructions were given to avoid contact with civilians, carry out the tasks and then exfiltrate. The forces employed consisted of eight sticks which were to drop on the night of 15 September. Two of the sticks failed to drop owing to thick fog over the DZ, and in spite of four further attempts they never did land.

The remaining six parties suffered appalling privations on account of the weather and severe lack of food. Being so near to the German border the local people were generally uncooperative and some of the men spent days on end in soaking wet clothing. A considerable number were captured and Privates Wertheim and Ashe were murdered by the Gestapo. Others were lucky and ended up in prisoner-of-war camps. Although scattered on dropping, the various small groups did make their way to their targets and managed to cut one railway line, destroy one locomotive and derail four trains. They also accounted for several vehicles, power cables and telephone lines before the survivors met up with American forces.

That ended the 2 SAS Regiment's contribution to the liberation of France, which had been a very real one and had been achieved at a comparatively high price in terms of men missing and killed. By and large, as was the case with 1 SAS, it was the experienced operators who survived to fight another day, and it was not immediately apparent just how many had fallen victim to the Gestapo.

10

The Final Phase of the War in Europe

We have already seen that by early September 1944, both Airborne HQ troops and the SAS Brigade, faced by the awful prospect of disbandment, had begun to consider the future employment of the various regiments. Three possibilities had been floated: working in a counter-intelligence role with the main armies in Germany; operating in the Far Eastern theatre; or disarming enemy formations in Norway and/or Denmark. Those discussions were clearly premature, as by the end of September it was obvious that the war was not going to be over by Christmas. Nevertheless, the question of employment still remained. Thus far the SAS had operated in areas where they had been able to count on some level of support from the local population, but this would not be the case inside Germany.

In early October, the brigade was in a state of flux, with units spread all over southern England. Tactical HQ was still at Moor Park, but Rear HQ and HQ 20 Liaison had moved from Oare House, Pewsey, in Wiltshire, to Sloe House, Halstead. 1 SAS had moved from Fairford to Nettlebed in Hampshire on 18 September and 2 SAS was at Shipton Bellinger near Tidworth. Both French Battalion HQs were in France, the Belgians were still at Fairford, and Station 1090 remained at Down Ampney. Through October and into November, there was a general move of all units into south Essex where they would be nearer to future operating areas in Germany and the Low Countries. At the same time, 38 Group RAF also moved its aircraft to East Anglian bases.

This chapter is concerned with the history of the SAS from the end of the French campaign to the last operational deployment of the war in the spring of 1945, in Holland and Germany. To avoid confusion, the staff discussions that took place during the winter of 1944–5 will be examined first, followed by the operations that ensued.

In a briefing paper for SHAEF issued on 5 October by Lieutenant-Colonel Collins, the brigade's situation was set out most succinctly in the form of a planning guide to run from October to the following January.[1] This was the first of a number of such appreciations that were designed to 'sell' the SAS to often sceptical higher headquarters. The strength of the brigade was listed as follows: 1 SAS, 520 men of whom 350 were operational; 2 SAS, 620 men, 380–400 operational; 3 French Para., 450–475 men, 450 operational; 4 French Para., 325–350 men, 350 operational; and Belgian Ind. Co., 110–130 men, 110 operational.

As far as 1 SAS was concerned, the jeep squadron assigned to the 21st Army Group for counter-intelligence could consist of between 120 and 180 all ranks (Major Marsh's C Squadron). A further 125 all ranks including the Houndsworth party (A Squadron) were exhausted after three months behind the lines and would not be available for SAS-type work but could be used as a police force. Excluding the above, all that remained was an operational strength of between 50 and 75 men, although for the Norway policing task, 200 to 250 men would be available.

2 SAS Regiment had around a hundred men still in the field on Loyton who, when relieved, would need a good rest. That left 250 parachute-trained personnel and up to 100 non-parachutists available for Norway, plus the Loyton people who would be available at the end of November. It was reported that 3 French Para. had been reinforced by 100-odd Resistance fighters who were not parachute-trained, and was to a certain extent mobile in requisitioned civilian transport. 4 French Para. was mobile in that it had forty armed jeeps and some 3-ton lorries. The Belgian company had sixty men being held in reserve to reinforce Portia (which will be discussed later) and other Dutch bases.

Colonel Collins stated that 1 and 2 SAS Regiments, less the jeep squadron earmarked for counter-intelligence with the 21st Army Group, were allocated to post-occupational duties in Norway, but would be available at short notice for operations, providing not too many personnel were required. As far as the French were concerned, it had been suggested that they be handed over to the French military authorities for use in an advance into Germany or for maintaining law and order in southern France. Collins's report stated, though, that 'Both battalions were very anxious to stay under British command if possible. The French military authorities had no real role for them nor were they yet in a position to operate and administer these battalions.'

As SHAEF thought it a waste for trained parachutists to be used in a ground role, they had proposed that both units should stay in France under SAS control and be held as a reserve for any airborne or jeep reconnaissance operations that might be required.

Collins then made the point that command levels such as corps and divisions had really very little idea of how to employ SAS troops and that in planning for Overlord and Anvil, comparatively little thought had been given to the possibility of SAS troops working in conjunction with the Resistance. He went on to suggest that small parties could be dropped along both sides of the Rhine to assist operations, staying in the field for up to seven days. To do that, 38 Group RAF aircraft would have to be established on airfields east of Paris together with an advanced Brigade HQ.

In a counter-intelligence role, the SAS could help to mop up parties of Germans who had been left behind and also assist in arresting known war criminals and Gestapo officials. Finally, he offered SAS troops to stiffen the Resistance in Denmark.

The whole winter period of 1944–5 was taken up at brigade level with preoccupations about finding a role – any role – for the SAS. The question of command and employment of the French also produced reams of paperwork. SHAEF decided that the two French battalions should concentrate in the Chalons-sur-Marne area and be prepared to take part in airborne operations, which angered General Juin who wanted to integrate them into the embryo French army. However, as they wished to remain under British command, they were left in limbo for several months. An element of farce crept into the proceedings on 17 October. An incoming signal to SHAEF G 3 from 6th Army Group HQ (the forces which had landed as Anvil in the South of France) stated:

3 and 4 French Para. Battalions mentioned in your signal are not part of 6th Army Group. This headquarters has no requests for their employment. Location of units not known. The First French Army has been contacted and has no knowledge of the whereabouts of these units. First French Army state they believed these units dropped in various places in France by the S.A.S.[2]

In mid-October, Brigadier McLeod stated in a letter to Airborne Corps HQ that it was unlikely that 1 SAS Regiment would be required in Norway before mid-April, which is the first real indication that the facts of the winter stalemate had really been understood. Another first mention in the same letter is his offer to make available part of 2 SAS for operations in north-west Italy if required.

An undated letter from Collins almost certainly written in early November to G 3 at SHAEF contains some idiotic suggestions for mass suicide missions for SAS troops by parachuting them into Germany. His idea was that this would cause parachute scares all over the country, thus tying down troops to guard lines of communications, as well as having a psychological impact on the local civilians. This seems particularly out of keeping as Collins's ideas were normally sensible.

Specifically, he suggested that troops could act as information parties for airborne drops or corps-level attacks, establish road and rail watches, or act as sabotage missions on specific objectives. 'Note. This could be done more easily at a later date when Allied troops are across River Rhine, but could be attempted now with party withdrawing through Switzerland.'[3] While calmly contemplating the misuse of that neutral country, his final suggestion was for raiding parties 'of some considerable strength' to be dropped into southern Germany to blow up installations, kill frontier guards and so on, and then withdraw into Switzerland. He at least had the grace to say that the latter plan depended on the parties – if there were any survivors – being exfiltrated from Switzerland as escaped prisoners of war.[3]

The above ideas might well be feasible today given the training, skills and equipment of the modern SAS, but they were certainly quite impractical in 1944. One can just imagine the diplomatic incident that would have been caused if a Swiss frontier post had been confronted by a bunch of heavily armed desperadoes, probably dragging an unwilling captive or two behind them, demanding political asylum as escaped prisoners of war. How would the British Embassy in Berne have reacted? Nobody who was in the regiment at that time to whom I have spoken had any recollection of the above plans, which was probably just as well.

Eminently more sensible was a SHAEF directive in late October on the employment of SAS troops. It began by making the point that in the post-Overlord phase, a number of operations had been successfully carried out in 'fair flying weather' and with the assistance of a friendly local population. These missions were of a strategic nature and took place far behind the lines, but with the advent of bad weather and hostile German civilians, future operations would of necessity have to be of a tactical nature. Thus planning would have to be delegated to corps level or perhaps even down to divisional level. The plain fact was that little was happening.

The whole strategic situation in north-west Europe in October–November 1944 mitigated against the use of SAS troops in an operational role, which was poor consolation to the men who, returning from leave, waited around for orders and were sent away on courses. In the north, the Germans were still firmly in control of most of Holland, and after Montgomery's failure to cross the Rhine at Arnhem in September, the 21st Army Group front had become bogged down. The Ardennes area in Belgium was unsuitable for the movement of large bodies of troops and was lightly held by the US First Army. In Lorraine, Patton was fighting a pecking campaign, trying without success to get over the Moselle around Metz. Further south still, determined German resistance had prevented the 6th Army Group from closing up along the Rhine.

The SHAEF directive recognized the facts of life and pointed out that SAS troops could be made available to gather information on immediate tactical objectives or to sabotage communications ahead of a planned attack. It was, however, noted that small SAS parachute parties could not carry enough explosive to demolish very large objects such as stone viaducts. A five- to six-man patrol could carry 100 lbs., sufficient for a steel-girder bridge. They could also be employed for security duty or in apprehending war criminals, but the point was made most strongly that they were not agents and did not operate in civilian clothes. SAS troops were, however, available for tasks requiring highly trained men with 'courage, initiative and individuality'.[4]

On 26 November, a signal was sent from SHAEF, signed by Eisenhower, to Allied Forces HQ (AFHQ) in Italy, stating that there was little possibility of employment for SAS troops in north-west Europe, and that a squadron could be sent to Italy if needed. It was suggested that a staff officer from the brigade should go out there to discuss the possibility. On the same date, SAS Brigade was asked for suggestions as to how it could help a Special Forces scheme to grab a German radio technician working on a V2 control site near The Hague. There is no evidence that this operation was ever carried out.

At the end of November Brigadier McLeod paid a visit to SHAEF and the two main Army Groups, Montgomery's 21st and Bradley's 12th, touting for custom. On his return he put pen to paper, once again lobbying hard for employment for his units. First, there was the perennial question of what to do with the French battalions which were still cooling their heels in the Reims–Épernay area. On 2 December he wrote to General Browning at Airborne Corps HQ explaining the situation and asking for instructions. A plan had been floated for one and a half squadrons to capture the east terminal of the causeway leading over the seaward end of the Zuyder Zee in Holland, but McLeod, being unduly pessimistic, felt it unlikely that that would be feasible before the end of June 1945. Another suggestion at the time was to drop a small recce party into the Eifel area. As one of the might-have-beens of history, had that operation been carried out at the end of November or early December, advance warning might have been provided of the massing of three German armies preparing to attack in the Ardennes on 16 December.

SHAEF had instructed that winter training should be given to the two battalions so that they could be employed on the Franco-Italian frontier, or in Austria, Northern Italy or Norway. McLeod pointed out, though, that in the long term no steps had been taken to regroup all French parachutists as a brigade, which was what the French authorities wanted. As there was no prospect of them being employed in an SAS role in the foreseeable future, he had issued orders for them to commence training as straightforward parachute battalions.

At present, the retention of the French S.A.S. Battalions does not help to win the war to any notable extent, and could only do so if proper employment were to be found for them in Germany, Norway or elsewhere. ... If handed back to the French they would rapidly deteriorate and their discipline and organization would become chaotic which will result in adverse political repercussions.

The brigadier finished by stating that from his knowledge of the authorities in Paris it was extremely unlikely that any rapid decisions would be taken. He therefore requested guidance as to the policy he should adopt pending a final decision on their future.[5]

In a further letter to Airborne Corps HQ, also written on 2 December, McLeod went into the future employment of the brigade in more detail, summing up what had been proposed to date. The two British regiments were still earmarked for Norway as Operation Apostle but planning remained nebulous. Various missions were being consi-dered for the Belgians once an advance into Holland got underway. What is interesting is the proposal mentioned above for a small recce party to go to the Eifel. This was envisaged as a three- or four-man mission consisting of volunteers wearing civilian clothes or German uniforms. The purpose would be to study the feasibility of SAS troops operating inside Germany, and could be mounted 'as soon as the necessary papers can be procured'. This seemed to be a complete reversal of opinion in view of the SHAEF circular which emphasized that the SAS were not agents and did not operate in civilian clothes.

It would also seem that Collins's earlier idea of operating in southern Germany had been seriously considered, because McLeod mentioned a mission to the Black Forest area that had been prejudiced by publicity given to an SOE operation close to the Swiss border. Apart from using the French for the job in the Eifel, to give them some employment, McLeod concluded that the most sensible idea would be to hand them back to their own national authorities.[6]

This was categorically knocked on the head by a set of notes for a meeting on 8 December between General Browning and General Whitely, G3 at SHAEF, in which it was stated that the two French battalions would remain under British control and would not be incorporated into a French airborne brigade.

On the same date, AFHQ in Italy signalled to SHAEF requesting the immediate posting of thirty SAS personnel by air transport, and stating that the remainder of a full squadron would be required in early January. A return signal informed them that, weather permitting, Major Farran would be arriving in Naples on 15 December.

Thus at the turn of the year, the only real prospect of action for the British regiments lay in Italy, and steps were taken to mobilize 3 Squadron of 2 SAS under the command of Major Roy Farran. The remainder of the British SAS had spent the intervening time in re-equipping, debriefing after the French campaign and undertaking mountain warfare training at Banchory in Scotland to prepare for operations in Norway. The latter area was the responsibility of Scottish Command, and through the autumn and winter a planning staff, with Captain Masters representing the SAS Brigade, ran through various scenarios without much urgency. C Squadron of 1 SAS sat around in southern Holland with nothing to do, except for a brief move to Antwerp to counter a threatened German paratroop landing that never materialized. The rest of 1 SAS was put on standby over the Christmas period to move to the Ardennes, but when the enemy attack was contained they were stood down again.

Thus the only unit actually employed on active operations was the Belgian SAS, although in very small numbers. To understand their activities it is necessary to return briefly to September. A mission code-named Regan and comprising a lieutenant (Kirschen) and three other ranks was dropped on the night of 15 September into Holland. This was purely an intelligence-gathering job and the party were given strict orders not to make any commitments about arming the Dutch Resistance. They were to obtain and radio back information about enemy activity between Antwerp and Maastricht and along the Rhine and Waal rivers. Almost immediately they became caught up in the bitter aftermath of the failed Arnhem operation and began organizing the escape of airborne personnel across the river. MI9 also became involved and a considerable number were assisted back to the Allied lines with the help of Dutch Resistance cells. The SAS party eventually changed into civilian clothes and continued to operate until 14 March, with the code-name changed to Fabian.

Operation Portia, which later became Gobbo, was inserted to the north of Regan. The aim was to explore the possibility of establishing an SAS base in the Drente area to hinder an eventual German retreat eastwards through Friesland towards their own border. It was commanded by Lieutenant Debevfe with five other ranks, two of whom were signallers. In addition, a number of weapons instructors were dropped to aid the local Resistance. The party dropped on the night of 26 September to an SFHQ reception and rapidly built up an information network enabling them to radio intelligence back to base. They also reported that the countryside was far too densely populated to be suitable for a larger SAS party. That simple factor was to hamper all attempts at widespread infiltration into Holland, added to which the terrain was also quite unsuited to jeep operations and was virtually devoid of cover. The Portia/Gobbo party, however, remained in Holland until March, wearing civilian clothes and continuing to send out useful information.[7]

These two small Belgian operations, while extremely useful, were hardly the sort of work for which SAS units were trained and could equally well have been carried out by SOE agents. The remainder of the Belgian squadron remained in Brussels through the winter, except for a brief foray into the Ardennes in support of British troops on the northern flank of the German attack. Operation Regent involved the whole company mounted in jeeps, acting in support of ground units and carrying out reconnaissance missions, in late December and early January.

The Ardennes affair also provided brief employment for 3 RCP

(4 French Para.). The main part of the battalion was moved north in jeeps as Operation Franklin to provide support on the flank of the US VIII Corps. They too acted in a reconnaissance role and carried out attacks in conjunction with ground troops.

At the end of January, the two French battalions were ordered back to Britain, together with HQ 20 Liaison, and moved into bases in East Anglia. 2 RCP (3 French Para.) was at Orwell Park, Ipswich, and 3 RCP at Rundlesham Hall, Wickham Market. In November, 1 SAS had moved to Hylands Hall near Chelmsford and 2 SAS to Wivenhoe Park just outside Colchester. Thus the entire brigade, apart from the Belgians, who became a full regiment in March, was concentrated in the east of England, together with Station 1090 which was now at a place called Mushroom Farm at Wethersfield.

In January there was little sign of operations along the main Allied front getting underway, and the Americans were still engaged in mopping up after their setback in the Ardennes. Montgomery planned a major offensive to start in early February out of the salient around Nijmegen which he confidently predicted would get his troops over the Rhine in two weeks, but this degenerated into a month-long slogging match. Those responsible for SAS operations, however, were still forging all sorts of plans, and trying to persuade higher headquarters to include them in the order of battle for any operation that was going. It is of course easy to criticize that attitude, especially in view of the fact that the more crackpot schemes would have cost the lives of the operators rather than those of the staff officers. To be fair to the latter, the alternative was disbandment or absorption into another, larger force. The end of the war was in sight and everyone concerned with the future of the SAS realized that they must be in at the finish, in whatever role, in order to be able to claim exemption from the inevitable post-war cuts in manpower.

At the turn of the year there was much discussion of aid to prisoners of war and civilian deportees in Germany which came to a head at a meeting at SHAEF on 2 January. The subject had originally been raised by the French authorities who naturally had a vested interest as their nationals formed the largest group of captives inside Germany. It was felt that anything precipitate could bring reprisals down on the heads of such prisoners, but it was decided to look into the possibility of dropping small parties near known camps. At about the same time, a suggestion was also floated that the two French battalions might be sent into Brittany to operate against pockets of German troops that were still holding out in some ports such as Brest. At the end of the month, Major-General Gale who was in command of 1 British Airborne Corps wrote to SHAEF asking for a statement of priorities on the employment of SAS troops in view of planned airborne operations in Germany in 1945. He had in mind an operation code-named Eclipse which would have involved extensive jeep patrolling in Germany, to the south of Kiel, and the seizure of an airfield in that area.[8]

With the general situation regarding the SAS as a whole still in a state of indecision, it is time to examine what was happening in Italy with the detached squadron of 2 SAS. Since returning from France, Roy Farran had been in Greece on what he himself admitted was a bit of a holiday, although he was attached to Land Forces Adriatic as an SAS observer. When Franks had gone over to France to take part in Loyton, he had left Sandy Scratchley and a certain Major the Hon. John Bingham in charge of headquarters. The latter had tried to prevent Farran from going to Greece, but he had simply caught an aeroplane after a row on the telephone. Bingham was one of the breed of non-operational officers who had insinuated themselves into minor staff positions with the brigade and 2 SAS and who were treated with scant respect by the fighting troops. The basis for such appointments often seems to have been that those concerned were old school chums or came from the same background of aristocracy and club membership. 1 SAS was relatively free of the breed, as Paddy Mayne simply would not tolerate them.

Farran flew out to AFHQ in Naples on 15 December accompanied by an advance party from 3 Squadron, their heavy equipment being sent by sea. He makes the point in his memoirs that this was not his own squadron, but one which had been raised when the regiment had returned to Scotland in the spring of 1944. It had been trained by Major Rooney who had injured himself in a parachute drop and the men were relatively inexperienced in operations. Right from the start, Farran was seen as the force commander and it was not envisaged that he should take part in operations.[9]

The advance party had been sent to mount an operation, commanded by Captain Walker-Brown and code-named Gallia, on the Italian Riviera between Genoa and La Spezia. The operation was to act in support of a proposed offensive in the area by US ground forces and also to persuade the enemy that there was an airborne battalion in Italy. Walker-Brown himself had served with the Highland Light Infantry in Libya where he had been taken prisoner. After two escape attempts he had regained the Allied lines in Italy and had joined the SAS in 1944.

The drop took place on 27 December when five officers and twenty-nine other ranks were parachuted in daylight north of La Spezia to operate with partisans against enemy rear concentrations. They landed to a reception organized by the British Liaison Officer in the area, and were divided up into a headquarters and five sections. On 3 January a message came through that the Genoa to La Spezia road had been attacked and some good bombing targets were sent. There was also a request for arms for approximately fifty partisans who had been recruited. In the meantime they attacked an enemy headquarters with brens and a 3″ mortar. The following day it was reported that a German prisoner had told them that the German offensive in the Serchio valley had not been followed up because of 'uneasiness caused by the Allied raid on the coast'. Farran felt that this was excellent proof of the value of such raids by SAS troops.

Walker-Brown and his men operated under almost Arctic conditions in mountainous country for nearly two months, achieving a considerable bag of enemy transport and personnel. At one stage the Germans were said to have employed 6,000 troops in an attempt to track down the SAS party. Although the SAS were on foot, they made extensive use of their 3″ mortar which was carried on requisitioned mules over the mountain ridges. Resupply was difficult owing to the weather and the lack of suitable DZs, and at one stage the squadron medical officer had to be dropped in to deal with several cases of exposure and frostbite. In spite of the privations suffered, the various sections kept up the pressure, mining roads, ambushing and creating alarm. By 10 February, Walker-Brown decided that the area was played out and determined on a withdrawal. He ended his report by stating:

German intelligence by that time had established that we were really fewer in number than at first reported, and I think we had exhausted the potential of surprise and exaggerated rumours. I thought it was time to withdraw from that particular operation with a view to being deployed in another area, where once again we could exploit surprise and rumour.

Walker-Brown was awarded the DSO for his courage and inspired leadership on this particular operation.[10]

The remainder of Farran's new squadron travelled out to Italy by sea, but he also undertook some local recruiting, collecting three officers and a few NCOs from the local replacement depot. Although the squadron had autonomous status, it was administered to some extent by SOE and for operations came under an American, Colonel Riepe, who was responsible for clandestine activities. When Walker-Brown returned to Squadron Headquarters from Gallia, he was placed in charge of the resupply of parties in the field, in which capacity he worked miracles. Squadron Headquarters was in a country house near Cecina, where Roy Farran instituted a thorough toughening-up programme for officers and men. Three relatively small operations and one major one involving the whole squadron were carried out.

The first of the small operations, Operation Cold Comfort, later renamed Zombie, was designed to drop a small ski-trained party to the north of Verona. From there they would attempt to block the main railway leading to the Brenner Pass by creating a landslide in a cutting. Had they succeeded they would have severely hampered the movement of German reinforcements south through the Alps. Twelve men under Captain Littlejohn were dropped at the end of February and became scattered on landing. Resupply proved extremely difficult owing to the weather, and movement was hindered by an unfriendly local population who were of Germanic origin and fervently hoped for a German victory. On 17 March it was reported that a section under Sergeant Lipscombe was in hiding and that efforts to drop Lieutenant Wilmers to him had repeatedly failed owing to aircraft problems. A week later the area was reported as being insecure, and on 31 March as 'very hot'. It was therefore decided to exfiltrate the party. The officer in charge, Littlejohn, and Corporal Crowley had by then both been caught and executed under the Commando Order.[11]

I have not been able to find any information about the other two smaller operations and for some reason the volume of reports on Italy does not contain any details. One was known as Blimey and consisted of twenty-five men under a Captain Scott. They were dropped into the same area as Gallia at the beginning of April with much the same mission. According to Farran, they failed to achieve anything worthwhile and most were taken prisoner. The other was Canuck, commanded by a Canadian, Captain Buck McDonald. Their mission was to harass German communications between the Riviera and North Italy. McDonald organized a group of efficient partisans and, equipped with a 75mm. howitzer, captured the town of Alba near Turin. In a SHAEF report there is also mention of Break II which I have been unable to identify.[12]

The main operation undertaken by the bulk of the squadron was Tombola which has been extensively written about, notably by Roy Farran himself. It is therefore only necessary to go into the highlights, although in terms of the history of the SAS, the operation is extremely important.[13]

It would seem that Roy Farran himself was the instigator of Tombola and that he had every intention of leading it himself in spite of orders to the contrary. What he had in mind was a large-scale tactical operation, rather than a raiding party, using partisan formations. There were considerable numbers of such irregulars, of varying political allegiance, under a central command based in Milan. Each area command had a British Liaison Officer from SOE attached, responsible for arming them and persuading them to fight Germans. The usual reservation was aired during the planning stage that infiltrating uniformed troops before the main battle started would bring down German reprisals and scatter the partisans before they could be of use. The liaison officer in Reggio Province, Michael Lees, however, had no such reservation and was keen to receive such uniformed support.

Farran described his squadron as 'an odd collection of toughs' who included two Spaniards, an Austrian named Stevens and a 60-year-old merchant seaman called Louis who had come out from Gallia with Walker-Brown. Without hesitation Louis agreed to parachute back behind the lines although he had no military status and was not even paid. Another character who had been on Gallia and who volunteered to return with Farran was Lieutenant Riccomini. Half Italian, he had escaped from a prisoner-of-war camp with a Scottish officer, Captain Eyston, who was appointed second-in-command. Many of the new recruits had not completed basic parachute-training and did their first jump on the operation. By that stage of the proceedings, Farran had assumed the name of Major Patrick McGinty. As an ex-escapee from the Germans, he had the right to do so and chose that particular pseudonym from the well-known song about an Irish goat who swallowed a stick of dynamite. His DSO, awarded for his deeds during Wallace, was gazetted on 29 March 1945 in the name of Captain (temporary Major) McGinty.

An advance party under the command of Captain Eyston dropped in daylight on 4 March, accompanied by Farran who was supposed to have acted as dispatcher. He naturally had worn a parachute in case the aircraft got into difficulties, and equally naturally he had used it, in a sublime gesture of Nelsonian blindness towards orders. Eyston badly injured his shoulder on the drop but later recovered sufficiently to be able to take part in operations. The area where they were to work was in the mountains south of Parma which overlooked the wide plain that runs east–west across northern Italy.

Farran's party was received by Lees on the DZ and an agreement was reached to form a Battaglione Alleata under SAS command, absorbing various partisan units but remaining separate from the local command structure. The new formation eventually consisted of fifty SAS from 3 Squadron. They were augmented by seventy Russians, most of whom had escaped from German prison camps, led by a former Red Army lieutenant, Victor Pirogov, known as 'Victor Modena'. They were well armed and efficiently led. The remainder of the force comprised 100 Italians commanded by a man named 'Tito'. They were a mixture of an ostensibly non-political unit leavened with 'Garibaldini' or Communists.

The first drop brought in supplies and weapons for the new battalion, plus three officers and the seaman Louis. Only one of them had ever jumped before, but Farran reckoned that parachuting 'must not be considered a bogey and is only a means of getting into the objective'. The arrival of the equipment boosted Farran's prestige to great heights and ensured that he had the confidence of the partisans, which was all-important in dealing with such irregulars. On 9 March, twenty-four more SAS arrived and were split up among the Russian and Italian groups as instructors. The following two weeks were devoted to weapon-training on 3″ mortars, brens and heavy machine guns.

Farran had been ordered not to begin offensive operations before 23 March, but to concentrate on training his force, which was rapidly welded together. With a great understanding of human nature and people's need to belong, he asked Walker-Brown to provide feather hackles in green and yellow for the Italians to wear in their khaki berets. This gave them pride, and they adopted woven badges with the motto 'Who Dares Wins' on their pockets. There was also a group of women who acted as couriers. They had 'McGinty' embroidered on their pockets and a badge consisting of a bow and arrow. The final touch of military swank, however, was the arrival of Piper Kirkpatrick, complete with kilt, dangling on the end of a parachute. He too had been provided by the indefatigable Walker-Brown in distant Florence and he was accompanied by a 75mm. howitzer which had been dismantled for dropping. The Battaglione Alleata had acquired its own artillery to supplement a number of Italian 45mm. cannon belonging to the partisans.

The initial disposition of the force was essentially defensive, to protect the base against a German attack, but neither Lees nor Farran was prepared to remain passive for long. They had received information about a German corps headquarters at Albinea, down on the plain where the foothills of the mountains ran into the Po valley, and resolved to attack it. The plot was hatched on 20 March and the plan was radioed back to Colonel Riepe at the 15th Army Group. The battalion received agreement and recent air photographs were dropped in. Farran dryly commented: 'Later they revoked their decision. It was too late. We were already on our way to the plains.'[14]

Behind that brief statement lurks a controversy and shades of the perennial problem of SOE fingers in the pie. The SOE presence was located in Florence as No. 1 Special Forces Headquarters, which controlled the activities of the British Liaison Officers working with the partisans. They were generally opposed to offensive activity until the main advance started, giving the usual reason that premature attacks would bring reprisals and scatter the guerrillas. Lees felt it was important that his partisans should taste action, as otherwise they would go stale and their morale would drop. His view was that they were in a war and should be fighting, hence his keenness to have Roy Farran's SAS party in his area.

The apparent reason for the attempt to cancel the raid was that information had been received that the Germans were about to mount a major drive against the partisans, known as a *rastellamento*. Lees, speaking to the author Laurence Lewis, said that he recalled receiving signals warning of such an action.

I told them that we were not concerned, our positions were strong enough to hold and at any rate we were at war to fight wars. I also seem to recollect being reproved for making life difficult for others. Specifically I recollect sending the cable 'rastellamento balls' when they kept on about it. I think this made me very unpopular, as did the fact that Farran's mission made me independent of S.O.E. Florence H.Q.[15]

Walker-Brown, equipped with his own radio link to Farran and SAS sources of supply, was the guarantee of that independence. In an interview given to the same author, he said that when informed about the proposal to attack the German headquarters, he consulted Colonel Riepe who urged postponement.

I was then sent for and interviewed personally by General Mark Clark, who gave me the date of the Fifth Army offensive, and said it was most important that the planned attack should be delayed, so that the two could be co-ordinated. However, I forcibly put over that partisan morale, having been wound up to a pitch, could only be unwound at substantial risk to the success of the operation and its security. This was not accepted by General Clark. I found myself in an extremely difficult position. However, by sending a carefully worded signal with ample scope – I hoped – for Roy to read between the lines, I urged him if possible to postpone operations. As subsequent events proved, this was not possible.[16]

Farran received that signal when his force was well into the approach march, and once again adopted the Nelson approach. Disobeying orders is of course reprehensible in any military situation, but against that must be set the fact that had he pulled back, his force might well have disintegrated. Accompanied by the piper, the Battaglione Alleata marched down from the hills, armed to the teeth and prepared to do battle. The actual German headquarters, enclosed within a military compound, were located in two houses, the Villas Rossi and Calvi. Farran's plan was that his Russians would guard the perimeter while the SAS forced an entry with the backing of the Italians.

The attack was made at night and initial surprise was achieved. Encouraged by the skirl of the pipes which could be heard over the crackling of small-arms fire, the men assaulted the two villas. The Germans inside reacted and a major battle developed with casualties on both sides. Riccomini, Sergeant Guscott (an SAS radio operator) and Corporal Bolden were killed and several of the raiding party were wounded, including Mike Lees. With the targets on fire and ammunition running low, Farran gave the order to retire. Carrying their wounded, the raiders set off on the long march back to the hills, through country which by then was alive with German patrols. The two Spaniards, Ramos and Burke, carried Lees for several days on a ladder until they found a safe hiding place for him, for which act they were each awarded the Military Medal.

Once through the German lines, in a show of sheer bravado as Farran described it, the force formed up in threes and marched to the tune of the pipes through the village of Vallestra, led by Corporal Layburn on an improvised stretcher. They had killed thirty Germans and destroyed both villas, but they later discovered that the corps commander, General

Hauk, had been absent that night. Back at base in Florence, though, there was trouble brewing, and Walker-Brown received a 'fairly sizeable rocket' from Fifth Army. Shortly afterwards, Farran's old *bête noire*, Major the Hon. John Bingham, arrived in Italy; on 16 April he wrote to Brian Franks.

> He [Riepe] has had considerable trouble with a turbulent member, who apart from disobeying orders forbidding him to drop – which authority took in the right spirit – also disobeyed a clear order from Riepe not to attack an enemy H.Q. He excused himself by stating he was away from the wireless set. However, S.O.E.'s representative with him has informed S.F.H.Q. that our friend did, in fact, receive the signal. They are quite naturally very cross and told me they intend to Court Martial their own people.

Bingham went on to write that he thought the reasons for forbidding the attack were good ones and that he had asked Lieutenant Colonel Baring (G1 at Brigade HQ) 'to send a sharp rebuke to our member. . . . Even if he were Court Martialled (4 to 1 against) I should think he would at worst be reprimanded and his career would certainly not be damaged.'[7]

The above report to the regimental commander smacks of a child telling tales to teacher, yet another letter from Bingham dated 1 May, this time to Roy Farran himself, presents a different picture. It should be noted that by that time Brigadier Mike Calvert had replaced McLeod. The letter starts:

> My dear Roy,
> Firstly all congratulations on another sensational performance, a regular 'Farrango'. Brig. Calvert is tickled to death. In case Riepe did not show you his most flattering signal to Calvert and the latter's reply, here they are:
> Calvert v Riepe.
> 'F256. Personal for Brig. Calvert from Riepe. Am convinced now that FARRAN premature action in attacking 51 Corps HQ in March was due entirely to misunderstanding of orders and largely fault of myself and others this HQ. Due to good fortune no harm resulted and much good was accomplished. FARRANS gallant action in subsequent operations have completely sold to American part of this HQ the tremendous value of SAS operations. Accordingly request you

remove any stigma attached his record resulting from this unfortunate occurrence.'

Riepe v Calvert.

'GO.534. your F256. from CALVERT. OK thanks stigma removed.'[18]

The above exchanges have been quoted at length as an illustration of the way in which facts could be oversimplified and then distorted. Farran himself in his subsequent writings did not dwell on the dispute in any detail except to hint that a British faction (led perhaps by Bingham) wanted him court-martialled. Yet it would seem that his decision to drop was overlooked and that the anger was caused by his refusal to halt the attack. There probably were mutterings about taking some sort of action against Farran but then Riepe seems to have changed his tune. Whatever the facts, Roy Farran was awarded the decoration of Officer of the US Legion of Merit. Mike Lees was replaced as Liaison Officer, a decision taken by SOE before he was wounded, and still feels that he was set up as a scapegoat because he had been too aggressive.

To return to Tombola itself, during the first week in April the enemy mounted a strong attack on the area, which was repulsed by Farran's defensive outposts. During the same period, orders were received to prepare to move the whole force down on to the plain to coincide with the main attack by the Fifth Army. A few jeeps had by then been received and on 5 April the party were informed that the main attack had begun. Their mission was to attack the main German line of retreat along Highway 12 on 10 April.

The Battaglione moved in four columns down on to the plain, their heavy weapons and equipment, including the famous 75mm. howitzer and a good selection of mortars, carried on mules and in bullock carts. They concentrated in the village of Vitriola where they feasted on fried eggs and red wine, their staple diet throughout the operation. Roy Farran described the scene, as a partisan band prepared for action.

Long, greasy-haired pirates were sitting on the steps, cleaning their weapons in the streets. Jeeps dashed about everywhere with supplies. The night air was broken by the tap-tap-tap of Morse from our wireless sets and the Russians sang as they refilled their magazines. At night one could hear Modena's tame accordionist and occasionally Kirkpatrick's pipes, which were now suffering from lack of treacle, an essential lubricant for the bag, I am told.[19]

Results of attacks on the road were at first patchy owing to the lack of targets and enemy opposition. Farran therefore decided on 16 April to take the jeeps and the howitzer into action himself. They merrily fired seventy shells into the town of Sassuolo, scoring direct hits on German concentrations. The whole force kept up a furious pace of ambushes and mortar attacks, until on 20 April, word was received that the main offensive had succeeded. Farran reorganized his force into a 'Victory Column' which consisted of twelve British SAS, thirty Italians, three jeeps and the howitzer, intending to attack targets between Reggio and Modena. The remainder of the SAS were deployed with various partisan bands, including a detachment with the 19-year-old Rhodesian, Lieutenant Harvey, who had been recruited from the replacement depot before the operation. He mounted a brilliant ambush on Highway 12, and was subsequently awarded the DSO for his part in the attack on the German corps headquarters.

The battalion stores were moved down on to the plain from Vitriola, in ox carts groaning under the weight of 75mm. shells, petrol and ammunition for the Vickers. Towing the gun, Farran set off to attack the provincial capital, Reggio. Having shelled it, Victory Column ambushed their way through to Modena, where they had a party and a sing-song and slept in beds. That was effectively the end of Tombola as orders were received for the SAS to return to Florence. With the wounded on board, accompanied by one of the Italian partisan girls, a convoy of four jeeps, two civilian cars, two captured lorries, a German ambulance and the faithful howitzer in tow formed up for the long drive. The gun was cloaked in a swastika flag. Covered with the grime of months in the mountains the Battaglione Alleata drove through springtime Italy, welcomed in every village they passed through. Sadly they had to leave the Russians behind, to be ignominiously disarmed and herded back to death at the hands of the Commissars.

The above necessarily brief account can do scant justice to an operation which in its conception, strictly speaking, fell outside classic SAS philosophy yet which proved that well-trained men from the regiment could rise to the occasion and, under an inspired leader, could themselves lead groups of irregular forces. It foreshadowed, perhaps, operations in Oman carried out by 22 SAS regiment in the 1960s in conjunction with locally raised tribal levies. As Farran put it:

It was extraordinary how successful the British common soldiers were as detachment commanders. They reacted to their sudden responsibility magnificently. .... Very few of them were non-commissioned officers or had ever had responsibility before. Parachutist Murphy commanded a section of ten Russians with a Browning heavy machine-gun and two Brens at Civago, which was the remotest and most dangerous outpost.[20]

With the war in Italy virtually over it is time to return now to the main front in north-west Europe, as the Allied armies prepared to cross the Rhine and begin the final assault on Germany. The two British regiments had completed their mountain training and had absorbed a considerable number of replacements to bring them up to strength. On 5 March, Brigadier McLeod had left to take up his appointment as Director of Military Operations in India. Subsequently he became saddled with much of the blame for the lack of understanding of SAS capabilities and for launching them on unsuitable operations. As has been shown, however, he did his best to resist idiotic demands from higher headquarters; in reading through the documents of the period, he emerges as a stout defender of SAS principles as well as being concerned for the future. He suffered from the fact that he was not 'family', and as a regular career officer had been wished on the SAS who would rather have had one of their own as brigade commander. McLeod was replaced by Mike Calvert who brought with him a reputation for daring and courage, won while fighting with the Chindits in Burma. Known as 'Mad' Mike, he was an able commander and perfectly sane, but was fated to preside over the SAS at a time when they were no longer able to act independently.

By early March, Montgomery's armies had closed up to the Rhine and had cordoned off the remaining Germans in the north of Holland. The 21st Army Group had laid plans to employ the entire SAS Brigade, less Farran's detached squadron, as reconnaissance parties in front of his main advance, and proposals to drop them deep into Germany had luckily been shelved. Planning began in February and Montgomery's Rhine crossing took place on 23 March. There were five separate SAS operations which ran more or less simultaneously during this final phase of the war. In the first operation, Archway, two squadrons, one each from 1 and 2 SAS under Franks (Frankforce), were to cross the Rhine and patrol in advance of the ground forces. In Operation Howard, two squadrons from 1 SAS under Paddy Mayne were to be similarly employed. In Operation Larkswood, the Belgian SAS Regiment was to provide reconnaissance and flank protection for the Canadian armoured division by jeep infiltration. The fourth operation, Amherst, involved both French regiments which were to drop in northern Holland to aid the advance of ground troops by seizing bridges and road junctions. Finally, in Operation Keystone, one squadron of 2 SAS was to capture bridges north of Arnhem, arriving by parachute and by jeep infiltration.

Brigadier Calvert took personal charge of the final stages of the campaign and established an advanced Tactical HQ at Nijmegen. The various movements and supply of his entire brigade were a remarkable feat of logistics by any standards. For Amherst alone, sixty-five aircraft were employed for the initial deployment on the night of 6 April, dropping jeeps, stores, personnel and dummy parachutists. They flew in Stirlings and Halifaxes from Great Dunmow, Earls Colne, Rivenhall and Shepherds Grove airfields with an average dropping error of three and a half miles on a cloudy night. It had originally been planned to drop the Keystone parties on the same night, but in the event this was postponed until 11 April. The actual parachuting, however, was only a part of the problem. The men and stores had to be concentrated at the right airfield in the right order and at the right time. Once there the actual aircraft had to be loaded, hot meals served, last-minute shortages made good and the inevitable changes of plan coped with. For instance, the jeeps loaded were not actually dropped, but were landed at an advanced airfield and driven through the lines. The two British regiments were transported with their vehicles by landing craft from Tilbury to Ostend, from where they drove to their concentration areas, accompanied by lorry-loads of stores. That this all actually worked, apart from the inevitable minor hiccups, is a tribute to the hard work of the brigade staff and the unsung heroes of Station 1090 at Mushroom Farm.

Larkswood involved 200 men of the Belgian SAS Regiment under the command of their original leader, Major Blondeel. The unit was organized into two squadrons, each of which had a troop of twenty jeeps carrying fifty men, and an assault troop of forty men in 15cwt. trucks. They advanced as a screen in advance of II Canadian Corps which was on the left flank of the 21st Army Group, moving northwards into Holland. They encountered difficult jeep country criss-crossed by dykes and waterways, and were never really able to fan out any distance away from the Canadians. In spite of that, they captured several bridges which they held until the main forces caught up with them. German resistance was tough. The regiment suffered severe casualties, but was able to sow considerable confusion among enemy formations. They were also able to relieve several of the Amherst parachute parties which had not been overrun by the Canadians as rapidly as expected. The men then carried on into Germany, acting as the spearhead for the Polish Armoured Division right up to the time of the final surrender.

Amherst was a large and extremely complicated operation. The following account is therefore based on Brigadier Calvert's summary appended to the operation report.[21] The first steps were taken on 28 March when Calvert, who was in Brussels, was asked by the 21st Army Group if he could provide troops to operate with the First Canadian Army in Holland. He offered the services of the two French battalions and flew up to see the Canadians. They indicated that the earliest they would wish to mount the operation was 15 April, although in fact it actually started eight days earlier. The intention was to drop the two units in the area of Groningen, Coevorden and Zwolle, forty-eight hours in advance of the planned Canadian arrival. Their task was to create maximum confusion, hinder the demolition of bridges, capture Steenwijk airfield and rouse the local Resistance.

Calvert issued a warning order and returned to his headquarters where he briefed Colonel Prendergast who was then the commander of HQ 20 Liaison. Prendergast flew out to see the Canadian corps staff in whose area the French would be operating, and the basic plan was agreed on 4 April. Meanwhile, the logistics were being sorted out and an air plan was prepared. In a postscript to the report there is a fascinating comment which characterizes much of what the SAS was, and still is, all about – except for the lack of security which does not apply to the regiment today!

The following incident gives a very clear insight into the character of these French battalions, their initiative, offensive spirit, courage and lack of security. The morning before the operation started, six French privates of the battalions were in hospital in Paris with injuries or sickness. Within six hours of having heard, unofficially in Paris that morning, that the operation was to take place the following night, they were at Earls Colne. They received no official assistance in their journey. They dropped that night. No one in the French battalions considers this incident anything out of the ordinary.

The drop took place on the night of 8 April through solid cloud. As it had been assumed that the sticks would be overrun within forty-eight hours, they carried only light personal weapons and food for that period.

In fact, many were to spend more than a week in open country, but a considerable number of ambushes were carried out. Prendergast moved forward and established an advanced HQ at Coevorden from where he operated the armoured jeeps which drove in to collect some of the parachuted parties and the Belgian SAS. By 21 April most of the French had been returned to their bases in Britain, having achieved the bulk of the assigned tasks. They claimed 269 Germans killed, over 200 wounded and 187 taken prisoner. Their own losses totalled 160 killed, wounded or missing, but of the latter, 67 were shortly recovered from a prison camp. The report commented wryly that 'some other men were last seen disappearing in the direction of Berlin, hot foot after the enemy'.

One interesting innovation was the use of Typhoon fighter-bombers to drop resupply containers in daylight, which proved highly successful. The ponderous nature of SAS communications, however, persisted, dictated largely by poor technology and the unreliability of the various sets. Direct information could still only be received by parties in the field by broadcast to their portable MCR 100 receivers, and all signals traffic still had to be routed via Moor Park, where it was decoded, translated into English and then retransmitted to Canadian headquarters. In the case of bombing targets this led to delays and missed opportunities. In his report Calvert suggested the inclusion of RAF liaison officers as forward observers with SAS parties, equipped with a direct ground-to-air link. This would have enabled air strikes to be called down more or less instantaneously, but it was to be several years before such an idea became reality. In the 1945 campaign, a start was made in equipping SAS jeeps with short-range radios enabling them to communicate with each other and their squadron or troop commander. This was an innovation, but again the sets were cumbersome and unreliable.

Operation Keystone was similar in intention to Amherst although on a much smaller scale. The force involved was Major Grant Hibbert's squadron from 2 SAS, although in the original outline plan of 24 February this was envisaged as a task for 1 SAS. The aim was to disorganize the enemy to the south of the Zuyder Zee (Ijsselmeer) and capture bridges over the Apeldoorn Canal. To achieve this, two advance parties were to be dropped to prepare DZs to receive the main force and some jeeps. In addition, a further jeep party commanded by Major Druce would penetrate through the lines and drive north to meet up with the rest of the squadron.[22]

One of the advance parties of three men under Lieutenant Stuart dropped successfully on 3 April and made contact with the Resistance, but unfortunately their radio set was smashed on landing. The other party, finding no reception signals on the DZ, returned to Britain. Captain Holland dropped with the main party of sixteen men on the night of 11 April and found the area suitable for operations. He sent a signal asking for jeeps to be dropped but for some reason this was never received. In spite of this, two attempts were made to parachute in more men and jeeps but these were aborted owing to cloud cover. Holland's force maintained an aggressive patrolling routine and accounted for a number of vehicles and enemy personnel. Major Druce met up with them finally on 18 April, and the following day they drove back to Nijmegen to rejoin Grant Hibbert. The combined squadron then drove north-east to catch up with Brian Franks and the Archway parties.

Major Druce's force consisted of ten armoured jeeps, which assembled near Arnhem on 12 April. The following day they set out to break through the German positions, but on that and successive days they were never entirely successful. They did not have sufficient firepower to break through the German opposition and then they were caught up by the tanks of the Canadian 5th Armoured Division. In spite of that, they managed to kill thirty Germans and take fifty prisoners. That part of the operation illustrated the frustrations encountered by SAS parties condemned to operate in the forward battle zone on tasks which could perfectly well have been accomplished by armoured car units.

To carry out Operation Archway, Colonel Franks had a composite force from both British regiments, the first time that they worked together in any numbers during the war. Frankforce as it became known consisted of A and D Squadrons of 1 SAS commanded by Major Harry Poat. This group was divided up into three large troops, commanded by Majors Tonkin, Fraser and Muirhead. The 2 SAS element comprised Major Power's squadron divided into two troops commanded by Captains Mackie and Miller, later to be joined by Grant Hibbert's squadron from Keystone. Major Verney, who had joined the SAS after his escape from the Italians following his SBS raid on Sardinia, commanded the force headquarters. Franks had 430 men under his command mounted on 75 jeeps with a supply tail consisting of a number of trucks. Little known is the fact that the 1 SAS component of the force were wearing black Tank Corps berets in the hope of avoiding execution as parachutists if captured.

Frankforce left Essex and were shipped out on landing craft to Ostend where they arrived on 20 March. Their mission was laid down in

SAS Brigade Operational Order No. 2, dated 15 March, and consisted
of two phases. On 23 March a large airborne operation, Varsity, was to
be carried out on the east bank of the Rhine in advance of the main
crossings between Rees and Wesel. Frankforce were to carry out
reconnaissance tasks for the airborne forces and then to achieve deep
penetrations into Germany ahead of the main advance north-eastwards.
Their ultimate destination was to be Kiel.[23]

The two squadrons crossed the Rhine at Wesel in Buffaloes, a type of
amphibious barge fitted with tracks, on 25 March and drove through the
ruins of the town which had been well and truly cratered by the RAF.
The subsequent actions of the force are difficult to piece together
coherently, as they consisted of numerous small-unit engagements in
villages along the way. Initially they caught up with the airborne troops
and had quite some difficulty in forcing a way through the crust of
German defenders. The jeep sections probed for a way through and
became pinned down for a couple of days, Bill Fraser being wounded in
the process. The opposition they faced ranged from crack German
airborne troops to teenage Hitlerjugend and the elderly men of the
Volkssturm (Home Guard). By that stage of the war, the SAS were well
aware of what had happened to many of their comrades and there were a
lot of scores to settle. Reading between the lines of what people have
written or have said in interviews, the last few weeks of the war were
fought quite savagely, especially after the men had been confronted with
the evidence of Nazi brutality. Frankforce was deployed initially as a
recce screen for 6 Airborne Division which was heading towards
Münster.

The Belsen episode is particularly strange. All those I have spoken to
in 1 SAS who were with Frankforce remember having gone into the
concentration camp before it had been properly liberated and there are
photographs to prove this. Yet oddly enough, the official report of
Archway does not mention the camp at all. A British Second Army
pamphlet records that a local truce was drawn up on 13 April between
VIII Corps and the German First Parachute Army whereby the
Germans would evacuate the area of the camp owing to the danger of
typhus, leaving the staff and inmates to be dealt with by the British. It is
recorded that the first troops to arrive at the camp were from the 63rd
Anti-Tank Regiment, although the probability is that they were pipped
to the post by the SAS, who were in the area on 14–15 April. Whether
this was by accident or design is difficult to determine. Johnny Cooper
states that they were issued with yellow armbands and inoculated against

infectious diseases, with specific orders to hold the area after the German combat troops pulled back.[24]

What they discovered beggars adequate description – between 40,000 and 60,000 living skeletons suffering from malnutrition and disease and still being brutalized by SS guards. A Hungarian unit under arms was patrolling the camp perimeter, shooting any inmates who tried to get out. Those who were there remember meeting Kramer, the Commandant, who was later hanged as a result of the first war crimes trial in the British Zone. In the recent biography of Paddy Mayne, his driver, Lance-Corporal Hull, admits to having shot some of the guards, but this is difficult to account for as Mayne's unit at the time was sixty-odd miles away to the west. Whatever the truth of the liberation of Belsen, the SAS were not there for long as their job was to move on towards Luneburg.

A few days previously, on 8 April, Fraser's troop, which had been taken over by Ian Wellsted, had become embroiled with some Germans near Nienburg. They were patrolling in advance of the armoured cars of the Inns of Court Regiment and, with Johnny Cooper's section in the lead, drove into some woods. There they ran into a German ambush which included three armoured vehicles. The result was three killed and five wounded, including Ian Wellsted who was shot through both legs. The jeeps were extremely vulnerable to ambush on roads running through woods, as the enemy remained invisible. At that stage of the advance there was no sign of a general collapse of the German army.

In spite of setbacks and casualties the indomitable SAS humour was never far from the surface. In the official report for Archway, there is the following little gem contributed by John Tonkin for 12 April.

This day will go down as being the greatest in the squadron's history. At 1500 hours alone and without any supporting arms, it captured, at great risk to the personnel involved, a German Baggage. This was an attractive corporal in the W.A.A.F. Sergeant Valentine showed great bravery in that he searched her kit. She was removed as rapidly as possible to a P.O.W. camp by the squadron commander. There were no casualties.[26]

In Luneburg, on 19 April, various patrols were detailed to carry out a dawn swoop against known Nazis who were in hiding in the town. Thus the regiment became the executive arm of a Field Security Section, the role for which it had originally been envisaged in Germany. Johnny Cooper remembers that the British authorities had put up posters in the town with photographs showing the horrors of Belsen, but the local people refused to believe what they saw and claimed that it was Allied propaganda.

As April progressed, Frankforce moved on northwards, crossed the Elbe and advanced into Schleswig-Holstein, heading for Lübeck and Kiel. Gradually the opposition slackened and there were several mass surrenders to small jeep patrols. An entire division tried to surrender to Tonkin, who took photographs of a jeep driving along an endless column of enemy vehicles parked beside the road. Who was first into Kiel remains a matter of dispute, but a group of naval technicians were taken into the dockyard city to lay their hands on the submarine base. Just before the final capitulation of Germany, Frankforce was ordered to pull out and make for a rendezvous in Belgium, prior to being shipped back to Britain on 10 May. They had lost seven killed and twenty-two wounded in the drive through North Germany.

The final operation in north-east Europe to be considered is Howard, which was carried out by B and C Squadrons of 1 SAS under the command of Paddy Mayne. They left from Tilbury on 6 April and the following day the long column of jeeps and lorries drove to Nijmegen. Mayne went on ahead and met Calvert at Canadian Army HQ where he was briefed. The mission assigned was to advance ahead of the Canadian 4th Armoured Division, on the right of the Belgian SAS, in the direction of Oldenburg. The two squadrons, commanded by Major Bond and Major Marsh, concentrated at Meppen, having motored through the ruins of Cleve and crossed the Rhine at Emmerich. They departed for action on 9 April, moving into terrain similar to that found in Holland, criss-crossed with dykes and waterways. This was far from ideal country for jeeps and some criticism was voiced at the time about the ponderous nature of the Canadian advance. The SAS were informed that the opposition was unlikely to amount to much and the general feeling was that they were off on a swan.

Mayne put the two squadrons on to parallel roads, and without any definite objective they set off, aiming to rendezvous in a forest about seventy miles to the north. Both squadrons travelled quite openly in columns with the jeeps bunched together. The bulk of the men were not particularly experienced and failed to realize that, compared with France, the roles were now reversed. In Germany it was the enemy who were lying in wait for any transport unwise enough to venture along open roads. Shortly after setting out, B Squadron became involved in an action that led directly to the award of Mayne's fourth DSO and in a recent biography, the authors claim that the citation was 'concocted' by the intelligence officer, Mike Blackman, and Derrick Harrison.[27]

It is an undisputed fact that Mayne should have been awarded the VC at some stage of the war, for any one of a number of courageous exploits. He had been given three DSOs for his leadership and bravery, but what was missing was one act of conspicuous gallantry which would have justified the VC. One traditional reason for the award has been the rescue of wounded comrades under fire. In interviews for the biography, three lieutenants who were part of the action, Schlee, Surrey-Dane and Scott, have given their version of events, and the latter two have stated that they were persuaded by more senior officers to suppress certain facts.

What actually happened was as follows. The leading patrol of three jeeps was commanded by Schlee. As they approached the small town of Borgerwald, they came under fire from a small group of houses and a wood. Two men were wounded and the crews dismounted and took cover in a ditch. The enemy were well concealed and there was not much that the jeeps could do, caught as they were in the open. Behind them on the road, the rest of B Squadron bunched up and came to a halt. As an indication of their lack of experience, there was indecision as to what to do. Major Bond and his gunner, a Czech Jew who used the name Lewis, got out of their jeep and walked down the road towards the houses. Just before they got there they both slipped into the ditch to make their way towards Schlee. Trying to crawl over a culvert, both men were shot dead by a sniper.

In the meantime, Mayne had been informed by radio and he appeared on the scene. As nobody seemed to have much idea as to what had happened, he took a bren and several magazines from his jeep and started to walk down the road, followed by Hull, his driver, with a tommy-gun. Firing from the shoulder, Mayne emptied several bursts into the woods and one of the houses, and then walked coolly back to the jeeps, having assessed the position. He asked for a volunteer to 'have a go' and picked Lieutenant Scott. With Mayne driving and Scott manning the twin Vickers in the back, they charged down the road towards the ambush scene, spraying the houses and woods. Once past the houses, Mayne turned round and Scott climbed into the front to fire the .5 Browning. Mayne then drove back to where the wrecked jeeps had been abandoned and stopped. With Scott firing away, Mayne climbed out and helped Schlee and his men out of the ditch. All eyewitnesses agreed that by then the Germans had ceased firing and had probably slunk away.

Blackman, who was not present, wrote the citation with the best of motives, intimating that Mayne had brought out the wounded under heavy fire, and generally embellishing his account. This was perpetuated by Derrick Harrison, who was also not present, in his book *These Men are Dangerous*, published in 1957.

Down the road from the rear of the column came Paddy's jeep in a swirl of dust. Flat out, he flashed past and headed downhill straight for the heart of the trouble. Alone, sweeping past the strongpoint, he raked it with fire, turned and with the guns still blazing swept back again, stopping only to lift the wounded men into his jeep. A second and a third time he returned, unscathed in the face of withering fire, to rescue the survivors of the trapped section, and to recover the two bodies.[28]

How he could have both driven the jeep at speed and fired the guns single-handed is not explained. The fact remains that those whose responsibility it was to decide on such things ultimately awarded a third bar to his DSO. If one considers that Mayne was only 29, his record was an exceptional one. Yet at this late stage of the war, he seems to have relapsed into melancholy often accompanied by heavy drinking. In the above mentioned biography, his driver gave the authors a somewhat colourful description of Mayne's activities in Germany in April 1945, and rather implies that he went swanning off on his own. Yet the official report is quite categoric that he made the decisions about the activities of the two squadrons and kept up the pressure on the enemy. He was far too experienced and responsible a leader to leave his men in the lurch, especially in view of what had happened in the ambush.

They buried the two dead men and Mayne then withdrew the whole force back to the shelter of the Canadian armour to refit. Since setting out they had advanced thirty miles in three days of hard fighting and had suffered casualties. It was clear that the lightly armoured jeeps were no match for determined German ambush parties. The two squadrons were amalgamated under the command of Tony Marsh, and once again set out, this time slightly more cautiously. Known by the Canadians as 'our little friends in the mechanized mess-tins', they fought their way forward through a number of vicious little actions. On 23 April they reached the Kusten Canal and were transferred from the 4th Armoured Division back to the control of the Canadian II Corps. They then moved forward ahead of an armoured brigade and on 3 May found themselves to the north of Oldenburg. There they received orders to move back to Belgium and concentrate at Poperinghe prior to returning to Britain. Laden with well-earned booty, the jeeps drove back along their line of advance, passing units moving up to the front as the war was still not finally over. Also in the column were a number of fine Mercedes and BMW motor cars that had been liberated from their previous owners. They crossed the Rhine and in Belgium there was one last excuse for a party.

Some troops hit Brussels in a big way, while others celebrated in Poperinghe, which during the First World War had been just behind the front line at Ypres, and other little towns near the Belgian coast. Captured pistols, medals and Nazi daggers were soon turned into hard cash from American rear echelon troops eager to have a 'souvenir'. Reg Seekings went into a garage just outside Brussels to refuel with petrol on the afternoon of 8 May.

I was getting filled up and debating whether to go into Brussels overnight and then go to Poperinghe the next morning. A young girl came running out and said, 'The war is finished.' I said, 'I've heard that all before.' She said, 'No, it's true. Your prime minister, Mr Churchill, is speaking now.' So I ran into the garage and sure enough, the war in Germany had finished. We stopped and had coffee with them and decided we wouldn't go into Brussels. We went to Poperinghe instead and took part in the celebrations there. I was glad I did, because it was just as my old man had described it, hadn't changed at all. They were all sitting outside on the pavement, having a drink. All those old girls were there and we kept running out to the gents. Then we heard this old girl say, 'They're just like their fathers, drink-drink-drink, piss-piss-piss.'[29]

11

Norway, Disbandment and Re-formation

The two British regiments making merry in Belgium were unaware of the reason for their hasty recall, but the brigade staff had been working around the clock to prepare for a rapid move to Norway. As we have already seen, the idea of using SAS personnel to disarm the German garrisons in Norway had been mooted as far back as September 1944, and ever since then planning had carried on in a desultory way. Various scenarios had been laid down depending on the war situation at the time and the other tasks on which the regiments were engaged. There had even been some ideas floated about inserting small parties to disrupt enemy communications and hinder the movement of troops out of Norway for use elsewhere. Attention focused on the proposed demolition of a railway bridge near Trondheim, code-named Operation Ibrox, to be carried out by ten men from 2 SAS who would then exfiltrate through Sweden. This was scheduled for the night of 28 March and the party actually stood by at the airfield, but it was cancelled by SHAEF.[1]

The 'Condition Apostle' for the employment of the SAS assumed that an unconditional surrender by the Germans in Norway had already taken place. This occurred at the beginning of May, and overall command of the operation was given to the 1st Airborne Division with SAS Brigade Tactical HQ plus 1 and 2 SAS Regiments attached. The operational instruction issued by the brigade on 8 May illustrates the air of confusion and the logistical problems involved in the move.

2 sqns 1 S.A.S. and 2 sqns 2 S.A.S are now concentrated at DIXMUDE awaiting transport to ENGLAND. 1 sqn 1 S.A.S. was

last heard of deployed in KIEL area and may take some time to concentrate.

Information has been received that those in DIXMUDE will possibly sail on 9 May but Belgian dockyard celebrations and other attendant problems are causing delays. It is unlikely, therefore, that they will be in this country before 10 May.

All these units have been operating from the RHINE across GERMANY during the last two months and their clothing, their weapons and their vehicles are correspondingly worn and shabby. It will take at least 3 to 4 days for them to be reorganised so that they can uphold the traditions of smartness and turn out of the British soldier in an occupied country.[2]

In spite of the celebrating Belgian dock workers, the various parties were shipped out of Ostend on tank-landing ships, but as they nosed their way into Tilbury, it was noticed that a welcoming committee of Customs officers was in attendance on the quay. Quite who gave the order is unclear, but many of those present state that it was Paddy Mayne himself. When the great bow doors swung open, the jeep engines revved up and roared off the ship at high speed like a swarm of bees. The Customs men leaped for their lives and the jeeps rapidly dispersed all over southern Essex still laden with their loot.

The following few days witnessed a flurry of activity. Sixty new jeeps were issued, clothing was replaced and both regiments re-stored. Briefings were held to inform everyone of the task, before the move began to the various airfields for departure. The mission, known as Doomsday, was defined as supervision of the disarming of German forces in Norway and the carrying out of internal security duties. It was estimated that there were 300,000 of the enemy still in Norway who had actually surrendered, but their attitude was unknown at that stage. An advance party from brigade staff was flown to Stavanger accompanied by representatives from each regiment on 12 May, and the airlift of the main party started three days later. By 26 May, 760 men, 166 jeeps, 68 trailers, 17 motor-cycles and 33 tons of stores had been offloaded in Stavanger. From there the two regiments and Brigade HQ moved to Kristiansand which was to be their area of responsibility. Shortly afterwards, however, the whole brigade moved to Bergen where they were to remain until the end of the Norway assignment.

For the troops, the work was hardly onerous and their four months in

Norway were regarded by all concerned as a well-earned holiday. It was summer, the weather was warm, and the British were popular. The future, though, was still uncertain. Brigadier Calvert returned to Britain in June and began lobbying hard for the SAS to be employed in the Far East. In this he was supported by the formidable presence of David Stirling who had arrived back from Colditz.

There was a firm proposal for 1 SAS to go out as part of Mountbatten's South East Asia Command, but while in prison, Stirling's mind had been mulling over other possibilities. He had arrived back in England on 15 April to a disappointing welcome.

It was too ludicrous. The psychologists were getting quite a grip within medical circles in the U.K. and they assumed that anybody who came out of Colditz required treatment before being allowed back into normal circulation. We were put inside a camp that had a wire perimeter and there were all the official nannies there. We were told we had to be there for two days and they patronized us rotten. Naturally when we got there we had dates that very evening in London. I don't think there was anybody left in the camp at all by eleven o'clock. We were all in London or had gone home.[3]

Shortly afterwards Stirling and Fitzroy Maclean lunched with the Prime Minister and discussed with him what was called the Chungking Project. Stirling's intention was to form a brigade, commanded by himself, consisting of 2 SAS Regiment, an OSS regiment (the American equivalent of SOE) and a third regiment to be raised from released prisoners of war, including friends from Colditz. Their job would have been to operate in China, shutting off supplies to Malaya, sabotaging industrial centres in Manchuria and seizing parts of the coast to enable American ground forces to land. The plan was vintage Stirling – he was always capable of seeing the wider strategic implications of an operation. To put the project into context it has to be remembered that only a very tiny circle, including Churchill, had been initiated into the secret of the atomic bomb. It was thus generally assumed that the war against the Japanese would last for quite some time. Churchill gave his support to Stirling and planning for the operation was well advanced when the first atomic bomb was dropped. The subsequent Japanese surrender on 15 August put paid to any SAS involvement in the Far East, and Stirling himself subsequently went out to Africa.

Their mission in Norway accomplished, the two British regiments sailed for Britain at the end of August, knowing by then that disbandment was inevitable. Their departure was certainly welcomed by the British diplomatic representatives in Oslo who begged the War Office to remove the SAS. The reason for this was the last action of the Second World War in which the regiment took part, and for which no battle honours were awarded to be embroidered on the Colours. The participants, none of whom are noted for their reliability or impartiality, still have fond memories of the Battle of Bergen. Sadly, no after-action report exists in the public records and it is thus impossible to give an exact date or list the casualties. All sources agree, however, that the lads from the two regiments were extremely popular with the local girls, a fact that was resented by many young Norwegian males and members of the Bergen police force. What started off as a minor brawl in the centre of Bergen one night erupted into a fairly major confrontation which the SAS won.

The actual move from Norway back to Britain caused some personal hardship to certain members of the SAS who had invested their pay in expensive furs. On the assumption that they would sail together with their vehicles, the extra petrol tanks of the jeeps had been disconnected and the furs had been stuffed inside. There was a howl of rage when the men were informed that the jeeps would be taken by a separate ship and delivered straight to a stores depot in England.

Safely back in the Chelmsford area, this time minus their contraband, all concerned had to consider the future. The brigade was being broken up as the foreign regiments returned to the control of their respective armies. On 21 September the Belgians were handed over, and the French left on 1 October. There was no place in the slimmed-down peacetime army for an SAS formation of any description, reflecting perhaps the antipathy of the War Office bureaucracy for irregular formations. 1 and 2 SAS were officially in 'suspended animation' and the only work for the men was to hand in stores. There was an air of relief that the war was over, but also one of sadness, especially among the small group who had fought right through from the beginning. Quite a lot of time was spent in celebrations of one sort or another, which usually ended in high jinks. In one famous escapade, Paddy Mayne drove a jeep up the stairs at Hylands Hall which was used as a mess by officers of 1 SAS. Unfortunately, he could not get it down again and the fitters had to dismantle it the following morning. On a more serious note, Colonel Franks, accompanied by the Revd Kent, 2 SAS padre, and several others, returned to Moussey for the inauguration of a memorial to the villagers who had failed to return from concentration camps. As a token of gratitude, an SAS guidon was presented to Moussey and still has an honoured place in the church. Great efforts were made to secure appropriate British decorations for those who had helped the Loyton party.

The official War Office orders for disbandment of the brigade headquarters, the two regiments and attached units were issued at the beginning of October. The final parades were held and on the 5th of the month, the SAS ceased to exist, except for small skeleton staffs disposing of the remaining stores and paperwork.[4]

Those officers and men who still had time to serve or were regulars departed for their parent regiments, where they often felt like fish out of water. Temporary majors with chests full of medals found themselves back as captains or lieutenants, having missed out on the promotion ladder, and it is a fact that none of the wartime officers in either regiment went on to achieve high rank in the Army. For some, the transition to civilian life was easy. Many of those who had joined the SAS comparatively late seem to have been able to shrug off the war and return to their civilian occupations. A few went to prison and others made brilliant careers.

For some, however, the transition from the war years was a difficult one. Tanky Challenor admits that by the end of the war he had had the first intimations of mental instability. He ultimately joined the Metropolitan Police, but his career as a detective was blighted by his illness, and after a trial for planting evidence on a suspect, he spent a considerable time in a mental hospital.[5] Others required psychiatric help to enable them to come to terms with normal life, while some never did. Drink sadly claimed a number of victims.

It is not possible to chart the post-war activities of everyone who has featured in this history but the following cross-section can perhaps be regarded as typical. Brian Franks returned to his job as General Manager of the Hyde Park Hotel, the bar of which became a sort of unofficial meeting place cum employment exchange for SAS personnel who were in the London area. Both Johnny Cooper and Bob Bennett resurfaced in the SAS when it was resurrected as a regular regiment in Malaya. Harry Poat returned to growing tomatoes in Guernsey. Paddy Mayne, John Tonkin and Mike Sadler went off to the Antarctic as part of a survey expedition. An old back injury caused Mayne to be invalided home and he retired to a legal post in Belfast. Never able to settle, his drinking and brawling became legendary. In the early hours of 15

December 1955, he crashed his car into a house in Newtownards, fatally fracturing the base of his skull. Reg Seekings joined the Rhodesian Police. Roy Farran became involved in counter-terrorist work in Palestine and was acquitted on a charge of murder. His brother was blown up by a terrorist parcel bomb which had been meant for him, and he subsequently settled in Canada where he became a cabinet minister in Alberta. Jim Almonds built a boat and sailed it across the Atlantic. Several others became doctors, entered Parliament or joined the 'firm'. One even became an assistant hangman.

In theory the SAS ceased to exist in October 1945, but in practice pockets of it survived for quite some time in strange places. For four years there was a small group in Greece with the British Military Reparations Committee. This included Alastair McGregor and Bob Bennett who continued to wear full SAS insignia. Their job was to investigate claims from Greeks who had helped forces personnel during the war and to arrange payment of outstanding debts. Inevitably some of them became tangled up in the Civil War there.

The investigation of war crimes also occupied a group of men from the SAS in various capacities, as there were a considerable number of scores to be settled. In late November 1944, Brian Franks had sent Christopher Sykes back to the Moussey area to try to discover the fate of the missing men from Loyton. He brought back enough evidence to establish that at least some of them had been murdered. John Tonkin had also journeyed to France on a similar mission. In December, thirty-one bodies had been discovered in some woods near the village of Rom in the *département* of Deux-Sèvres. Subsequent post-mortems proved them to have been those of British service personnel who had been captured during Bulbasket. All had been shot.[6] Owing to the escape of Vaculik and Jones, the fate of the other members of the Garstin stick was well known, but by the end of the war there were still several men who had not returned from any prisoner-of-war camp.

The War Office displayed little interest in the fate of missing army personnel and it was not until the liberation of Belsen that a war crimes investigation unit was set up. This remained persistently understaffed and was finally wound up in 1949. The lack of official enthusiasm for finding those guilty of crimes against members of the SAS angered Brian Franks, and when in May 1945 information was received from the French occupying forces that some bodies of British servicemen had been discovered at Gaggenau in Germany, he decided to act. He sent his intelligence officer, Major Eric 'Bill' Barkworth, with a small detachment over to the French Zone of Germany to investigate.[7]

The Barkworth party, known as the SAS War Crimes Investigation Team, established that the bodies found at Gaggenau included men from Loyton who had been murdered at the nearby concentration camp of Rotenfels. From there they concentrated their search in the Moussey area, uncovering more bodies and evidence as to the identity of the perpetrators. By the autumn of 1945 they had built up an impressive dossier concerning the fate of the missing men, but their efforts were threatened by the disbandment of the regiment.[8] Brian Franks used his considerable political connections to keep the unit in being, and as late as 1949, the team was still at work, wearing SAS insignia. Their brief had been extended to investigate not only Loyton, but also the deaths of men from both regiments. At the British Zone military trials at Wuppertal, many of the guilty were brought to justice and several were hanged.

In the immediate post-war period, there was a small group of people who were determined that the SAS should survive, and that in doing so it should return to the original principles laid down by David Stirling. There is little in the way of documentation on this period and much of the lobbying was carried out over lunch tables and in Pall Mall clubs. As all those concerned at a senior level between 1945 and 1947 are now dead, it is difficult to piece together the story.

The War Office did show some interest, as evinced by an approach to Calvert by the Director of Tactical Investigation in October 1945. Calvert's letter is given in full in Appendix D, as it is an interesting refutation of many of the criticisms usually levied at 'private armies' by the establishment. I have in my possession a comprehensive report entitled 'Notes on the Organisation, History and Employment of Special Air Service Troops'. This is undated, but may well have been prepared in response to the above. Quoted below is the section on 'principles'.

a)   Intervention by S.A.S. Troops must have a strategic or tactical effect on operations. The degree of risk that should be accepted depends on the nature of the task.

b)   It is invidious to state that such a task is or is not an S.A.S. role, but it is essential to consider whether the task allotted cannot be carried out with greater chance of success by other military units or other branches of the Services (Air Force etc.).

This applies particularly to diversionary tasks or attacks on specific pin-pointed tasks in a tactical area.

c) The very high degree of collective and individual training makes it possible to operate in smaller parties than troops not specifically trained for this role, with equal or greater effort.

d) Where troops are operating behind enemy lines, they should be scattered in as many small parties as possible, though having where possible good communication by signal or courier with a small central base.

e) Good signal communications are essential and only under very exceptional circumstances is it sound to land parties without some form of signal communication.

f) Parties must have a firm plan for their eventual withdrawal, however vital the target.

g) S.A.S. Troops can rarely achieve their objective if landed in the face of immediate and alert ground opposition.

h) The initiative must be retained as long as possible by operating in an offensive manner. The psychological importance of keeping the morale high, both of own troops and of local partisans and civilians who may be assisting them, is enormous.

j) Surprise should be achieved and exploited fully. For this reason operations are normally carried out at night.

k) Casualties can and should be kept at a low percentage, bearing in mind that all personnel captured may be shot.

The report is extremely comprehensive and was obviously designed to sell SAS theories based on experiences during the latter part of the war. The War Office concluded its investigation into the role of raiding forces and decided that there was a need for a small unit of highly efficient troops able to operate behind enemy lines. It was felt, however, that in the post-war climate of austerity there was no justification for the raising of a new regular regiment. Instead, it was decided that a Territorial Army unit would be founded in 1947. Initially this was to be attached to the Rifle Brigade as its parent formation, but it finally merged with the Artists Rifles, becoming known as 21 SAS (Artists).

The Artists Rifles had started life as a volunteer battalion raised from among the London artistic community in 1859, and during the Second World War had functioned as an Officer Cadet Training Unit. It too was in search of a new role after the war, and as it owned its drill hall in Duke's Road, Euston, Brian Franks suggested the merger. The new regiment's first commanding officer was, deservedly, Lieutenant-Colonel Brian Franks DSO, MC, who had done so much work behind the scenes to keep the SAS tradition alive. Major L. E. O. T. (Pat) Hart, a regular Rifle Brigade officer, was appointed second-in-command. It is an irony that Pat Hart, who had served on the staff of the SAS Brigade, was the last officer to leave in 1945, having been responsible for winding up the affairs of the SAS.

The rebirth and subsequent campaigns of the SAS will have to wait for a further volume to do them justice. But the original principles of David Stirling remain just as true today as they did in 1941. It is difficult to sum up the wartime history of the regiment in terms of hard and fast statistics. Some I have quoted in the text where appropriate, but in a history of this sort there are factors to consider other than just numbers of the enemy killed. Above all in a small unit, there is the human factor, without which it could not function. From hours spent in the pleasant company of those who served and from reading the documents, the one element that has emerged most strongly in my mind is the essential sense of humour, often black, of the SAS. They always retained the ability to laugh both at themselves and at their misfortunes, and then get on with the job in hand.

It is difficult to quantify the characteristics that made up the typical SAS member, but service in the regiment seemed to break down the barriers of class that were so very real in even the wartime army. Most of the SAS officers came from the public schools system, with a few notable exceptions like Bill Cumper who had risen from the ranks, and there was always a contingent from the aristocracy. Yet internal promotion worked well, with Johnny Cooper, Jim Almonds and Pat Riley all receiving commissions and continuing to serve with the regiment. The officers themselves included a considerable number of artists and thinkers, as well as sporting types. Of the other ranks, there were a few of the thug variety, a number of rascals, but by and large they formed a cross-section of men from all parts of the British Isles. These were leavened with Spaniards, Polish and German Jews, Frenchmen, Czechs and members of almost all the combatant nations, who were made equally welcome. They were proud of being in the SAS and would not tolerate 'bull'. They kept themselves smart without having to be ordered to do so. Officers and men all underwent the same training and had to meet the same high standards, which engendered mutual respect. That was vital for the successful functioning of a small patrol on an operation, when privations and danger had to be equally shared between officers and men. Those who did not fit in were ruthlessly weeded out, especially during the earlier stages of the war. It was unfortunate that during 1944–5 the standards of recruitment were allowed to slip.

A belief has grown up that those who make the grade in the SAS are in some respects supermen. This is not so, and most of those who were recruited during the war possessed only average physical fitness. As few of them had much in the way of previous combat experience, it was the training programme that gave them their ability to conduct operations so successfully. What was required was an innate mental toughness and an absolute determination to succeed. Every one of them I have spoken to willingly admits to having experienced fear, yet as Jock Lewes taught them, 'the man who runs away has stopped thinking'.

What does emerge is a composite individual who could only be led by example and who had learned to be in full control of himself at all times. He was trained to kill and given the opportunity and equipment to practise his skills. In this more squeamish age, the actual business of killing is regarded with horror, yet in a war defeating the King's enemies meant eliminating them. That was what the SAS was there for, to fight against an awful tyranny, and most of them enjoyed what they had to do, but felt no rancour afterwards. What all the survivors have in common is an immense zest for life, an enduring capacity for strong drink and a dislike for those who 'winge'. The same applies to the French and Belgian veterans who are still proud of their links with the SAS and wear their beret and medals with distinction at reunions.

The SAS fought right through from the open spaces of the desert to the woods and towns of Germany. In four short years they created a legendary *esprit de corps* and enjoyed a remarkable series of successes as well as a few resounding failures. The aim of this book has been to present the history of the SAS without any gloss at all, and to make the point that where blunders occurred they were not necessarily the fault of the SAS themselves. David Stirling was right to insist that those who carry out operations should also plan them. During his period in command he enjoyed a very free rein, yet his high-handed way of riding roughshod over any opposition made him few friends. It is interesting to speculate what might have happened had he not been taken prisoner. Would he have been given command of an SAS brigade including the SBS and his brother's regiment? That is probable, yet the question remains as to whether he would have been able to cope with the necessarily static life of such a command. He always delegated paperwork to others and would not have taken kindly to acting as ringmaster of a large team of staff officers.

It is easy to look back on the desert period as a kind of golden age, when one just went out and raided with little in the way of official control. L Detachment did account for 400 enemy aircraft at very little cost, but was operating in an ideal environment. When it was turned into 1 SAS Regiment, the writing was already on the wall, as the unit had become too unwieldy and was finding it difficult to recruit enough men of sufficient calibre. As proof of this one only has to look at the disasters that befell B Squadron. It was unfortunate that Stirling was captured, but he only had himself to blame and, as a result, left the regiment in a vacuum.

It is to the credit of Paddy Mayne that he emerged as a fine leader of men in battle, but he never had the personal charisma of Stirling in dealing with higher authorities. Bill Stirling, too, found himself out on a limb in his relationship with headquarters in Algeria. The war had moved into a new phase of professionalism in 1943, and it is doubtful if even David Stirling could have retained control of the SAS as being only answerable to the Commander-in-Chief. One inescapable fact is that once they had left the desert, the SAS required the use of aircraft or ships for infiltration into target areas, and thus became dependent on the goodwill of those who could provide them. It was no longer possible to mount an operation by charming an RAF squadron commander over a meal in Cairo. The SBS, operating in the Aegean, retained far greater control over their activities simply because they owned the caiques and schooners which were their principal means of infiltration.

Using the SRS in Sicily and Italy as a mini-Commando was a total waste of such highly trained personnel, yet they coped magnificently. 2 SAS was never really allowed to develop its potential in that theatre, and as a result many of its operations were only half successful. The sad truth is that memories were short, and without the dynamism and contacts of David Stirling the various staffs involved never understood the potential uses of SAS formations. The time to rectify that was when the brigade was formed at the beginning of 1944, yet as we have seen, the SAS became a pawn in a much wider game. Instead of co-operation in defeating the common enemy there was a sorry tale of staff rivalries and intrigue, for which SOE must shoulder much of the blame. Many of the veterans criticize the brigade, and in some respects it was an unwieldy organism owing little to SAS principles. Yet it performed miracles of logistics and its two commanders, McLeod and Calvert, did their level best to preserve the SAS intact. It was not their fault that regiments were committed to poorly planned operations, and in retrospect Bill Stirling's resignation remained an empty gesture.

Yet in spite of the criticism, the SAS did survive and, with principles intact, continues to serve. The mute testimony of the wartime years has to be sought by the traveller, in small village cemeteries in France where the odd standard-issue headstone with the winged dagger badge can be found among the more ornate offerings to the local dead. That same traveller might by chance arrive on a summer's day and encounter a small procession of mainly elderly men, their flags hanging limp in the morning sunlight, as they make their way to the graveyard. There they pause for a moment and lay their wreaths, at the tomb of a young man – a Jock, a Paddy, a Taff, a Geordie, a Cockney perhaps, or a gallant dashing officer, '*mort pour la France*'. They remember, over a few glasses afterwards, the nights waiting for the aircraft, the arrival of the strange men who always seemed to be joking, the gaiety amidst the fear, and the staccato roar of the Vickers K. They remember, too, their own dead. The small memorials beside country roads list a few names, and underneath, '*Fusillés par les Allemands*'. Nobody who has attended such a ceremony will ever forget the gratitude that is still felt by these simple country people for '*les SAS*'. Disorganized the Resistance may have been, and even exasperating at times, but they still tend the flame of memory and pass it on to their grandchildren.

On the clock-tower at Hereford is inscribed:

> We are the pilgrims, Master we shall go
> Always a little further, it may be
> Beyond that last blue mountain buried with snow.
> Across the angry or glimmering sea . . .

Appendix A:
The Organization of the SAS
1941–1945

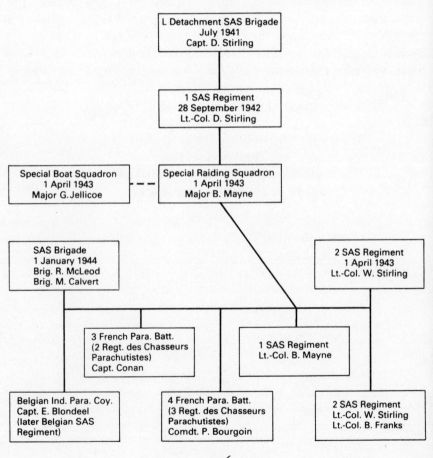

L Detachment SAS Brigade
July 1941
Capt. D. Stirling

1 SAS Regiment
28 September 1942
Lt.-Col. D. Stirling

Special Boat Squadron
1 April 1943
Major G. Jellicoe

Special Raiding Squadron
1 April 1943
Major B. Mayne

SAS Brigade
1 January 1944
Brig. R. McLeod
Brig. M. Calvert

2 SAS Regiment
1 April 1943
Lt.-Col. W. Stirling

3 French Para. Batt.
(2 Regt. des Chasseurs
Parachutistes)
Capt. Conan

1 SAS Regiment
Lt.-Col. B. Mayne

Belgian Ind. Para. Coy.
Capt. E. Blondeel
(later Belgian SAS
Regiment)

4 French Para. Batt.
(3 Regt. des Chasseurs
Parachutistes)
Comdt. P. Bourgoin

2 SAS Regiment
Lt.-Col. W. Stirling
Lt.-Col. B. Franks

Appendix B:
The Post-Operation
Report on Operation Wallace

Major Farran's post-operation comments on Wallace, taken from PRO
WO 218/197, are quoted in full as they form an excellent summary of
operational conditions in France. Many of the comments could equally
well apply to other operations. Roy Farran probably had the best grasp
of military realities of any of the more senior officers in the wartime
SAS.

Strategy and tactics

It had been proved again that jeeping is not only possible but easy
when the front is unstable. As soon as the front becomes firm,
however, jeeping becomes difficult. The concentration of enemy
troops on the line of the Moselle made penetration by vehicles very
dangerous. It might have been possible with strict control of troops by
wireless from a squadron HQ and with a firm line of supply. In this
operation lack of previous training made it necessary to move the
jeeps from one area to another in large parties under experienced
officers. If sufficient troop leaders of high quality, reliability and
experience had been available, I believe that more damage could have
been inflicted on the enemy by widely dispersed troops, only regroup-
ing periodically for resupply. Three jeeps could have penetrated to
areas impossible for nine. A firm base is not necessary for jeeps and it
is better to maintain mobility by aiming at complete independence,
without being tied to dumps. This of course is contrary to our
previous ideas when we thought jeeps should always operate from a
fixed base where refitting and refuelling could be carried out. When

an enemy is withdrawing our type of troops do the most damage when they are placed directly across his axis of withdrawal. In this operation we were faced with two enemy centre lines, one from the west and one up the valley of the Rhone from the south. It was necessary therefore to move our area of operations about fifty miles south east at least once a week. It was not always easy to find a forest large enough to conceal a base for nine jeeps. On the other hand there were always plenty of small woods adequate for concealing a troop. A troop could move daily with the greatest ease. Movement of a squadron column was always fraught with grave risk. It is possible to equip a troop to be independent of supply for a period of a week and to have a range of 200 miles. I believe that our operations were most effective during the last two weeks in the area of the Vosges, although during this time the enemy was very sensitive to our attacks and made our life very uncomfortable. I take this as proof that he disliked our presence more there than in other regions. During this period we actually knocked out a smaller number of vehicles but our patrols covered a wide area and knocked out important vehicles from large convoys. Another explanation of the enemy's dislike of our activities, apart from the fact that he was thicker on the ground, was that we had reached the point where the axis of the western and southern armies converged.

The best tactical team is two jeeps, but a troop of three jeeps means that there is always one vehicle in reserve in the event of a breakdown. A trailer carrying a 3″ mortar is valuable to a squadron but the strain on a jeep's clutch over bad country makes more trailers inadvisable. In any case, in view of the tremendous weights carried on D.Z's, spare clutches must be taken. In ambuscades it is better to sacrifice cover to enable the jeep to take on targets at close range. The twin Vickers gun will cut a truck in half at under fifty yards, but at greater ranges is too inaccurate. The principles of a good ambush are as follows. A position where the jeep cannot be seen until the target is within range but where the jeep is certain of getting a long burst into the bonnet of the truck as soon as it appears. A burst in the front part of the vehicle will set it on fire nine times out of ten. A good covered withdrawal. No banks or undergrowth which enemy troops can use for retaliatory fire. As soon as sufficient damage has been done, the jeep must disappear. It is not necessary to stay long enough to count the bodies. We were very pleased indeed that we had decided to take a Bren gun on the rear mounting. It was invaluable for accurate fire and foot parties. Fifty percent of our bags were obtained by the Bren when the Vickers had failed. If the Bren is fired from a dismounted position, it must not be so far away from the jeep as to prejudice a quick withdrawal. Other jeeping principles remain unaltered. Firing on the move again proved to be a waste of time.

Jeep modifications

Although the modifications were quite sound, the workmanship was so bad that the welding gave way in many places. The following are the chief suggestions. The rear mounting should be on the back of the jeep in the centre. So many air-locks were experienced in the pipes from long-range tanks that it is thought that it would be better to carry three jerricans on each side. This would also eliminate the total wastage of petrol if a tank is hit. The clips for Vickers magazines must be secured more firmly. The spigot swivel on the twin Vickers mounting frequently snapped. This was due to the standard mounting being too heavy. A lighter, strong, firm mounting must be designed immediately. The weight of the mounting also hindered accurate firing, being balanced on such a weak small centre point, it was top-heavy and unwieldy. A big iron rack should be fixed on the back of the jeeps for carrying personal kit. The following modifications were unnecessary – spotlights and smoke dischargers.

Personnel

The men and NCOs were all absolutely first class and their standard of discipline was high. Most of the newly arrived officers require training especially in handling men of this type. I suggest that no officers who have not had previous active service experience in a service unit should be recruited. Extremely young officers are usually an embarrassment in operations of this nature, which call for a great understanding of men and unshakeable self confidence.

Resupply

On the whole was good. The only criticisms are the delay in sending articles demanded. Essential goods should not be put in one plane, i.e. one plane carrying all petrol, all cigarettes etc. Too much ammunition and explosive was dropped when not demanded. There has been practically nothing to blow up in France since D + 7. The method of dropping panniers, the irregularity of lever messages.

Wireless

Wireless worked perfectly well. The night emergency frequency seemed hopeless. Many encoded fatuous useless messages were sent on the broadcast which used up signallers' time unnecessarily. More use could be made of the broadcast to ease the strain on control by sending messages when reception on the Jedburgh set is bad. The tendency of No. 22 sets to wander off frequency made them useless for jeep intercommunication. I think a No. 19 set would have been better.

Appendix C:
The French and Belgian SAS
Units in France

This book has essentially been concerned with telling the story of the two British SAS regiments but, as we have seen, the SAS Brigade in the run-up to D-Day included two French parachute battalions and a Belgian independent parachute company. Their deeds alone would warrant an entire book and I have not had the space to do them sufficient justice. Therefore this appendix must suffice.

In terms of basic training and equipment, both the French and the Belgians were identical to the two British regiments. They were directly under the command of SAS Brigade and were not subject to control by their national armed forces authorities. Where they perhaps differed was in temperament and outlook, which in the case of the French frequently exasperated those British who came into contact with them. The French were so often foolhardy and immensely brave, thus suffering commensurate casualty levels.

In keeping with General Montgomery's initial aim to use SAS troops to isolate the battlefield, it was obvious that the large German garrisons in the Brittany area had to be hindered from moving round the corner to reinforce the front in Normandy. It was decided to drop a large force from 4 French Para. into Brittany on D-Day to establish two bases and also to send in a number of small parties to cut rail communications. The Samwest base was located near St Brieuc in northern Brittany and was commanded by Capitaine Le Blond with Flight-Lieutenant Smith as British Liaison Officer. The Dingson base was to the south of the peninsula in the Vannes area, under the command of the one-armed Commandant Bourgoin, the regimental CO. The advance parties for both bases were successfully parachuted in on 6 June and were able rapidly to build up their numbers to around 100 men at each, plus four jeeps at Dingson.

The French detachments got a rapturous welcome from the local population who naturally believed that liberation was at most a matter of days away. Samwest soon found itself in difficulties, partly caused by poor security in that men went out openly to eat in restaurants. The SAS Brigade war diary noted sourly that the French were far too fond of fraternizing with civilians and cadging food. Even worse, however, was the state of the Resistance which consisted of a number of disparate groups who refused to work together and lived in an atmosphere of mutual distrust. Each clamoured for priority in the supply of arms and they could not be formed into a cohesive force. They were only too keen to supply information, but as Le Blond noted in his report: 'Don't believe every tale you hear. E.g. A small motor car arriving in a village with three Boches has been magnified by the end of two hours, to two lorries and thirty Russian cavalry.'

The upshot was that the Germans struck on 12 June, mounting a major attack on the base. A battle developed which caused the enemy considerable casualties, but the SAS and the Resistance were dispersed. A number of the French paratroopers stayed on in the area, however, and with the help of Jedburgh teams managed to arm and train a worthwhile Resistance unit. The rest joined up with the Dingson base.

By 18 June, Bourgoin had managed to organize and equip three battalions of Resistance and a company of gendarmes. This sounds impressive, but his force of around 2,500 men was armed only with rifles and Stens. They were generally without military training, had no communications and little transport. On that day the base was attacked and the force scattered. It had been far too large to escape detection and was not sufficiently well armed to protect itself. About forty SAS men established themselves in a new base near Pontivy which became known as Grog.

Cooney consisted of eighteen three- to six-man parties which were dropped into Brittany on 7 June, on a line from St Malo to Vannes, to cut rail communications. They had some success and most of the men joined up with Dingson.

Although much was achieved and the Germans were forced to divert forces to deal with the SAS in Brittany, the operations showed that it was too early in the campaign to arm large parties of Frenchmen. Once the fixed bases were scattered, the smaller groupings hid themselves away and got down to some serious work while concentrating on minor operations. By the end of July it was estimated that 15,000 Resistants were at varying stages of military readiness, and the enemy had suffered 2,000 casualties. On 5 August, eleven jeeps were flown in to Bourgoin in the only SAS glider-borne operation of the war. When the Americans finally moved into Brittany in mid-August, the scattered detachments were pulled in and 4 French Para. was reorganized, making up its numbers with recruits from the Maquis.

3 French Para. had to wait until 16 July before getting into action, when a troop was dropped south of the Loire to disrupt rail communications in the Nantes–Saumur area. The force, known as Dickens, remained there until early October, and although they were inserted far too late, they managed to achieve a total breakdown in the railway network in the area. They were credited with 500 Germans killed and 200 vehicles destroyed.

For some strange reason the Belgians were not initially employed in the liberation of their own country. Their first drops were at the end of July and early August in the areas around Le Mans and Chartres (Chaucer, Shakespeare and Bunyan). Their job was to harry the retreating Germans but they were dropped too late and only encountered the tail end of the enemy. They rescued a large number of shot-down aircrew, but several of the parties were overrun within two days of landing. The commander of the Chaucer party, Captain Hazel, made a typical report about the calibre of the Resistance units he encountered. 'They were quite excited to see us but had only just been assembled a few days ago and had no training, no unity of command and did not want any.... They promised to collaborate, but as seen later, they were eager to chase the Germans by themselves when things were easy, but came to us for help when things were bad, and then too late.'

Once the break-out from the constriction of the Normandy beach-head was achieved, General Patton's Third US Army crossed the Seine and headed north-east towards the German frontier. This left him with a vast open flank to his right which was threatened by German units also retreating in the same direction. This flank was mainly guarded by various SAS parties, both British and French. During the first two weeks in August the 3 French Para. Battalion got down to business with a whole series of drops across central France. Moses started off by relieving Bulbasket in the Vienne and was built up to a force of fifty-odd men with a number of jeeps. Other similar troop- and half-troop-sized parties dropped into the Massif Central, Corrèze and Creuse, and as far afield as the Franche-Compté. Wherever they went, their dash and enthusiasm swept up the local population, obsessed as they were with killing Germans and liberating their country. The French operated best as the spearhead of an Allied advance, as they had little talent for lying low and observing. Between 16 July and 7 October, 3 French Para. lost ninety-six men killed, wounded or taken prisoner which was 20 per cent of their effective strength. On the other hand, they were officially credited with 2,340 Germans killed, 2,976 wounded and 1,090 taken prisoner, plus a vast amount of damage to material. In late August they were located as follows:

Barker	Half-troop, Saône-et-Loire.
Samson	Half-troop, Haute-Vienne.
Marshall	Half-troop, Corrèze.
Harrods	Half-troop, Saône-et-Loire.
Snelgrove	Half-troop, Creuse.
Jockworth	Half-troop, Loire–Rhône.
Abel	One squadron, Doubs.

The Moses party in the Vienne found itself without any enemy to pursue by mid-September and was moved to the area south of the Loire estuary where pockets of Germans were still holding out in places such as La Rochelle. The Dickens and Samson parties were also redirected there, but by the end of the month the mopping up was left to the Resistance. The troops from Jockworth were the first into Lyons on 3 September where they became involved in street fighting. Harrods personnel moved west into the Doubs *département* at the end of September and linked up with the various groups from Abel, fighting with the advancing Americans towards Belfort. By the end of September the work of 3 French Para. had been virtually completed and the various sub-units were collected in the Épernay area to reform.

The reconstituted 4 French Para. went back into action in full strength on 29 August. In Operation Spencer, the whole unit of over 300 men in 50 jeeps was infiltrated on land to act as a blocking force along the Loire to the east of Bourges. The purpose of the mission was to hinder German formations moving north-east, ahead of the Allied forces moving up from the south, from crossing the upper reaches of the Loire. They were credited with the destruction of over 100 vehicles and took 2,500 prisoners. More important, though, their presence directly contributed to the surrender of over 20,000 of the enemy to the Americans. At a conference held at Orléans on 5 September, presided over by Brigadier McLeod, Bourgoin reported that the majority of his forces had concentrated around Briare on the north bank of the Loire.

Numerically much smaller than the French units, the Belgian company tended to be used for small-scale operations of a reconnaissance nature. After their forays into the Le Mans area, their commanding officer, Captain Blondeel was parachuted with forty men and some jeeps into the French Ardennes on 16 August to report on enemy movements. This drop was known as Noah, and the small force was credited with 138 Germans killed in a couple of weeks of active ambushing. The Belgians' first entry into their own country was on 2 September, when a small force dropped to the east of the Meuse as Brutus to contact the Belgian Secret Army, arrange for supply drops and then join up with Captain Blondeel. The advance party was reinforced by fifteen men and three jeeps, but by mid-September they had been overrun and retired to Brussels.

The Belgians also had the dubious honour of being the first SAS troops to enter Germany – by accident rather than design. The purpose of Operation Bergbang was for a small force to observe communications in the Liège–Aachen–Maastricht area, ahead of a proposed airborne drop. On the night of 5 September, a party of reinforcements was actually dropped inside Germany. They had some difficulty in getting back into Belgium but operated successfully for a few days in the Spa area before being overrun.

Thus by the end of September the liberation of France had been virtually completed and Allied forces were also established well inside Belgium. But all along the line from the Channel to the Swiss frontier the Germans were digging in, determined to stop incursions into their own country and to hold on to as many of their ill-gotten gains as possible. The men of the various foreign SAS units had achieved much, but were tired and in urgent need of refitting. Gradually they were gathered together into concentration areas for leave and to absorb replacements, while over their heads the controversy about their future employment raged on.

Note: This appendix is based on sources from PRO WO 218/114, PRO WO 218/193 and PRO WO 277/2.

Appendix D:
The Future of SAS Troops
1945

Subject: Future of SAS Troops

HQ SAS Tps/80/17/G

Lt-Col W. Stirling
Lt-Col D. Stirling, DSO
Lt-Col R. B. Mayne, DSO
Lt-Col B. M. F. Franks, DSO MC
Lt-Col I. G. Collins
Lt-Col E. C. Baring
Lt-Col The Earl Jellicoe
Lt-Col D. Sutherland
Lt-Col D. Lloyd Owen, MC
Major J. Verney, MC
Major R. Farran, DSO, MC

The Director of Tactical Investigation, Maj-Gen ROWELL, has been ordered by the Chief of Imperial General Staff, that his directorate should investigate all the operations of the Special Air Service with a view to giving recommendations for the future of SAS in the next war and its composition in the peace-time army. The actual terms of reference were:

'An investigation of SAS technique tactics and organisation without prejudice to a later examination of all organisations of a similar nature which were formed and operated in various theatres of this last war'.

Brigadier Churchill is Deputy Director of Tactical Investigation and lives at Flat 110, 4 Whitehall Court, London, S.W.1 (Whitehall 9400 Ext 1632), just behind the War Office. The officer immediately concerned is Lt-Col C. A. Wigham. Lt-Col Wigham has in his possession all the reports on SAS operations in W. EUROPE. The reports on SAS operations in ITALY and in the MEDITERRANEAN Theatre are also being obtained and forwarded. I have given Lt-Col Wigham your names so that he may either have a talk with you to obtain your views and to find out about incidents which are not clear in the reports, or to ask you to write your views to him.

We all have the future of the SAS at heart, not merely because we wish to see its particular survival as a unit, but because we have believed in the principles of its method of operations. Many of the above-named officers have had command of forces which have had a similar role to that of the SAS, as well as being in the SAS at one time.

The object of this investigation is to decide whether the principles of operating in the SAS manner are correct. If they are correct, what types of units should undertake operations of this nature, and how best to train and maintain such units in peace, ready for war. I will not start now by writing about the principles of SAS, which have been an intrinsic part of your life for the past few years, but I will mention what I think are some of the most important points which need bringing out. The best way to do this is to consider the usual criticisms of the SAS type of force.

1. 'The Private Army'

From what I have seen in different parts of the world, forces of this nature tend to be so-called 'Private Armies' because there have been no normal formations in existence to fulfil this function – a role which has been found by all commanders to be a most vital adjunct to their plans. It has only been due to the drive and initiative of certain individuals backed up by senior commanders that these forces have been formed and have carried out their role.

2. 'The taking up of Commanders' valuable time'

This has often been necessary because it has very often only been the Comds of armies who have realised the importance of operations of this nature, and to what an extent they can help their plans. The difficulty has been that more junior staff officers have not understood the object or principles of such forces. They have either given us every help as they have thought us something rather wonderful, or they have thought we were 'a bloody nuisance'. I feel that the best way to overcome this is, that once the principle of the importance of Special Raiding Forces operating behind the vital points of the enemy's lines is agreed to, it should become an integral part of the training of the army at the Staff College, military colleges, and during manoeuvres, etc. Students should be asked not only what orders or directives or requests they have to give to the artillery, engineers, air, etc. but also what directives they would give to their raiding forces. There should be a recognized staff officer on the staffs of senior formations whose job it is to deal with these forces, i.e. the equivalent of a CRE or CRA. This should also be included in the text books FRS, etc.

3. *'These forces, like airborne forces, are only required when we pass to the offensive, which – judging by all previous wars – is when the regular army has been nearly wiped out in rearguard actions whilst the citizen army forms, i.e. about 3 years after the beginning of the war.'*

The answer here, I feel, is that it is just when we are weak everywhere that forces of this nature are the most useful, and can play a most vital part in keeping the enemy all over the world occupied. Also there is little difference between the roles of SAS and 'Auxiliary Forces' who duck when the enemy's offensive rolls over them and then operate against the enemy's L of C from previously constructed bases. An SAS formation, by its organisation and training, is ideally suited to operate in this defensive role.

4. *'Overlapping with SOE and other clandestine organisations'*

My experience is that SOE and SAS are complementary to each other. SAS cannot successfully operate without good intelligence, guides, etc. SOE can only do a certain amount before requiring, when their operations become overt, highly trained, armed bodies in uniform to operate and set an example to the local resistance. SOE are the 'white hunters' and produce the ground organisation on which SAS operates.

All senior officers of SOE with whom I have discussed this point agree to this principle.

5. 'SAS is not adaptable to all countries.'

This has already been proved wrong. SAS is probably more adaptable to changes of theatres than any regular formation. Also, as I have said in 4 above, SAS work on the ground organisation of SOE. It is for SOE to be a world-wide organisation with an organisation in every likely country. Then when necessary, SAS can operate on this organisation using their guides and intelligence knowledge, etc.

6. 'Volunteer units skim the regular units of their best officers and men.'

Volunteer units such as SAS attract officers and men who have initiative, resourcefulness, independence of spirit, and confidence in themselves. In a regular unit there are far less opportunities of making use of these assets and, in fact, in many formations they are a liability, as this individualistic attitude upsets the smooth working of a team. This is especially true in European warfare where the individual must subordin-ate his natural initiative so that he fits into a part of the machine. Volunteer units such as the Commandos and Chindits (only a small proportion of the Chindits were volunteers although the spirit was there) have shown the rest of the army how to fight at a time when it was in low morale due to constant defeat. A few 'gladiators' raises the standard of all. Analogies are racing (car, aeroplane, horse, etc.), and test teams.

7. 'Expense per man is greater than any other formation and is not worthwhile.'

Men in units of this nature probably fight 3 or 4 times more often than regular units. They are always eager for a fight and therefore usually get it. If expense per man days *actually in contact with the enemy* was taken into account, there would be no doubt which was the more expensive type of formation. I have found, as you will have done, the 'old familiar faces' on every front where we have seen trouble. I consider the expense is definitely worth it without even taking into account the extra results. One SAS raid in North Africa destroyed more aeroplanes in one day than the balloon barrage did during 6 years of war.

8. *'Any normal battalion could do the same job'*

My experience shows that they definitely cannot. In NORWAY in 1940, a platoon of marines under a sgt ran away when left on its own, although they had orders to stay, when a few German lorries appeared. Mainly owing to the bad leadership of this parade ground Sgt, they were all jittery and useless because they were 'out of touch'. A force consisting of two Gurkha Coys and a few British troops of which I was one was left behind in 1942 in Burma to attack the enemy in the rear if they appeared. The Commander, a good Gurkha officer with a good record, when confronted with a perfect opportunity (Japs landing in boats onto a wide sandy beach completely unaware of our presence), avoided action in order to get back to his Brigade because he was 'out of touch' and could not receive orders. By avoiding action, the unit went into a waterless area and more perished this way and later by drowning than if he had attacked.

My experience with regular battalions under my command in Burma was that there were only 3 or 4 officers in any battalion who could be relied on to take positive action if they were on their own, and had no detailed orders. This 'I'll 'ave to ask me Dad' attitude of the British Army is its worse feature in my opinion. I found the RAF and dominion officers far better in this respect. I have not had experience with the cavalry. They should also be better. Perhaps cavalry could take on the SAS role successfully? I admit that with training both in Burma and North Africa there were definite improvements amongst the infantry, but in my opinion, no normal battalion I have seen, could carry out an SAS role without 80% reorganisation. I have written frankly and have laid myself open to obvious criticism, but I consider this such a vital point I do not mind how strongly I express myself. I have repeated this for 5 years and I have nowhere seen anything to change my views, least of all in Europe.

I have mentioned some points above. You may not agree with my ideas but I write them down as these criticisms are the most normal ones I know. Other points in which the D.T.I. wants to obtain information are:

1. *Obtaining of recruits.* Has anybody got the original brochure setting out the terms and standards required?
2. *Obtaining of stores and equipment.* Here again, I imagine SOE has been the main source of special stores. My own HQ is producing a paper on this when in England.

3. *Signal communication.* This is of course one of the most important parts of such an organisation and it has, as in other formations, limited the scope of our operation.
4. *Foreign recruits and attached civilians.*
5. *Liaison with RAF and Navy.*
6. *Command.* How is an organisation of this sort best commanded and under whom should they be?
7. Suggestions re survival in peacetime including auxiliary formation, command, technical development, etc.

You may expect a communication from Lt-Col Wigham. Please give your views quite candidly. They certainly need not agree with those I have written down. I am sending Lt-Col Wigham a copy of this letter so that it may give you something to refer to if necessary. I hope, from the army point of view, and for all that you have worked for and believed in during the last few years, that you will do everything you can to help Lt-Col Wigham to obtain all the information that he requires. We can no longer say that people do not understand if we do not take this chance to get our views put before an impartial tribunal whose task it is to review them in the light of general policy, and then make recommendations to the C.I.G.S. Send along any reports or documents you have got. Lt-Col Wigham is thirsting for information.

[Mike Calvert]
Brigadier,
Commander,
SAS Troops.

Sloe House,
Halstead, Essex.
12 Oct 45.
JMC/LGM.

Notes

At the end of the Second World War, when the two British SAS regiments were disbanded, their accumulated papers were crated up and sent to the Army Air Corps records office in Edinburgh. After some time they were presumably disposed of, as the present-day units of the regiment do not hold them. Casual inspection of the indexes at the Public Record Office (PRO) reveals that there is little in the way of documents filed under SAS as such. Examination of certain classes, however, reveals that there is a lot of material filed under less obvious headings. The main PRO classes used have been:

WO 202   Miscellaneous Middle East and Mediterranean papers
WO 218   War diaries and miscellaneous files
WO 219   SHAEF files

In addition, I have used various original papers from my own collection (auth. coll.), which have kindly been made available to me by former members of the regiment. A further source of original material consists of documents and first-person accounts printed from time to time in *Mars and Minerva* (*M & M*), the journal of the Special Air Service Regiment. Such primary source material has been supplemented by a series of interviews carried out during 1987 by myself and my then colleague for a proposed television series (AK/GS i/v).

1.   The Birth of an Idea

1. *M & M*, 1984.
2. J. Cooper, 'The Originals' *ms.*
3. Waugh, Letters, p. 149.
4. AK/GS i/v, David Stirling.

5. PRO WO 218/173.
6. AK/GS i/v, David Stirling.
7. Stirling, 'Memorandum on the Origins of the Special Air Service Regiment', November 1948 auth. coll.
8. AK/GS i/v, David Stirling.
9. Stirling, 'Memorandum'.
10. *Ibid.*
11. Cowles, *The Phantom Major*, p. 12 *et seq.*
12. AK/GS i/v, David Stirling.
13. AK/GS i/v, Bob Bennett.
14. J. Cooper, 'The Originals' *ms.*
15. Stirling, 'Memorandum'.
16. AK/GS i/v, David Stirling.
17. Stirling, 'Memorandum'.
18. *Ibid.*
19. *Ibid.*
20. AK/GS i/v, Reg Seekings.
21. J. Cooper, 'The Originals' *ms.*
22. AK/GS i/v, Reg Seekings.
23. J. Cooper, 'The Originals' *ms.*
24. AK/GS i/v, Pat Riley.
25. J. Cooper, 'The Originals', *ms.*

2. Early Raids in the Western Desert

1. AK/GS i/v, David Stirling.
2. Lloyd-Owen, *The Desert My Dwelling Place*, p. 110.
3. J. Cooper, 'The Originals' *ms.*
4. AK/GS i/v, Jim Almonds.
5. *M & M*, September 1987 and June 1983.
6. PRO WO 201/2261.
7. *Ibid.*
8. Artemis Cooper, *Cairo in the War*, p. 219 *et seq.*
9. AK/GS i/v, David Stirling.
10. Byrne, *The General Salutes a Soldier*, p. 21 *et seq.*
11. AK/GS i/v, Reg Seekings.
12. AK/GS i/v, Mike Sadler.
13. PRO WO 201/731.
14. *Ibid.*
15. *Ibid.*
16. *Ibid.*
17. J. Cooper, 'The Originals' *ms.*
18. *Ibid.*

3. Expansion and Regimental Status

1. PRO WO 201/732.
2. PRO WO 201/731.
3. *Ibid.*
4. *Ibid.*
5. *Ibid.*
6. *Ibid.*
7. J. Cooper, 'The Originals' *ms.*
8. *Ibid.*
9. James [Pleydell], *Born of the Desert*, p. 91.
10. Cowles, *The Phantom Major*, p. 176 *et seq.*
11. J. Cooper, 'The Originals' *ms.*
12. Auth. coll.
13. PRO WO 201/732.
14. *Ibid.*
15. Auth. coll. Translator unknown.
16. PRO WO 201/753.
17. *Ibid.*

4. Last Days in North Africa

1. AK/GS i/v Stirling.
2. PRO WO 201/728.
3. *Ibid.*
4. *Ibid.*

5. James, *Born of the Desert*, p. 210 *et seq.*
6. PRO WO 201/738.
7. PRO WO 201/2257.
8. Deighton, *Alamein and the Desert War*, reprinted in part in the *Sunday Times*, 17 September 1967.
9. *M & M*, insert, June 1968.
10. PRO WO 201/743.
11. PRO WO 201/732.
12. PRO WO 201/743.
13. PRO WO 201/752 and 753.
14. PRO WO 201/752.
15. Cowles, *The Phantom Major*, p. 244 *et seq.*
16. PRO WO 201/743.
17. *Ibid.*
18. James, *Born of the Desert*, p. 282.
19. PRO WO 201/743.
20. PRO WO 201/747.
21. J. Cooper, 'The Originals' *ms.*

5. The SRS in Sicily and Italy

1. *M & M*, September 1985.
2. PRO WO 218/97.
3. PRO WO 218/98.
4. PRO WO 218/97.
5. AK/GS i/v, Reg Seekings.
6. *M & M*, September 1985.
7. Bradford and Dillon, *Rogue Warrior of the SAS*, p. 79.
8. Report of Operation Baytown, reproduced in *M & M*, June 1984.
9. AK/GS i/v Reg Seekings.
10. Report of Operation Baytown, reproduced in *M & M*, June 1984.
11. AK/GS i/v, Pat Riley.
12. AK/GS i/v, Reg Seekings.

6. 2 SAS in Sicily and Italy

1. Challenor, *SAS and the Met.*, p. 33 *et seq.*
2. Quoted in Strawson, *A History of the SAS Regiment*, p. 137.
3. PRO WO 218/175.
4. Farran, *Winged Dagger*, p. 167 *et seq.*
5. PRO WO 218/177.
6. Report by Major Barkworth, 'Two Escapes in Italy', auth. coll.
7. *M & M*, December 1982.
8. PRO WO 218/177.
9. Challenor, *SAS and the Met.*, p. 53.
10. *Ibid.*
11. PRO WO 218/176.
12. *Ibid.*
13. PRO WO 218/181.
14. PRO WO 218/178.
15. PRO WO 218/182.
16. Hughes, *Who Cares Who Wins*, p. 176.
17. Strawson, *A History of the SAS Regiment*, p. 143.
18. PRO WO 218/183.
19. PRO WO 218/184.
20. PRO WO 218/185.
21. PRO WO 218/185 and Hughes, *Who Cares Who Wins*, appendix.
22. Report by Major Barkworth, 'The Commando Orders of 11.10.42 and 26.6.44. Wuppertal. 23 June 1948', auth. coll.

7. The SAS Brigade

1. PRO WO 227/2, 'Airborne Forces', compiled by Lt.-Col. Otway DSO, War Office, 1951.
2. PRO WO 218/114.
3. Letter from the late Major Eric Barkworth to Major John Tonkin. Copy in auth. coll.
4. PRO WO 218/114.
5. PRO WO 277/2.
6. Vaculik, *Air Commando*, p. 134.
7. Bradford and Dillon, *Rogue Warrior of the SAS*, p. 94.
8. Vaculik, *Air Commando*, p. 139 *et seq*.
9. McCluskey, *Parachute Padre*, p. 44.
10. J. Cooper, 'The Originals' *ms*.
11. PRO WO 277/2.
12. *Ibid.*
13. Typescript, 'Notes on the organization, history and employment of Special Air Service troops', n.d., auth. coll.
14. PRO WO 218/186.
15. PRO WO 218/114.
16. *Ibid.*
17. Farran, *Winged Dagger*, p. 222.
18. PRO WO 218/114.
19. *Ibid.*
20. PRO WO 218/194.
21. *Ibid.*
22. *Ibid.*
23. PRO WO 218/195.
24. PRO WO 218/194.
25. PRO WO 218/196.
26. PRO WO 218/194.
27. *Ibid.*
28. *Ibid.*
29. *Ibid.*
30. PRO WO 218/193.
31. PRO WO 277-2.

8. 1 SAS, in France

1. PRO WO 218/193.
2. *Ibid.*
3. PRO WO 218/114.
4. Auth. coll.
5. AK i/v, John Tonkin.
6. Bulbasket signal log and report by Major Tonkin, auth. coll.
7. Account in Hastings, *Das Reich*.
8. La Chouette, *La Résistance dans la Vienne*.
9. AK i/v, John Fielding.
10. Hastings, *Das Reich*, p. 227.
11. Letter from Camille Olivet to Max Hastings, photocopy, auth. coll.
12. Marnais (ed.) *L'Odyssée des Parachutistes SAS du Capitaine Tonkin et des Maquisards du Capitaine Dieudonné*, p. 25.
13. *Ibid.*, p. 62.
14. PRO WO 219/2389.
15. J. Cooper, 'The Originals' *ms*.
16. 'Reception of personnel and stores dropped by parachute', SAS Brigade document, 6 June 1944, auth. coll.
17. McCluskey, *Parachute Padre*, p. 68.
18. PRO WO 218/114.
19. J. Cooper, 'The Originals' *ms*.
20. PRO WO 277/2.
21. PRO WO 218/193.
22. *Ibid.*
23. Harrison, *These Men are Dangerous*, p. 224 *et seq.*, and PRO WO 219/5092.
24. PRO WO 219/5092.

9. 2 SAS in France

1. PRO WO 218/114.
2. *Ibid.*
3. Flamand, *L'Inconnu du French Squadron.*
4. PRO WO 219/5092.
5. Farran, *Winged Dagger*, p. 227.
6. *Ibid.*, pp. 237–8.
7. PRO WO 219/5092 and 218/197.
8. Flamand, *L'Inconnu du French Squadron.*
9. PRO WO 218/194.
10. *SAS Brigade Operational Reports,* Vol. 7, Sect. 8, Vosges, auth. coll.
11. Kemp, *The Secret Hunters*, p. 28 *et seq.*
12. AK/GS i/v, Henry Druce.
13. For an account of the wider campaign in the area, see Kemp, *The Unknown Battle – Metz 1944*, Frederick Warne, 1981.
14. Sykes, *Four Studies in Loyalty.*
15. *Ibid.*, p. 198 *et seq.*
16. *Ibid.*, p. 207.
17. *SAS Brigade Operational Reports,* Vol. 7, Vosges, Appendix C (1).

10. The Final Phase of the War in Europe

1. PRO WO 219/2877.
2. *Ibid.*
3. *Ibid.*
4. *Ibid.*
5. *Ibid.*
6. *Ibid.*
7. *SAS Brigade Operational Reports,* Vol. 10, Holland, auth. coll.
8. PRO WO 219/2877.
9. Farran, *Winged Dagger*, p. 262.
10. PRO WO 219/2977 and 219/5092.
11. PRO WO 219/5092.
12. *Ibid.* and letter from Bingham to Franks, 16 April 1945, auth. coll.
13. For this operation see PRO WO 219/5092; Farran *Winged Dagger;* and an article by Colonel Harvey in *M & M*, Vol. 6, Nos. 2 and 3.
14. Farran, *Winged Dagger*, p. 291.
15. Lewis, *Echoes of Resistance*, p. 102.
16. *Ibid.*, p. 104.
17. Letter from Bingham to Franks, 16 April 1945, auth. coll.
18. Letter from Bingham to Farran, 1 May 1945, auth. coll.
19. Farran, *Winged Dagger*, p. 317.
20. *Ibid.*, p. 288.
21. PRO WO 219/5092.
22. *Ibid.*
23. PRO WO 218/117.
24. J. Cooper, 'The Originals' *ms.*
25. Bradford and Dillon, *Rogue Warrior of the SAS*, p. 207.
26. PRO WO 218/117.
27. Bradford and Dillon, *Rogue Warrior of the SAS*, p. 169 *et seq.*
28. Harrison, *These Men are Dangerous*, p. 269.
29. AK/GS i/v, Reg Seekings.

11. Norway, Disbandment and Re-formation

1. *SAS Brigade Operational Reports,* Vol. 12, Norway, auth. coll.
2. File of miscellaneous papers regarding Norway, auth. coll.
3. AK/GS i/v, David Stirling.
4. File of miscellaneous papers re-

garding disbandment, auth. coll.

5. Challenor, *SAS and the Met.*, p. 117.

6. Copy of report by the local *gendarmerie*, auth. coll.

7. For a detailed account of the investigation of war crimes, see

Kemp, *The Secret Hunters.*

8. Barkworth, 'Interim report on missing personnel of 2 S.A.S.', Gaggenau, 15 July 1945, and Barkworth, 'Missing Parachutists', Gaggenau, 14 November 1945, auth. coll.

Bibliography

General Histories: The SAS

Geraghty, Tony, *Who Dares Wins*, Arms and Armour Press, 1980; Fontana paperback edn. 1983, with additional chapter on the Falklands.
—— *This Is the SAS – A Photographic History*, Arms and Armour Press, 1982.
Ladd, James D., *SAS Operations*, Hale, 1986.
Macdonald, Peter, *The SAS in Action*, Sidgwick & Jackson, 1990.
Seymour, William, *British Special Forces*, Grafton Books, 1986.
Short, J., *The Special Air Service*, Men-at-Arms No. 116, Osprey, 1981.
Strawson, John, *A History of the SAS Regiment*, Secker & Warburg, 1984.
Warner, Phillip, *The SAS*, William Kimber, 1971; Sphere Books paperback edn. 1983.

General Histories: The SBS

Courtney, G. B., *SBS in World War Two*, Robert Hale, 1983.
Ladd, James D., *SBS: The Invisible Raiders*, Arms and Armour Press, 1983.
Pitt, Barrie, *Special Boat Squadron*, Century, 1983.
Warner, Phillip, *The SBS*, Sphere Books, 1983.

Biographies

Bradford, Roy, and Dillon, Martin, *Rogue Warrior of the SAS*, John Murray, 1987.
Cowles, Virginia, *The Phantom Major*, Collins, 1958.
Marrinan, Patrick, *Colonel Paddy*, Ulster Press, 1960.

First-person Accounts

Appleyard, J. E., *'Geoffrey'*, Blandford Press, 1947.

Byrne, J. V., *The General Salutes a Soldier*, Robert Hale, 1986.

Challenor, Tanky, with Draper, Alfred, *SAS and the Met.*, Leo Cooper, 1990.

Cooper, John, with Kemp, Anthony, *One of the 'Originals'*, Pan, 1991.

De Souza, Ken, *Escape from Ascoli*, Newton, Publications, 1990.

Durnford-Slater, John, *Commando*, William Kimber, 1953.

Farran, Roy, *Winged Dagger*, Collins, 1948; reissued by Arms and Armour Press, 1986.

—— *Operation Tombola*, Collins, 1960; reissued by Arms and Armour Press, 1986.

Harrison, D. I., *These Men are Dangerous*, Cassell, 1957.

Hills, R. J. T., *Phantom Was There*, Edward Arnold, 1951.

Hislop, John, *Anything but a Soldier*, Michael Joseph, 1965.

Hughes, J. Quentin, *Who Cares Who Wins*, privately published, 1989.

Johnston, Charles, *Mo, and Other Originals*, Hamish Hamilton, 1971.

James [Pleydell], Malcolm, *Born of the Desert*, Collins, 1945.

Maclean, Fitzroy, *Eastern Approaches*, Jonathan Cape, 1949.

McLuskey, J. Fraser, *Parachute Padre*, SCM Press, 1951.

Newby, Eric, *Love and War in the Apennines*, Hodder, 1971.

Pringle, Jack, *Colditz Last Stop*, William Kimber, 1988.

Sykes, Christopher, *Four Studies in Loyalty*, Collins, 1946.

Verney, John, *A Dinner of Herbs*, Collins, 1966.

—— *Going to the Wars*, Collins, 1955; reissued in paperback by Anthony Mott, 1983.

Vaculik, Serge, *Air Commando*, Jarrolds, 1954.

Waugh, Evelyn, *The Letters of Evelyn Waugh*, ed. Mark Amory, Penguin, 1982.

Young, Irene, *Enigma Variations*, Mainstream, 1990.

The Long Range Desert Group

Constable, Trevor, *Hidden Heroes*, Arthur Barker, 1971.

Crichton-Stuart, Michael, *G Patrol*, William Kimber, 1958.

Kennedy-Shaw, W. B., *Long Range Desert Group*, Collins, 1945.

Lloyd-Owen, David, *Providence Their Guide*, Harrap, 1980.

—— *The Desert My Dwelling Place*, Cassell, 1957; reissued by Arms and Armour Press, 1986.

Secondary Sources

Boehm, Boettcher, Reuter and Weingardt, *Sicherungslager Rotenfels, Ein Konzentrationslager in Deutschland*, Suddeutscher Paedogogische Verlag, Ludwigsburg, 1989.

Buxton, David, *Honour to the Airborne*, Part 2, Elmdon Publishing, Solihull, 1985.

Calmette, A., *Les Équipes Jedburgh dans la Bataille de France*, Paris, 1966.

Chouette, La, *La Résistance dans la Vienne*, privately published, n.d.

Cooper, Artemis, *Cairo in the War*, Hamish Hamilton, 1989.

Deighton, Len, *et al.*, *Alamein and the Desert War*, Sphere Books, 1967.

Flamand, Col. Roger, *L'Inconnu du French Squadron*, privately published, 1983.

Foot, M. R. D., *SOE in France*, HMSO, 1966.

Hastings, Max, *Das Reich*, Michael Joseph, 1981.

Kemp, Anthony, *The Secret Hunters*, Michael O'Mara Books, 1986.

Lewis, Laurence, *Echoes of Resistance*, Costello, 1985.

Marnais, A. (ed.), *L'Odyssée des Parachutistes SAS du Capitaine Tonkin et des Maquisards du Capitaine Dieudonné*, privately published, n.d.

Racault, Gaston, *La Vienne pendant la Seconde Guerre Mondiale: Vol. 3, Les Maquis, la Libération*, CRDP, Poitiers, 1987.

Ricatte, René, *Viombois, haut lieu de la Résistance*, GMA–Vosges, 1984.

Rousselet, Maurice, *Occupation et libération d'un coin de Bourgogne*, privately published, 1980.

Swinson, Arthur, *The Raiders*, Pan, 1968.

Warner, Phillip, *Phantom*, Kimber, 1982.

Index